14-

How to Help
Children
Through a Parent's
Serious Illness

Twelve-year-old Lois Colvin shows how her mom's breast cancer affected her family, which she sees as a happy heart before the diagnosis, then a heart broken by the cancer diagnosis. Finally, the family works to put its heart back together.

How to Help
Children
Through a Parent's
Serious Illness

Supportive, Practical Advice
from a Leading Child Life Specialist

REVISED AND UPDATED

Kathleen McCue, M.A., C.C.L.S.

with Ron Bonn

St. Martin's Griffin ✖ New York

HOW TO HELP CHILDREN THROUGH A PARENT'S SERIOUS ILLNESS.

REVISED AND UPDATED EDITION.

Copyright © 1994, 2011 by Kathleen McCue, M.A., C.C.L.S., with Ron Bonn. All rights reserved. Printed in the United States of America. For information, address St. Martin's Press, 175 Fifth Avenue, New York, N.Y. 10010.

www.stmartins.com

Library of Congress Cataloging-in-Publication Data

McCue, Kathleen.
 How to help children through a parent's serious illness : supportive, practical advice from a leading child life specialist / Kathleen McCue, Ron Bonn. — 2nd St. Martin's Griffin ed.
  p. cm.
 ISBN 978-0-312-69768-6 (pbk.)
 1. Parent and child. 2. Sick—Family relationships. 3. Parents—Death—Psychological aspects. 4. Family psychotherapy. I. Bonn, Ron. II. Title.
 BF723.P25M33 2011
 649'.1—dc23   2011027055

Revised and Updated Edition: December 2011

10 9 8 7 6 5

To Mom, Marjorie, and Debbie
Strong women, strong family
—KATHLEEN MCCUE

For my family
and
For all the families—
"Our family is our fort."
—RON BONN

Contents

SPECIAL SITUATIONS

Foreword

My wife died of breast cancer in 1977, after a three-year struggle. When I came home from the hospital and told my two young children the tragic news, they were relieved when they realized we would all stay together. "We thought we'd be adopted," they said. I realized then how little I had prepared them for what would be the worst event of their lives. Shuttled back and forth between grandparents, they understood only that something was gravely wrong, that their world was coming apart.

As I read *How to Help Children Through a Parent's Serious Illness,* it all came back. I just wish this book had been available then. Remarkably insightful, it will be a gentle hand to help those who otherwise would have to face personal tragedy alone.

I thought no one could understand terminal illness within a family without having been there. Well, Kathleen McCue has been there.

I hope you never need this book, but if you do, use it, trust it. It could help your children for the rest of their lives.

—Bill Kurtis

Preface

A Quick Look Forward

It's the aim of this book to help you help your children, from the moment one parent is diagnosed with a serious or life-threatening illness, or the moment you begin *looking* for help, right through the resolution of that illness, whatever it may be. We may find ourselves together for weeks, months, or years.

If, however, you've picked up the book for help with an immediate problem, or an emergency with your children, here is a quick guide to what each chapter contains. (At the end of most chapters, you'll find more detailed subject listings, to take you to whatever page you may need.)

Chapter 1, "The First Day of the Rest of Your Life," starts from the moment of diagnosis. It explains what and how you should tell your children about the illness, what questions they'll probably have, how children of different ages are likely to react, and how you can help them. The central message of this chapter—and of the book—is absolute honesty.

Chapter 2, "Getting It Together," helps prepare your family for the long haul. It discusses how to minimize stress on the well parent, how to rally and organize the support that's available, what kind of help you can expect from your children, and what kind of help they'll need from you.

Chapter 3, "Early Warnings," details the early warning signs you may see when your children *aren't* handling the crisis. It explains how to look for signs of trouble in their drawings and their play, a series of specific warnings in behavior—sleeping, eating, school failure, and more—and how you can begin to handle them: what to ask and what to say.

It warns strongly against permitting any pattern of failure to develop. The final section deals with children who seem to be trying to injure themselves.

Chapter 4, "Help! How to Give It, Where to Get It," goes into much more detail on how you can help your children when they show you they're in trouble. It covers how to understand what the trouble is, how to decide whether a child needs outside help, the different levels of support available—from friends and family all the way up to psychotherapy—and where and how to find it.

Chapter 5, "The Wonderful, Terrible Internet," looks into perhaps the greatest change in our lives since this book was first published: the explosive growth of the Internet. The Web today, perched just inside your home computer, poses both great opportunities and grave dangers to your children in this time of family crisis. This chapter explains how to use the Internet to enhance both your children's well-being and their understanding of your situation, and shield them from the many dangers of *bad* information, *frightening* information, and *too much* information that are now just a mouse-click away. We look as well at the use and misuse of social networks like Facebook.

Chapter 6, "Preparing Children for Hospital Visits," explains how to prepare children for visiting a sick parent: how to decide whether or not a visit is a good idea and how to ready them for the frightening sights. The chapter explores how to take children through two entirely different situations: a parent in intensive care and a parent hospitalized for a serious but non-life-threatening condition.

Chapter 7, "Coming Home," offers the briefing I give a well parent when the sick parent is about to come home—how to prepare your children, how to involve them, how to deal with their too-glowing expectations, avoiding big celebrations, what the well parent and the sick parent can expect from their children, and what the children will need from both of you.

Chapter 8, "When It Won't Get Better," deals with illness that will not go away—chronic, degenerative diseases that will persist or grow worse over years. It explains how to help your children understand what such an illness feels like and to cope with the permanent change in your family's life and adapt to this partial loss of a beloved parent.

Chapter 9, "Dealing with a Parent's Mental Illness," changes and re-adapts some of our earlier emphasis, particularly on when to bring in professional help for your children. A parent's mental illness can be far more damaging to her children than any physical problem; the children, and the crisis, require special understanding and special handling by adults.

Chapter 10, "When Things Get Very Bad," looks at dying—and living. Some of the subjects: children's last times with dying parents; to visit or not to visit the hospital; dying at home; legacies of love—on paper or on tape—that can live on with your children after you leave them, and how the surviving parent and the children can help each other through their grief to an undamaged future.

SPECIAL SITUATIONS

Chapter 11, "Children and Trauma," explains how to cope with the traumatized child who has witnessed something shocking—a father falling from a ladder or struck by a car, a burn victim. Such shocks trigger the "freeze/fight/flight" reflex in the deepest part of our ancient brain and require new techniques to help the child get beyond them and back to emotional health.

Chapter 12, "Single Parenting, Multiple Households," addresses the new reality that many if not most American children today either live in single-parent households or divide their lives between two households. We discuss the strength and selflessness this new family structure imposes on parents when one falls gravely or fatally ill. And we look at a number of true stories of how single parents have dealt with the crisis, and how those decisions impacted, for good or ill, their children's future.

*A special note for single parents: In this chapter, under the heading, **"If Yours Is a Single-Parent Family,"** you'll find important suggestions for selecting a special friend or relative who can help you and your children through this medical crisis.*

I suggest you read that section carefully now, and begin to decide whom you want to enlist for this crucial role. You and your helper should use this book together, with the helper taking the role of "well parent" for your children from here on.

Chapter 13, "Genetic Diseases: 'No, but . . . ,'" looks into the other field that has exploded since our first edition: the science of hereditary disease. New DNA tests can identify hundreds of genetic anomalies that may foreshadow future diseases, but only a handful of those diseases can be treated and controlled if they actually appear. What should a parent tell a child, do for a child, who may (or may not) carry a mutated gene that could surface as a serious or potentially fatal condition a decade or two from now? What do your children (and you) need to know? And sometimes most important of all, *when* do you all need to know it?

Chapter 14, "Some Other Special Situations," looks into special family or medical situations that may affect how the principles of the book apply: Among them:

- when the patient is *not* a parent
- contagious diseases
- the vulnerable child
- when the child had a role in "causing" the parent's condition

Chapter 15, "Emily's Hero," shows us, in a child's own words, just how healthy and strong children can emerge from even the ultimate family tragedy.

Note to the Reader

The family stories that appear throughout this book are based on my case notes. I did not record conversations with children, parents, or medical professionals. Therefore, the conversations that accompany the stories are reconstructed and reported to the best of my memory

The names and certain characteristics have, in most cases, been changed to protect the privacy of those people with whom my work as a child life specialist have brought me in contact. I also note that many of the stories included in this book are composites, based on two or more real case histories.

Chapter illustrations are by children I've worked with. These names are real. I thank them for their artistry and their courage.

Two Readers' Forethoughts

Dear Ms. McCue and Mr. Bonn:

I am convinced it was an angel that led me to your book in the patient/family "library" in the gift shop in the hospital where my husband was being treated.

I couldn't sleep one night and began to read your truly extraordinary book. I read your suggestions for what was age appropriate for my sons, and discussed them with my sons the next morning (which was exactly two weeks after my husband had been admitted). I told them that their father's illness wasn't anyone's fault, it wasn't contagious, etc.

Three hours later my son Sam's eyes filled with tears (this is a child who rarely cries, even when physically hurt). He began, "You know, Mom, I asked Dad to play basketball with me and he told me he was too tired. I asked him again, and even though he only did the rebounds . . . and THEN HE WENT INTO THE HOSPITAL!" at which point he *really* started to cry.

Needless to say, for two weeks my son had carried the burden and responsibility of feeling he was responsible for his dad being hospitalized. Your book, with its guidance, anecdotes, and concrete, empirical suggestions, not only alleviated the obvious pain and guilt of one nine-year-old child but also helped me lay the groundwork for an ongoing avenue of communication that continues to this day. Within the last two weeks, we have discussed everything from illness to God, etc. My son and I have forged a wonderful bond and relationship that was unthinkable and inconceivable to me only a few weeks ago.

Not only am I a parent, but I am also an educator by profession. Your book is clear, concise, "reader-friendly," and I am sure will aid countless other families in the future.

My family was blessed to have been able to be helped by your book and we will always be grateful. I have extolled the virtues of your book to countless professionals in the past few weeks (and I have spoken to many). In fact, I am buying a copy for my son's school to have for future reference. I hope and pray that your book becomes a mainstay in every library and every school so that if (God forbid) other families should need it, it will be there for them.

Thank God, our story appears to have a happy ending—we hope my husband will be home within a few weeks—and that he will continue his recovery at home and resume work, fatherhood, etc., with the same gusto and *joie de vivre* as he enjoyed in the past. In the meantime, my sons and I will be different, stronger, and better able to communicate and weather whatever storms the future may have in store for us.

So once again, from the bottom of my heart, a sincere thank-you. May you live to enjoy a full and healthy and happy life!

—Jane and Josh, Sam and Matt

If there is one thing I wish I could tell other parents in the same boat, it is that, although this sucks, you and your kids will be okay.

—Joyce Callahan

Introduction to the First Edition

This book began without any of us realizing it.

As resident child life specialist at the Cleveland Clinic Foundation, I'd get a call, usually from the intensive-care unit.

A child has come in, seen his mother or father lying in a bed, pale as death, hooked into a battery of life-support drips and monitors, and the child has gone berserk, run screaming down the corridor. Could I come?

Or the child is sitting stiff and silent outside the intensive-care unit, refusing to speak. Could I come?

Or the child is behaving perfectly well, only the nurse thinks he should be crying his heart out. Could I come?

These things happen again and again in every big hospital. But gradually we came to realize:

As surely as the parents of sick and dying children need help and support, *the children of gravely ill parents need help and support*. Yet while almost every good hospital has a continuing program for parents of sick children, *there didn't seem to be any programs to help children whose mothers or fathers were seriously ill*.

With all our advanced techniques for treating serious disease, for saving or prolonging life, we in medicine have forgotten one very important affected group: the children of our patients.

We have a great deal of knowledge about children and stress. Yet there was no organized effort to pass that knowledge on to the parents, *to help them help their children.*

In most hospitals no counselor, no manual, was routinely at hand to tell parents what to expect from their children, and to work with the children from the moment of diagnosis through months or years of a parent's treatment. There was no continuous guidance on how to address children's questions and fears, from the darkest puzzlings about separation, change, pain, and death to the most mundane worries of "Who'll tuck me in?" "How will I get to soccer practice?"

There was no day-to-day counseling for the sick or the well parent about how to interpret their children's conduct and how to help children who were showing signs of trouble. What is "normal"? What is dangerously *not* "normal"? What signs can you look for? What warnings do children give? What can you say and do to maintain the mental and emotional health of your children through months or years of medical crisis, no matter what the final outcome?

Your Children: Part of Your Treatment

Out of that realization has come first our program and now this book.

From 1987 until 1995, if you, a parent, were admitted to the Cleveland Clinic with a serious or life-threatening illness, then as part of your treatment your children were entitled to the continuing services of our Child Life program for as long as they were needed. Over those nine years we worked with hundreds of families. We helped well over a thousand *normal* children survive and prevail through a terribly *abnormal* situation in their lives.

(That situation has changed; it's brought up to date in the Introduction to the Second Edition.)

Yet even when the children of Cleveland Clinic patients still had access to the free Child Life program, for other parents across America the problem remained: There was no guidance on how to bring their children through these devastating family medical crises. Parents had nothing in print they could routinely consult when they wondered about their children's reactions, their emotional well-being.

What was needed, I felt, was a *manual*—a book that would summarize the very best of our own and others' expertise, and guide Mom and Dad step by step through all the many turnings of how children respond to a parent's serious illness.

Perhaps, as you read this, you are thinking, "She's not really talking to me. *My* illness is treatable, it's curable." Please think again. If the illness is serious, if it will change you in some way, if it is causing you high levels of worry or stress, then it *will* affect your children. Most of you who read this will survive your medical crisis and return to a full, normal life. For you the aim of this book is to bring you and your children through even stronger, united, and ready to challenge the future. But please indulge me for just one moment: I want to tell you a story that involves a death. I tell it now, because it seems to me to make two vital points:

1. **Even in the face of ultimate tragedy, children can be prepared, can weather the trauma, can emerge whole and healthy and ready to go on with life.**
2. **On the other hand, children who are not prepared, not given the kind of support and understanding we'll be talking about throughout this book, can be permanently scarred by a parent's medical crisis, *even if the parent survives and returns eventually to full health.***

A Family Returns

You may remember it from the NBC Television report about our program. Nine months before, a young mother I'll call Samantha Marks had died after a long struggle with cancer. I'd been seeing her daughters—Annie, nine, and Carlie, six—all through her illness and after her death. But today was the first time their dad felt strong enough to return to the hospital where his wife had died.

Here is what he told a television audience about Annie and Carlie, and about Samantha's death:

"I told the kids the next morning. They cried for, I would say, a good twenty minutes. But then they . . . it seemed like they were prepared for it. Then they started comforting *me,* instead of losing it, as I thought they would."

Annie said this:

"She never goes out of my mind. But sometimes I'm not thinking about her; I'm having a good time. But she never left my mind."

I said, "She never leaves your mind, but it's okay for you, right, to have a good time, and play, and have friends, and laugh?"

Annie said, "Yeah. *That's what she probably wants us to do.*"

At our very first meeting, Samantha herself told me she thought she could let go of life a little more easily, knowing her children would be helped and supported through her death and afterward.

Helping You to Help Your Children

If you are reading this manual, something terrible and frightening is happening to your family. It is happening to you, it is happening to your partner, and it is happening to your children, and you're worried about them. You want them to come out strong and sound, ready for future happiness and success, whatever the medical outcome.

There are no "right" answers, but there *are* answers—there are questions your children will certainly ask; there are reactions, healthy and unhealthy, that you can observe and deal with. There are situations you can handle and resolve, and there are signs that can warn you your child needs professional help. Age is an important clue to what children may think and feel, so some of our discussions will be divided into age groups. You can see where your own children fit in. Of course, there are no sharp dividing lines between groups.

This handbook is drawn from the great and growing body of knowledge of how children think and react, from our own years of experience, and from the insights and experiences of other child health professionals. If, as I hope, our manual can help you now, please remember this:

It really belongs to all those other mothers and fathers who live with us, who have allowed us to share their struggle, who have died with us. Most of all it belongs to the children: the Survivors.

Introduction to the Second Edition

Very little has changed.

Everything has changed.

In the years since *How to Help Children Through a Parent's Serious Illness* first appeared, my continuing work with children, and your response to the book, have only deepened the truth of our first principles:

- You *must* tell your children the truth, however painful. You must never lie to them.
- Children are stronger than you think.
- Mistakes made with love are easy to correct.

These ideas, these guideposts for bringing your children safely through a family medical crisis or a family tragedy, have not changed, will not change. But how much else has changed!

What's New

When this book first appeared, the Internet was primarily a useful tool for adults running governments and corporations. Today just about every child goes to it unhesitatingly for information and, all too often, misinformation. And they tell each other all their secrets on their Facebook pages.

The science of genetics was a lusty, promising infant, but most of that promise was unfulfilled—biology still hadn't unraveled the human genome. In our first edition we emphasized the need to tell your children, "You can't catch this from me." But what do we tell them now, when science might say, "You may *already* have 'caught' this from me. *You may have inherited it*"?

In 1995, the family norm in America was two parents, living together—the first edition did offer some guidance to the single parent, but today the single parent has become America's new normal, and a great deal more attention must be paid.

HIV/AIDS then was an almost inevitably fatal disease, and in the first edition we treated it as such. Today, as I write, it's still not curable, but with proper treatment it's become a chronic disease, no longer a fatal one. Cancer—my own field of practice for the past ten years—remains a frustrating killer, but the number of survivors has vastly increased— one medical estimate suggests that three-quarters of a million cancer victims who would have died twenty years ago are alive today thanks to early diagnosis and advances in treatment. Partly as a result of that good news, more than a million and a half cancer survivors today are parents with children under age eighteen. Half a million American children today are living with a parent who's in the early stages of treatment for cancer.

The list goes on. Today's parents, facing a family medical crisis, confront a vast array of dangers and of opportunities undreamed of when this book first appeared. And so we felt the need to bring *How to Help Children* . . . into the twenty-first century. The core of the book, its central philosophy, remains unchanged. But new chapters and new sections address these new realities of parenting through a family medical crisis.

(The original text has been expanded and updated throughout this second edition.)

A Little Background

If you've read the previous introduction, you know how our Child Life program began—at the Cleveland Clinic Foundation, one of America's leading medical centers. There we found ourselves coping with hysterical children, terrified and out of control because of the sudden shock of seeing what a gravely ill parent looked like in a modern hospital room that might just be saving her life.

In the program we developed, your children were actually *entitled* to our care, at no additional cost, if you were a patient at the Cleveland Clinic. Other good teaching hospitals matched our program. But then came the financial crisis of the mid-'90s, with a particular squeeze on health care. How do you assign a dollar value to a healthy child—a child who survives a parent's grave illness or death and grows up to be a productive member of American society? How can you prove that child wouldn't have turned out just as well without a Child Life program? Our program, and others like it, could not show a bottom line—and so they were among the first to be cut back or cut out in that recession.

Along with those dramatic improvements in treatment of some of our dread diseases came, inevitably, a decline in the human factor—emotional and psychological support for the patients, their families, and particularly their children.

The new medical technologies required enormous investments of time, machinery, and technical skill—human contact had to suffer. Yet patients were becoming more and more aware of new, complementary ways of coping with their disease. They were asking: What should I be eating? What exercises should I be doing? Should I try yoga, massage, relaxation therapy, guided imagery? But their doctors and nurses, steeped in the protocols of Western medicine, had neither the time nor the training to provide answers.

Filling the Gap: Support Centers

As these human needs became painfully evident, dedicated health-care professionals and philanthropists around the country began devising community-based support centers, to provide the personalized, family help that the hospitals were retreating from (recently, many major hospitals have begun reinstating the family and child life programs).

In Cleveland, Eileen Saffran, a social worker in oncology whose parents had both died of cancer, got the idea for something she called "The Gathering Place—for individuals and families touched by cancer." In just eighteen months she brought it from an idea to reality; we opened our doors to the community as a new century dawned: January 2000. I became its first director of children's programs, and continue in that job today.

At The Gathering Place

Since The Gathering Place, and this century, opened, we've served some twenty-two thousand patients and their families, all at no cost to them. And a central focus has been treating the children of gravely ill parents—our goal is always to assure that, no matter what the outcome of the family's medical crisis, the children emerge whole, healthy, and ready to live full, rewarding lives.

Let me tell you of a moment that still makes me proud: A few years after The Gathering Place opened, we were nominated for a prestigious prize rewarding innovations in mental health. As a finalist, we got a visit from the chief of psychiatry at one of Cleveland's major hospitals. We took him through our Child Life program, documented to whatever extent we could our outcomes with the children of cancer patients, living and dead. I have never forgotten his words as he ended his visit:

> "I have been in the mental-health profession for forty-five years. I've seen all kinds of agencies, hospitals, clinics, outpatient services. They all called themselves 'mental-health' facilities, but really, they have all been about mental *illness*.

"I have to say: This is the first true mental-*health* program I have ever seen."

The Gathering Place won the prize.

The Bottom Line

Now, as you and I take this new journey together, to help your children through whatever the coming weeks, months, even years hold, perhaps you will be able to do what the medical profession has struggled so long to do: Place a bottom-line value on emotionally healthy children who are prepared to face a rich future, and enjoy brimming, fulfilling lives.

Taylor Haase, seven, draws two ways she copes with her dad's cancer—she's a "sunshine girl," playing outside in the sunlight, and a "chocolate girl"—eating her favorite treat.

I.

The First Day of the Rest of Your Life

You hear the words: "You have cancer."
"You have MS." "You have a brain aneurysm."
"You need a heart transplant." "You have AIDS."
The first thing you think about is your own life.
And the second thing is:
"What will happen to my children?"

Balancing Your Needs and Your Children's Needs

Here are two things that happened in our program at the Cleveland Clinic:

A young mother was being treated for cancer. She and her husband decided not to tell their nine-year-old son any details—too disturbing; why worry the boy? We'll just say Mom is sick; she'll be better soon.

But then he began "acting out" in school—fighting with classmates, disrupting classes, falling behind. So the parents brought him to our program.

When I met him, the boy was grumpy—angry with his family, annoyed at being haled before a child life counselor. Yet behind all that he wanted to talk, and very soon he did talk.

He'd overheard his father on the telephone, speaking gravely with a relative. He'd heard the words "malignant melanoma" and suspected they had something to do with cancer. And he was furious. He explained why in three sentences: "They didn't tell me everything. She's *my* mother. *I have the right to know what's going on.*"

The boy was absolutely correct. And what he said points up one of the central themes of this book: *The children of seriously or gravely ill parents always have the right to know what's going on. Not only is that knowledge their right*; it is one of their greatest *needs*.

The second story involves a father, a successful and self-assured businessman who was recently diagnosed with lung cancer. Once again, the parents decided not to tell their children, a nine-year-old girl and a six-year-old boy. The parents were pretty sure the children knew anyway, and they were right:

> ### *The children always know.* Or, at least, they always know *something.*

The normally cheerful little girl was constantly sad, suddenly breaking into tears. One night she begged her mother, "Whatever you do, tell me the truth. Tell me Daddy's going to be okay." Neither one realized that the little girl was asking for two different things. So the mother did what she thought right: She told her daughter something she wasn't at all sure of: "Of course he's going to be okay."

The boy's symptoms were even more disturbing: While previously he'd never shown much interest in toy guns and warfare, suddenly all his play was about killing. He ran around, indoors and out, making finger guns, shouting, "Bang, bang, you're dead." Death was the constant message; of his sister he said, "I just wish she was dead." The boy was now totally indifferent to his father; it was as if the father were not there.

Counseling the parents, I told them what to me was obvious and what is the central message of this book:

You must tell your children the truth.

We'll talk a good deal throughout this manual about why that's so. But for the moment, here are three reasons:

1. **Your children are affected by everything that happens in the family.**
2. **The more serious the situation, the more they will be impacted.**
3. **Lying to your children, in any way, will inevitably make things worse.**

But this father resisted. He was adamant that his children not be told of his lung cancer, *even though they obviously already knew.* And finally, he told me why:

"Don't you understand? If I tell the children I have cancer, *that means I really do.* How can I fight this thing, keep a positive attitude, do what the doctors say I must do, if I acknowledge that?"

Like the reaction of the boy in the first story, the father's reaction was absolutely normal. For *anyone* diagnosed with a serious illness, the first thought is for self: How can I live and fight, how will I handle the long, intense, perhaps painful course of treatment? How can I cope with the possibility, however unlikely, that I may not survive?

For a while, *everything revolves around self.* Only afterward come thoughts of family, of how this most personal crisis may impinge on the people we love. Yet the needs of those loved ones, particularly of our children, are immediate and pressing.

(In this case we reached a compromise: The father agreed that his wife should tell their children the full truth about his lung cancer. But she would also tell them, "Daddy can't talk about it now." Frequently, in the first days and weeks after diagnosis, it is the well parent who must deal most directly with children's needs and questions. We found an acceptable interim solution, until the father could deal both with the disease and with his children—until he *can* "talk about it now.")

Two needs collide: the patient's need to do whatever it takes to try to survive (if that includes fantasy and magic, so be it) versus the child's absolute, inescapable right and need to know the truth.

The tension between those two needs is where this book begins.

Making Your Children Part of Your Treatment

We believe very deeply that when a parent is seriously ill, the children must be treated right along with the adult. Indeed, the children's treatment is *part* of the parent's treatment.

Ideally, treating your children should begin on the day of diagnosis—the day you learn that you or your spouse or partner has a serious, possibly life-threatening illness. But as we'll see, the parents MUST get control of their own emotions, their own response to this looming medical crisis, before they can help their children toward what they need to understand. So we will offer continuing guidance on *what* to tell your children, *how* to tell your children, and, no less important, how to pick your moment: *when* to tell your children.

Keep this in mind:

It is almost never too late to start doing things the right way. Specifically, whatever point you may now have reached in your family medical crisis, whatever has already happened that may be creating problems for you and your children, *right now* is not too late to start handling things better. And that's because:

Mistakes made with love are easy to correct.

Avoiding the Biggest Mistake

The guiding principles, from the beginning to whatever the end may be, are *openness* and *honesty*.

Being honest can be painful. Nevertheless, dishonesty, even with the honorable goal of protecting the children, *may be the single biggest mistake you as a parent can now make.*

(Here's something to remember: Telling the truth doesn't necessarily mean telling *all* the truth, *right now.* We'll find instances where it's wise to delay some information. Whatever you do tell your children, whenever you tell them, it must be "the truth and nothing but the truth." But unlike the courtroom oath, it won't necessarily be "the whole truth"— not right away.)

Why?

We are looking at the rest of your children's lives. If they are deceived, lied to, "protected" from the truth, they will learn a lifelong lesson of distrust. There may be nothing more important in their lives than that they continue to trust the two people they love the most—the parent who is sick and the parent who will continue to care for them.

Counselors, psychologists, psychiatrists see them in their thirties and forties. And they say, "Doctor, I can't love anyone." And so often, when you look back, there was a real break in that love, during that person's childhood. Very often the break can be traced to the illness or death of a parent—a break never brought out and handled by the child.

Children Are Stronger Than You Think

There is one thing I count on absolutely in my work with families, and that you can count on now: Your children love you. Because they love you, they can handle what is coming; they are much stronger than you think possible. What we must do now is build on that love and so build that strength.

As this medical crisis forces its way into your life, and your children's, what we will try to do is maintain a sense of trust and continuity of parenting—so that, whatever happens, your children retain their trust in the world and in the people who care for them and care about them.

Three Things to Tell Your Children

Whatever your children's ages, what you are going to do at this point is

- **Tell them you are seriously ill.**
- **Tell them the name of your disease.**
- **Tell them your best understanding of what may happen.**

(As we'll see shortly, being honest does *not* mean telling everything. Children can absorb different levels of complexity at different ages, and you are the best judge of what your own child can understand. What it *does* mean, simply, is never telling anything but the truth.)

Before we go on to *how* to tell children at different ages, let me tell you one story that illustrates *why* they must be told.

A young mother was diagnosed with cancer. It was a kind of chronic leukemia whose treatment causes few visible symptoms; the parents decided they'd spare their nine-year-old daughter the worry. All the child knew was that Mom was going to the hospital now and again to get some medicine, not even staying overnight. No big deal.

One night, about two weeks after the mother was diagnosed, her daughter woke up in the middle of the night screaming.

She couldn't move her legs.

The little girl was rushed to Children's Hospital and evaluated thoroughly. There seemed to be no medical reason for her paralysis. The pediatrician, fortunately a very good one, asked the mother whether anything was going on in the family: A new baby? Marital problems? A move to a new house?

Nothing like that, she said, but there is this one thing.

The pediatrician, who'd had no idea the mother was ill, told her she *must* tell her daughter about the leukemia, tell her *right now*.

So together, Mom and Dad told her the truth: Mom has cancer. It's treatable and being treated. Mom honestly expects that she'll be okay.

And we're sorry to tell you this while you're sick, but we thought you should know.

The little girl said, "I'm glad you told me. I knew something was wrong. *I thought maybe you were getting divorced.*"

Within twelve hours she began to move her legs; two days later she was discharged from the hospital, and she has never had a recurrence. She still doesn't understand why she became paralyzed, *but she doesn't have to understand it.* She just needed to be treated with honesty.

A child can imagine much worse things than the truth.

The Three Ages of Childhood

As we begin to talk about how and what to tell your children, we'll divide them, very tentatively, into three overlapping age groups. Here as elsewhere, though, remember this: *You are the expert on your own children.* You know how they react, how mature they are, how they handle tough situations. When you think something's wrong, *something's wrong.* Follow your instincts; usually they won't lead you astray.

The three age groups, which require somewhat different handling (though always within the framework of total honesty), are:

- **Toddler to preschool,** from about age two to six. To help preschoolers understand a parent's cancer, I've written *Someone I Love Is Sick,* a children's book that you can customize to your own family's situation. It's available at The Gathering Place website, touchedbycancer.org, or at Amazon.com.
- **Latency,** or school-age, from about five or six years to twelve years.
- **Adolescence,** those terribly complicated teen years.

Generally, the first and third group need the most delicate handling. Latency age is usually just that; the child's potentials are *latent.*

He or she tends to be a little better adjusted, a little better able to cope, than an older or younger sibling.

But remember, there are no neat divisions in children's growth or behavior; these age divisions are anything but absolute. Your child may, probably will, slip back and forth between responses, may not even seem to fit his or her age group at all. These are general guidelines, and *wherever your child fits in is normal for your child*. And you, Mom or Dad, are the best judge.

Think about how we might tell a youngster in each group that a parent is seriously or gravely ill.

Explaining Your Illness to Your Preschooler

The family: father, mother, six-year-old boy, three-and-a-half-year-old boy. The father was diagnosed with a brain tumor.

The younger boy was bright and verbal; his parents thought he could understand the situation. Each time we met, both boys were present. Naturally the big brother was the little one's hero and role model. If the big boy looked sad, the little one knew he should look sad, and did.

At the first meeting, we talked about the brain, and how it is like a computer, how it runs everything else. Both boys understood that and how important it was; you could tell by watching their faces.

We maintained their concentration, particularly the younger boy's, by keeping everything very short—get the computer idea across, then play a little. With young children, that's extremely important; they can understand, but their attention span is like a hummingbird's.

And playing can be a marvelous tool. Take a doll or a stuffed animal. Say, "This is Daddy. Daddy's sick. What's the matter with Daddy?"

Use the language your child uses. If an injury is a booboo, talk about booboos:

"Daddy's got a booboo."

"Where?"

"Up here, in his head."

Take a nice bright Band-Aid, stick it on; the doctors are going to try to fix Daddy's booboo.

A parent can use a doll or stuffed animal just as well as a psychologist can. If the sick parent can do the explaining himself or herself, that is simply wonderful for the child. Hard on the parent, perhaps, but good for the child. And perhaps good for the parent as well. If you are the one facing that gravely uncertain future, everything you can do for your children will probably add to your own comfort. That's a thought we'll keep coming back to.

There's a difference between the three-and-a-half-year-old and the six-year-old. The parents told the older boy a little about the planned surgery, about the fact that the doctors were going to make a cut into Daddy's head to try to make him better. The younger boy wouldn't have understood about the incision; we left that out. Remember, being honest does not necessarily mean telling *everything* all at once. It means never telling anything but the truth. You can offer more of the truth as your child becomes ready.

(In later chapters, we'll talk about infants. You can't "tell" them what's going on. But in some very simple, important ways, you can make sure their world remains warm and secure in the midst of crisis.)

"I Think I've Ruined Her Life"

Before we leave this earliest age group, let me tell you one of the stories that gives me my absolute conviction: It's never too late to get things right for your children:

A young husband was beginning radiation therapy for lung cancer. In the corridor outside the treatment room, a nurse discovered his wife, sobbing. The nurse asked what was wrong. The woman murmured something about her five-year-old daughter. Then, quite clearly: "I think I've ruined her life."

The radiology people called me. I asked the mother what had happened. This was her story:

The family had not told the little girl anything about her father's illness. Five years old, they thought, was just too young. The morning before, Sunday, the family had gone to church. And the little girl had lit a candle and said this prayer: *"God, please make Daddy's cancer go away, so Mommy will stop crying."*

Mom and I sat and talked in the corridor for an hour. I told her what she might tell her daughter about her husband's cancer:

- Daddy has a bad sickness.
- The sickness is called "cancer."
- The doctors are treating Daddy now, and Daddy and I truly believe he will get better.

I assured her that a five-year-old could handle the situation. And I suggested some questions her little girl would almost certainly ask, questions we'll consider in the next section.

Afterward, the three of them went home and held a family meeting. They cried a lot, but they talked it all through, honestly. The mother called me several weeks later and said, "That was all we needed. We're communicating."

I never saw the little girl. I didn't have to.

Three Inevitable Questions

Sometimes I can predict the future.

I met with a young man about to undergo radiation therapy for cancer. He had two children in the preschool and school-age range. I told him they would have three immediate worries that he and his wife would have to confront:

1. **The children would suspect that somehow, because of something they had done or hadn't done, they had "caused" his cancer. This is called "magical thinking"; we'll meet it again and again. Young children believe in their own**

omnipotence; what happens around them happens *because of them*. *They can be overwhelmed by feelings of guilt for a situation totally outside their control.*

2. **The children would be afraid the illness was contagious, that by being with the parent, they too could "catch" cancer.**

3. **The children would want to know who would take care of them, who would do the "Daddy things," while Daddy is sick.**

The father called me several weeks later and said, "I can't believe my kids did all three of those things you said they'd do." Not all at the same time or the same place, but in those weeks, all three of those questions came up, repeatedly. *They are the three universal concerns of children in those years.*

The Three Right Answers

How do you handle the three universal concerns? Head-on, with unequivocal answers. And be prepared: They'll come up again and again.

You don't need to go into detail for the first two; you can say something perfectly straightforward, along these lines:

"I don't know for sure how I got it. But I do know two things:

"*Nothing you ever did made me get it.*

"*You can't get it from me. No one else can catch this cancer.*"

For the third concern, you *will* want to go into detail. And you'll want to give it some thought.

Remember that, especially for younger children, *routine equals security*. The family's routine is about to be disrupted, and you want to keep the disruption to a minimum for your children. Think about how you'll maintain their routine: Who'll babysit when Mom takes Dad to the hospital; how will your children get to and from band practice, soccer practice, the party on Saturday night? Tell them, in detail.

At the same time, reassure your children that they have a role to play in taking care of the sick parent. In the next chapter we'll talk about what some of those roles may be, but remember: They're entitled to help.

Explaining Your Illness to Your Six- to Twelve-Year-Old Child

In addition to wanting answers to the three inevitable questions, this latency-age group is going to want some detail about the illness. Starting at about age six, children become intensely interested in bodies, their own and other people's. You can expect some pretty close questioning as to exactly what is wrong with you and what the doctors are going to do about it.

Tell the truth, without embarrassment. And try to get your medical people to cooperate.

Want to See?

Ask the child: Would you like to see how the doctors are going to try to help Mom or Dad? Most young children jump at the chance; some of the older ones are a little more leery. Don't press; the child must *want* to go and see.

In many hospitals, when a parent is to receive radiation treatment or chemotherapy for cancer, or is awaiting an organ transplant, the staff will allow or even encourage you to bring your children to the evaluation session. Check with the hospital staff on who can help orient your children: "My husband is waiting for a liver transplant/prostate surgery/radiation—can you help my children understand what's going on?" That's when the technicians and the nurses can show the children all around the floor, explain how the doctors and nurses will be taking care of Mom or Dad. Often they'll take a doll or stuffed animal into the treatment area and "treat" it just as they will the parent.

Ask whether your hospital has a child life program in its pediatrics department, and if the staff is available to help you. These professionals are the people best equipped to introduce your children to the treatments their parent will undergo.

If the intensive-care unit is viewable, it's a good idea to take the children there, to give them an idea of what will be done for Mom or Dad and to get them accustomed to what goes on, so they'll be prepared and will understand what's happening when their own parent is lying there, surrounded by drips and monitors. (This kind of visit must be handled with great care and timing, so the children are *not* exposed to scary scenes that will add to their anxiety.)

If you will be treated on an outpatient basis, frequently the outpatient staff and even your treating physician will welcome a visit by your children to their clinic and will help them understand your treatment program.

All this is important right now, but it's also important in the long run: Whatever the outcome of the parent's treatment, the child offered this kind of respect and understanding is less likely to resent and fear the medical professionals, less likely to resist treatment and so jeopardize his own life, years from now.

Explaining Your Illness to Your Teenager

On the other hand, sometimes you *can't* predict the future. Usually the first thing I say to the parents of adolescents is, "If I could predict how your teenager will respond to this, I'd be a miracle worker. Nobody *ever* knows how a teenager will respond."

The fact is, a teenager facing a parent's illness may go off in all kinds of different directions, and that's okay—that's normal.

A parent's grave illness brings demands that most teens don't even begin to know how to handle. As adolescents, they're struggling to move away from the family. Now what should they do? Move back and help? Or run as fast as they can in the other direction? A parent's illness can create acute levels of psychological and emotional conflict.

Information, Please

Most adolescents seem to need an enormous amount of information; they want to be treated pretty much as adults. Not only will they want the basic information of the diagnosis, they'll also ask for the technical terminology, the statistical information on survival rates. The depth of their questioning may astonish you. And you mustn't duck. If you don't know, say, "Let's find out."

Today there is a new source of information literally at your children's fingertips—a source undreamed of fifteen years ago. Used properly, the Internet can be enormously valuable in helping your children cope with this family medical crisis. But used improperly, or without supervision, the same Internet can terrify—can pose grave dangers to your children's mental and emotional well-being at this moment of great stress. Chapter 5 aims to help you use, and prevent your children from misusing, this razor-sharp two-edged sword.

Keeping the Faith

Of all the age groups, adolescents are the most sensitive to deception and dishonesty—and so the most likely to lose faith in adults. In a way, *they want to lose faith in adults*—it's part of that normal process of moving away, into their own adulthood. So it's very easy for them to pick up an evasion or a white lie, and say, "Well, Dad's a liar; I'm not going to believe anything he tells me."

Privacy: Theirs and Yours

Privacy is a very important issue to teenagers; you can't force yourself inside their heads. You give the information and then wait: They may or may not talk to you. What's important is that they have *someone* to talk to. So if you know your teen talks from the heart to a best friend, the parent of a pal, a teacher, a coach, a minister or rabbi, then encourage him or her to share this new crisis with a surrogate.

You might promise your child: What she tells the surrogate will be confidential; the surrogate won't be reporting back to you. But both child and surrogate must understand: If your child starts contemplating harmful behavior—to herself or others—or if she's starting to think suicidal thoughts—then the surrogate *must* report that to you.

There's another consideration here: your own privacy. Probably you do not want the news of your illness "spread all over town." And you have every right to set guidelines: It's *your* family, *your* body, *your* illness. On the other hand, your teenager *must* have someone other than you to talk to. Within those two sets of needs—your need for privacy, your teenager's need to talk—is there someone you can personally share this illness with, tell him or her that your child knows what's happening and may want to talk?

If you particularly do *not* want your son or daughter talking to teenage friends, *then you must be very clear about that from the outset*—and you must give the child another outlet. A teen's natural behavior is to go to other teens.

You can say quite honestly, "This is a very private illness. I don't want everyone in town talking about me. I'll be embarrassed if people treat me differently. So: I love you, I want you to know the truth, I know you need to talk, and here's who you can talk to. But I don't want this all over town, at least not yet."

This is not dishonesty. It is family privacy. And it's perfectly all right.

Giving Your Children Hope

However grave the illness, hope comes along with every diagnosis. And it is neither wrong nor dishonest to pass this hope along to your children. Your physician may tell you there is a 15 percent chance of survival. That gives you a *chance*; there is treatment and you're determined to make the most of it. Other people have licked this thing, and you will too. That is what, being totally honest, you can tell your children. Give them *your understanding* of what's happening and what can happen.

If you tell your children what you yourself truly believe and hope, even if there's a somewhat different spin from what the doctors may have said, then there is no dissonance; it fits. Only when you tell them something you *don't* believe does the dissonance overwhelm their security, and their confidence in you.

Fears of Dying: First Thoughts

Faced with the news of a parent's grave illness, many children are going to wonder: *Will you die?*

They may or may not ask the question. I've found in my practice that only about half the children actually ask it out loud. They may ask it now or months from now. Nevertheless, however far the idea may be from your own thoughts, you must be prepared for the question. And to be prepared for it, *you need to know what your child thinks death is.*

A two- or three-year-old child may talk about death, may have a sense of its sadness. But a very young child can never really discuss it, never understand its consequences—above all, its finality.

By the time children are mid-school-age, around nine, ten, or eleven, they have come to grips with the central idea of death. Most children know, by this age, that death is final, that you don't return from it, and that it is inevitable. It will happen to everyone.

Having an ill parent, who may die, probably forces children to tackle the issue sooner than they might otherwise. So what do they need from their parents?

First, what they do NOT need is a promise you cannot keep. If your disease *is* potentially fatal, it's an easy, tempting thing to say at this moment—you may want to hear yourself say it—but it's a serious mistake:

"I promise not to die."

Instead, once again, tell them the truth: "Well, I hope I won't die. I'm going to do everything I can to not die from this."

Don't be afraid to tell school-age children, "Everybody dies some-time, you know that. But I'm going do my very best to get better and stay with you guys."

It is never wrong to have hope and to give your children hope. But it *is* wrong to make a promise to a child that you may not be able to keep.

What children do need is to understand their parents' beliefs about what death is and what may or may not come after. That means, for one thing, you will have to understand and be able to articulate your own beliefs. And, whether the subject comes up immediately, on that day of diagnosis, or months later, you will want to be careful.

Marcy's Monster

On the next page is a picture and its story.

A young father had died of cancer. He'd been treated in a local hos-pital, diagnosed as terminal, and simply sent home, with no support for him, for his wife, or for Marcy, their eight-year-old daughter. It was ap-palling care.

A few days later, at home, he died.

The hospital staff had given the mother virtually no meaningful in-formation; she hadn't known what to tell her daughter and so had told her nothing. Now, night after night, Marcy would wake up screaming: She was sleep deprived, almost out of her mind with fear.

Because Marcy herself had once been a patient at our institution, we brought her into our program. In trying to find out what was wrong, I asked her to draw a picture.

What she drew was shocking: A little girl is alone in her bedroom. In through the window floats a demon figure.

And then her story came out. Marcy's father had once been in trouble with the law. It wasn't a major infraction; he'd been picked up and briefly jailed on a charge of driving under the influence of alcohol.

But the family, deeply law-abiding and religious, had made a great fuss. And Marcy had picked up the idea:

When Daddy died, he'd go to hell.

Now the father she'd loved had become the monster of her picture. Every night, all night, she dreamed he was coming to take her to hell with him. She would try to run to her mom, but his fingers would aim a magic beam at her door, and it wouldn't open. She would dream she was pulling at the door, screaming, as her demon/father flew down to grab her. And she would wake up screaming.

In the end, we worked through it. The mother explained to Marcy that her father had been a good man, that mom herself deeply and truly believed he was now in heaven. (They also worked past another piece of bad advice. Someone had told the mother it would be wrong to let the troubled little girl sleep with her. We decided, under the circumstances, it was okay, at least until Marcy felt more secure. Follow your own instincts, not other people's ideas.)

Feeling Free to Question

Above all, when the subject of death arises, your children will need the topic to be completely open, so that at any point from the first day on, they feel free to ask any question and have it answered honestly, without evasion, without embarrassment.

At some point, if a parent is truly at risk of dying, children need to understand the permanence of death, and that someone who dies does not come back. It's acceptable, it's normal, for children to wish, to hope, to imagine that this time death will somehow be different. All you can do is remind them that it's okay to wish, but the truth of the matter is that when people die, they don't come back. And when your children are ready to make that leap, they will.

Something to Think About Now

All life is terminal. Even if one's own timetable is tragically shortened by a medical diagnosis, the end is not yet. There is still time, time for children and parents who love each other to make the most of. Don't try to shield your children from making the most of that time.

TELLING YOUR CHILDREN: A SUMMARY

All Children, All Ages (page 18)
Tell them these three things:

- Mom or Dad is seriously ill
- The name of the disease
- Your best understanding of what may happen

Preschool Age (page 20)

- Explain the disease on the child's level
- Use dolls or puppets to help
- Don't go past the child's attention span
- Don't go beyond the child's ability to understand

School Age (page 24)

Tell them three things, and keep telling them:

- Nothing they did caused the disease
- They can't catch the disease from you
- Who'll take care of their needs—who will do the "Mommy things" or the "Daddy things" now

If possible, let them talk to the doctors and nurses, and see where and how Mom or Dad will be treated.

Teenage (page 25)

- Give lots of detailed information; answer every question fully
- Make sure there is someone outside the immediate family with whom they can talk on a continuing basis
- Be prepared for anything

Jackie Schmauch, thirteen, pictures herself animé-style, as she thinks about the questions raised in her mind by a double blow—her father undergoing a bone marrow transplant for leukemia as her mother is diagnosed with breast cancer.

2.
Getting It Together

BOINGG!

She told me, "I feel like the rope in a tug-of-war."

She was a young mother; her husband was in the hospital just beginning chemotherapy before a bone marrow transplant—he'd be there at least five or six more weeks. She looked terrible. And this is what she said:

"I feel like a rope, with a lot of tentacles coming out. My husband needs me available all the time. My in-laws, and the people in my own family, want information; they're constantly coming to me with questions and, 'Well, tell him this, ask the doctor that.' And the children need me more than ever before; there are three of them and they're pulling three different ways.

"And all these people have hold of these tentacles, and here I am in the middle, and I'm being stretched out in so many directions—I'm stretched as far as I can go. I don't even know how to pull back in; there's just nothing left . . .

"Kathleen, I'm going to go BOINGG!"

So now, as you and your children begin preparing for the first, acute period of a loved one's illness, the primary aim of this chapter is to keep *you* from going *"BOINGG!"*

The Next Few Weeks or Months

We're talking now about how to cope with the first few weeks or months of a medical crisis, a time of intensive treatment and vast disruption of family life. (Chapter 8 deals with long-term chronic illness, when a parent's medical condition must become a *routine part* of your family's life.)

Once again, let me make a prediction:

You and your family have just had a terrific shock. One spouse has been diagnosed with cancer and must begin a tough series of radiation or chemotherapy treatments. Or the diagnosis calls for an organ transplant, and now the patient must wait—in the hospital or at home—until one becomes available. Or there's a brain aneurysm, a leaking blood vessel, calling for immediate, delicate surgery.

You will find that this acute medical situation divides itself into two phases.

The First Phase

Whatever the diagnosis, the first few days, the first phase, will almost arrange itself. You'll find yourself putting your normal life on "hold." Of course the well spouse can have two or three days off from work—take a week!—to cope with the situation. If the kids are out of school for a couple of days, so be it. Family members rally 'round; they even come in from out of town to help in any way they can, or just to be there for you.

And then everything changes.

The Second Phase

You and your children must begin to settle in for days, weeks, or months of continuing crisis. The well parent has to go back to work; the kids must return to school. Some of the help disappears; family from out of town goes back home.

And yet the medical crisis is unresolved; the chemotherapy, the wait for a heart or liver or kidney, the delicate and frightening surgery, and the slow recovery are *still at the core of your family's existence*. You and your children must find a way to take your lives *off* "hold" *amid a continuing crisis*.

The Roller Coaster

This opening period is one of the hardest for families; everything is new and everything has to be invented as you go. And now, for the first time, parents and children are going to encounter the emotional roller coaster ride of acute illness. The ups and downs are going to be wrenching at first; later on, you and the children will become more used to them.

But right now you'll find that the patient feels good one day, lifting your spirits, then feels rotten the next, bringing everyone down. The prognosis will be optimistic, then pessimistic, then optimistic again. You, the well parent, will think you've finally got everything under control—and the next morning all your careful planning will fall apart.

Families who come to me in these early days tell me how the unpredictable ups and downs are simply tearing them apart emotionally, and I have to say to them, *"It's going to be like that. What you're going through now is the norm."* This first, acute period of a medical crisis is one of the hardest times for families, and it's what we're going to try to prepare for now.

Preparing Your Children

One of the first things you'll want to do is give your children a kind of warning: The sick parent *and the well parent* are going to be distracted, maybe a little shaky emotionally. Sometimes the children will find one or both of them grumpy. The children may feel ignored, and they may be right; at times neither parent will be able to pay attention. If you let your children know these moments are coming, and why, they'll handle them a lot better when they do occur. *Your children do want to help.*

Explain too that the relationship is going to be especially tough for the sick parent. Go into a little detail about exactly how that parent is feeling now. Yet even as sick as that, Mom or Dad is still your mom or dad, and still wants to be involved in whatever happens in your life now. You'll have to cut each other a little slack.

Some Helpers to Relieve the Stress

First, let's see about cutting off some of those tentacles that can make you feel you'll go *BOINGG.* The fact is, some of those well-intentioned people who are stretching you can become part of the solution.

One of the quickest ways to find relief is to designate a *family communicator.* Draft a brother, sister, cousin, grandmother to keep in touch with you and with all those circles of concerned relatives, friends, and acquaintances. Politely steer all calls for information, advice, chitchat to the communicator; explain that he or she will have the latest medical reports and will pass on messages to you every day. *Get yourself off the phone.*

There's another ally you probably already have: your phone answering machine or your voice mail.

"Hi, thanks for calling. John's latest medical reports look good; he may be up to some visiting next week. We're a little busy around here now, so please leave a message, and I'll update this information every couple of days." Again, the important stuff will get through, but *you stay off the phone.*

And at some point you may simply have to tell it the way it is: Let friends and relatives know how stressed you are, and say, "We really appreciate your help and concern, but, please, *lay off us for a while.*" If you don't feel like saying that right out, perhaps your communicator or even a hospital social worker can do it for you.

New Help: The Web

Today there's a new, powerful, and tremendously useful tool for family communication: The Internet.

A series of organizations now sponsor user-friendly websites where you can set up your own pages to communicate with family, friends, well-wishers. Here are three:

MyLifeLine.org
CarePages.org.
CaringBridge.org

These sites offer families and friends a whole new way to stay in touch. Go to any of them, and you'll find clear, click-by-click instructions on setting up your own website. All three offer videos of how you can use the site to your advantage.

You can coordinate care and help; you or your "web supervisor" can even set up rotating lists of who'll take the kids to what activities, who'll bring a casserole on which night. You can post family pictures along with your medical updates and comments.

The sites are interactive; not only do you get to put up regular, timely updates on what's going on, but the folks you love and like can post their own messages of comfort, encouragement, and hope. Caregivers can ask for volunteers when some part-time help is needed.

And you control access. You can open your site so anyone can read and post notes, or restrict it by password so only the people you designate can read and write on your website.

As we'll see in chapter 5, the Internet can be a two-edged sword when it comes to serious illness in the family. But these family websites seem to me to have no downside; try one and see what you think.

Volunteers: Grab 'em!

So often a stressed parent will tell me at the beginning of a medical crisis, "Everybody *wants* to help, but nobody *helps!*" That urge to help is real, but it's transient—after a while, it goes away. So now, at the beginning, is the time to grab it, focus it, and put some lines out for the future.

Figure out specific things that will help, and ask for them. You're not imposing; people like to feel useful, and after all, they *did* bring it up.

- "Could you make a casserole?"
- "Gosh, I've got three loads of laundry sitting by the washing machine—could you possibly . . . ?"
- "It would be wonderful if somebody could take the kids to McDonald's tonight . . ."

All of this can provide immediate relief and help bring you back to your center. And a little more thought can extend the help into the future.

Remember, while the *will* to help is going to continue, people eventually stop *offering*. At first, when a family member goes to the hospital or comes home with a new disability, people rally round to offer assistance. That impulse usually doesn't last too long: People are not always generous over the long run. After a while, they fade back into their own lives and you find yourself living alone with the crisis.

So in those first, generous days, try to think of some of the help you'll need *in the future*, and start to put some strings on it. The outpouring is there: Grab it! "We're in good shape right now, but soccer season starts in two weeks, and Danny's going to need some rides; may I call you then?"

It may be a little difficult to think that far ahead, but anything you can take care of now, while friends and family are eager to help, will certainly pay dividends in the future—when, three days before Danny's first soccer game, you can simply pick up the phone and say, "Hi. Remember your nice offer to drive Danny . . . ?"

As Time Goes By

Of course you can't think of everything in that first, frantic week or two. You're going to continue to need help, but as days become weeks and months, you'll receive fewer and fewer offers. Yet that helping impulse is still there; it's just that people are thinking about other things. Those tentacles are still tugging at you, so now you have to reach out for the help. Many people are a little timid about *asking* for help, and that's unfair to the helpers: They *want* to be there for you. Helping makes people feel good.

And if you're still shy, think of getting someone else to ask for you. That's where the professionals at your hospital can come in. Counselors and social workers can be pretty insistent on behalf of clients.

"How Would You Feel . . . ?"

I met with a young couple. The mother was beginning chemotherapy for her cancer. First, of course, we talked about their two children and the need to be absolutely truthful with them. They agreed on a family meeting to do that. But then, as I thought we'd about wrapped things up, the mother said:

"You know, there is something else I need to ask about: How about the rest of my family? I haven't told anybody about this thing, and I come from a big family: I have six brothers and sisters. But I don't know if I can tell people about it; *I don't want them to feel they have to do stuff for me,* and I don't want them to hang around looking sad all the time. I need them to be happy, not worried about me. I don't want them to be different."

It came pouring out, all the ambivalence about what to tell the family, and whether to impose—the same kind of concerns you may be having right now. And after she got it all out, I asked her, "If this happened to one of your sisters, if she were dealing with this and she didn't tell you, *how would you feel?*"

She said, *"I'd be furious."*

And that, of course, was the right answer.

People diagnosed with serious diseases, and their immediate families, need support from the people who love and care about them. The love is there, the help is there.

So: If it happened to people you love, and they *didn't* call on you, *wouldn't you be furious?* In a sense, you owe it to your family and friends to let them in and let them help.

Everybody wins.

Getting Help from Your Children

Start with three ideas:

- When the family is in crisis, most children *want* to help. But:
- They want to do what *they* want to do.
- The help you can expect will depend on your children's ages, their personalities, and your own family style.

You need to be creative about the assistance you ask from your children, and you need to make sure they still have time and space to do their own things.

The amount of help and the *kind* of help will differ from child to child, age group to age group, family to family. It will depend on

- The personality of each child
- The child's relationship to the sick parent
- The child's tolerance of the yuck quotient

One child's being helpful might be carrying out the emesis basin, while another's is just staying out of the way and not being too demanding. Both can be equally helpful, can chop off tentacles. Remember, children, whatever the task, *need to be praised for their help.* The praise will make them feel good and appreciated, and will encourage more help in the future.

Don't Assume

A lot of parents, in my experience, seem to assume their children will somehow *know* what's needed from them, *know* they have to be good now. *Wrong.* Children are by nature focused on themselves; their world revolves around them, and that world owes them growing up. Only as they do grow up will they become more outward-oriented, less self-centered.

So it's very healthy for your child to be self-oriented and self-protective. But this means that, when your children are in that stage, any request for change is a big one, and their help should be praised. It should never be taken for granted.

A Promise

Before we go into the specifics of the help you can ask of your kids, let me make you this promise:

> **Your children have reserves of strength and character that you have never called on, and never dreamed of.**

Parental illness shakes up a family, provides an opportunity for new behaviors, and *some of those opportunities are wonderful.* They can actually help children to grow in ways they might never have grown without the crisis.

I've seen children become more self-sufficient, develop self-confidence and independence. I've seen brothers and sisters learn to get along with each other.

I've seen them learn to cook!

So a great deal of good for your children can come out of this crisis if you *use* them, *encourage* them, *expect* the help you need, and *praise* them for giving it.

Everyone Has a Job

Right from the beginning, make it clear to the kids "In this time of trouble for our family, *everyone has a job.* Mom's job is to get treated and get well; anything beyond that, we'll all have to divvy up. Dad's job is to go to work and to be there for Mom and you kids.

"For you guys, the first job is school. Even with all that's going on here, even though you're worried about Mom, even though I'm going to need your help around the house: *The first job is school.* Mom and I expect that, no matter what's happening, you'll continue to work, keep up your grades, keep making us proud of you. Failure is not an option."

Help from Toddlers and Preschoolers

At preschool age, the help is probably more *for* them than *from* them. Can your four-year-old tell time? Ask him to remind you when Daddy needs to take his medicine. Send him in to ask Dad, "What would you like to drink with the pills?" Keep in mind that the child will want to do something that involves *direct contact* with his sick parent—asking him to vacuum the rug won't do it.

Help from School-Age Children

At this age you can start to look for some real help. Get the children involved in the planning: Have a meeting with them and divide up the chores the sick parent can't do. Make a list together.

Mowing the lawn
Laundry
Pet care
Sorting the recyclables
Cooking
Doing the dishes
Washing the car
House cleaning
Shopping
Snow removal

Write down all the things that must continue to be done, medical crisis or no, then parcel them out among yourselves. You can start by asking for volunteers, then divvy up the jobs nobody really wants but that have to be done.

Help from Teens

Our list is cumulative. So in addition to all of the above, you can ask the teens to help care for younger siblings. This is a huge sacrifice—which is why, after some complaining, they'll feel very good when they do it, especially when you tell them what a terrific help they are.

But be prepared to head off the opposition:

"Aw, Ma, I don't want to stay with the little dork again."

"Well, it has to be done—do you have a better idea?"

"Sure. Hire a sitter."

"Honey, you know how tight money is right now, with Dad so sick. I really need you to do this. But—maybe I can do something for you?"

Saying Thanks

Any little extra privilege is a good way to say thank you. Permission to stay up an extra half hour weeknights. An afternoon with Play-Station or Xbox at a friend's house. Watching *Vampire Diaries* even *before* homework is done. An hour past curfew Saturday night.

Trying to Be the Grown-Up

Sometimes, knowingly or not, a child will try to take on a parental role, almost seeming to step into the shoes of the sick parent. You may notice your child

- Becoming a disciplinarian for younger siblings
- Becoming overly protective and overly concerned for the *well* parent—assuming a role as surrogate wife or husband
- Becoming generally bossy, trying to run the household

All this is a matter of degree, and both parents will have to make judgments. Taking on some level of responsibility is a good thing for a child and for the family in crisis; it's to be encouraged. But the parents must draw a line that their children are not to cross. Generally, children should be expected and encouraged to take over necessary *jobs* in the household; they should *not* be expected or encouraged to take over a parental *role*.

The well parent should make a mental check: Am I *expecting* my son or daughter to take on the role of semiparent? If that's the case, the well parent must consciously back off from those expectations.

Try to avoid catchy phrases like, "Well, Timmy, looks like you're going to be the man of the house for a while." And make sure well-meaning relatives don't lay that kind of message on Timmy.

Even if a child must take on some kind of a parenting role temporarily, be very clear when that job will end: "I know, sometimes when I'm away with Mom at the hospital, you have to tell your little brother what he should and shouldn't do. But remember, that's just for now; when Mom comes home, she'll still be Mom. You won't have to be in charge anymore."

It's wise to put that positive spin on the prospect, because sometimes children (just like the rest of us) don't want to give up authority. So it's important that they know, right from the start, that any grant of power is temporary. Mom will still be the mom; Dad will still be the dad. That's the best way for the whole family.

Help: How Intimate?

Just how helpful can your children be in actually caring for their bedridden parent? There's no absolute answer; what you can ask of them depends on your family's own style and your children's own sensitivity. Most children will want to be involved; they'll be both curious and interested in some of the intimate details of medical care.

Children are intrigued by medical equipment; they like to watch what's going on, and watching can lead to participation. Young children may like to sit there while you change the central line or an ostomy bag for the patient. They'll want to hand you things, to "help." They won't necessarily want to *do* the hands-on things, *but they like to think they're helping in some way.* And as long as they're not getting in the way of proper medical procedure, that's fine—let them. But:

Don't push them to do anything they're uncomfortable with. If a child doesn't want to do some intimate chore, and there's someone else available (including you), then get it done without the child. Over time, the child may *want* to get more involved, if you don't push now.

But if and when your child expresses an interest in helping with a personal function—emptying a bedpan, changing a bag—that's fine.

A Matter of Style

Think about your family style with regard to privacy, intimacy, nudity. If you've taught your children all along that bodies are private, and then you want them to change the pants on an incontinent parent, *you're violating what you've been teaching all along,* and that's going to set up serious conflicts.

The family that sits in a hot tub together with little or no clothing on will have fewer boundaries than the family whose motto is, "Shut the door."

Curiosity

Remember, *children are fascinated with bodies*—their own and yours too. Many children are extremely curious about surgery; they want to *see* what happened! This will be a matter of the *parent's* comfort level: If you can describe what the doctors did to you, so the child is prepared for what he's going to see, then "seeing" will probably be a good, uniting experience for both of you . . . an intimate memory to share.

What will probably happen is, "Oogh, that's really gross!" and then you'll both be fine—down comes the shirt, and it's still the same old Dad lying there. If the child doesn't ask to see, it's okay to offer.

For younger children, before you show them the real thing on the real body, it's a good idea to represent it on a doll, stuffed animal, or drawing.

And of course, if the child chooses not to look, that's fine—don't press.

More on Helping

When we find ways for the children to help—*really* help—we're doing the best job for them. It's not just chores. There can be little—or even pretty big—sacrifices: postponing a birthday party, or having it over at Grandma's house, nobody coming to Parents' Night, not enough money for band camp this year.

If your child's normal behavior is to slam doors, roar through the house, generally drive even a well parent crazy, then just acting differently—acting against her normal behavior—is a way for the child to help.

Rather than follow your natural impulse, which might be to scream, "Don't you know I'm sick? You're the most thoughtless child!" put it in a positive light:

"Look, just for a while, I need you to think about being quiet—not running, not slamming things. That's going to be a big help." Anything that gives your child a concrete task to fulfill is going to make him feel great about himself, now and in the long run.

In a way, it's like training a puppy: A little praise is going to buy you a lot of good behavior. When a puppy happens to make his puddle where you want him to make his puddle, it's, "Goooood puppy; oh what a gooood doggy you are!" And when you notice that your child has done something helpful without being reminded, tell him, "I've been feeling so crummy; I couldn't even think about taking out the trash; it's *wonderful* that you did that!" Very few children—very few of the rest of us, either—really hate being a bit overpraised.

Helping Your Children

So that's how they can help you. Now, how can you help them? Because a lot of things about a parent's illness can make your kids go *BOINGG*! too.

In the next chapter, we're going to look for signs of trouble in your children. But here, at the beginning, we can try to head off the trouble.

Helping Your Infants, Toddlers, and Preschoolers

For the smallest members of your family, the three most important issues are:

security, security, and security.

From the moment of diagnosis, their house is not their home—not the home they knew. There's a flurry of activities; people coming and going; phones ringing and endless murmured phone conversations. It's all scary, and it's bad for your children's stability. And you can't really control it.

What you can control is *routine* and the security it represents. Try to keep your children on their old schedule:

- Preschool
- Mealtimes
- Naptimes
- Story time
- Bedtime

If *you* can't handle keeping the routines going, get help from friends and relatives who can. Ideally, your *toddler's* life will stay the same; all the other stuff is grown-ups' problems.

Home and Away

At some point, you may have to farm your young children out for a while—you may have to spend days or weeks with your husband or wife at a hospital in a different city. Here again, the wisest course is the least disruption.

You'll probably have a lot of offers from friends and family to take your kids. *Pick one.*

There's a natural tendency to set up a rotation, to say, "Well, Grandma can have them from Friday through Sunday, and then Cousin Marge will do Monday and Tuesday . . ." Your idea is not to impose too much.

But for the good of the children, you're going to *have* to impose.

For a baby, moving out of his own home is hugely disruptive. After that, every additional move is still more disruptive, and the pattern can have long-term consequences. Moved and moved again, your infant learns to distrust his environment. Just when he's taught one grownup which cry means "I'm hungry" and which means "I'm wet," he must start all over again, training a new stranger. The lesson he begins to learn is, "I can't really trust people to meet my needs."

Constant house shifting during a crisis can damage a child's ability to trust and be close to others later in life. So when your kids—especially your littlest kids—must go away to someone else's house, they should stay in that house until they can come home.

Doing it that way also chops off a couple more tentacles for the future. You'll have more help available the next time you need someone to take care of them, from all the folks you didn't impose on this time.

Helping Your School-Age and Teenage Children

For your older children, you'll want to make sure the school—which means teachers, guidance counselors, and school nurse—knows what's going on. These people will be your allies in watching over your children's emotional health and looking out for signs of trouble. Get them on board right at the start.

If your children will be living away from home, make sure the school people know that they won't be able to get back in the house for a while, won't be able to dig out old notes or use the family computer.

Doing Their Thing

At the same time you and your children are divvying up the jobs that have to be done, you'll want to look out for another set of needs—theirs.

What's going on in their lives over these coming weeks and months? What has to be done to keep *their* routines going?

Are exams coming up? Will they have the time and materials they need for studying?

How is Tommy going to get home each Tuesday and Thursday after band practice? Who'll get Sheila to her girlfriend's birthday party—with a present!—on Saturday night, and who'll get her home on time?

And how about Sheila's own birthday, three weeks from now? Can she still have the party? Could we possibly switch it to someone else's house? That would surely be a big help!

Work together, with a datebook or one of those calendars that have big blocks to write in.

It's hard for kids to plan for the future, but now is a good time to get them started. They'll feel responsible—feel good—working with you to make up a schedule. And the better they get at looking ahead, the more certain it is that the things they want and need will still be there for them.

Thinking of You

When a parent is going into the hospital for more than a night or two, we like to suggest they stay in touch with their children, just to let them know Mom or Dad is thinking about them. One way, of course, is little notes sent home from the hospital. But more than that: While you're packing, tuck away a few messages your kids can discover as they go through their days. An "I miss you too" in a bookbag, or "Blow 'em away, Babe" in a trumpet case or "Sorry I'm missing the game, but I'm rooting for you guys" in a gym bag can give that little lift, provide the occasional reassurance that we're still all together in each other's hearts.

For the younger kids, inexpensive little toys, with little love-ya notes, can show up unexpectedly in the mailbox or under a pillow.

It really doesn't take much to maintain the bond, and these little surprise love taps will provide as much of a lift for you as for your children.

Doing Your *Thing*

All we're talking about is part of *parenting*—your children's central need; usually it's automatic, but in this time of crisis, *you have to deliberately parent your children.* In the midst of all those tentacles pulling at you, you must stay conscious of their needs. And sometimes, that's just going to get to be too much.

Take your children into your confidence. Tell them, straight out, that in order to help them, you must first help yourself—that means taking some time to yourself, taking some time to rest, or making the simple decision occasionally to say "No."

And if, sometimes, you have to say, "I can't," "I don't have the time," "I'm too sad" *that's okay.* Don't beat yourself up or think you're a terrible parent. That kind of honesty isn't bad parenting—it's good parenting. Your children *can* cope; they really are willing to live a day at a time. Knowing they're helping you out makes them feel like goooood puppies! And they *can* recover from a temporary lack of parenting.

Find someone to talk to. Nothing seems quite as bad or unmanageable once you get it outside your own head. Find a confidant among friends or family; talk with a friendly nurse or doctor. If the crisis is going to continue for a while, find a support group. Sometimes listening to other people's troubles, and having them listen to yours, is the best therapy of all.

Life After *BOINGG!*

And sometimes, under the kind of continuing stress you are going to be dealing with, the best of us snap . . . we do go *BOINGG!*

Usually for a parent, the snap comes not from doing too little but from trying to do too much—from refusing to recognize our own limits. That's what Callie did.

Callie had a twelve-year-old daughter Miranda: tough age. Callie's husband had been discharged from the hospital after a severe first round of radiation and chemotherapy for his cancer. He still needed a lot of care, day and night; the doctors may have sent him home a bit early. I'd seen the mother and daughter while he was hospitalized, but not since.

One morning I got a call from the girl's school counselor: She was in his office. The night before, she and her mother had had a terrible fight. It started small. Callie asked her to bring some medicine; Miranda had better things to do. Finally she brought the medicine and slammed it down on the bedside table—whereupon Callie slapped her across the face, chased her out of the room, and slapped her again.

Pretty obviously, this was a family at its wit's end.

So after talking to Callie (who was devastated by what had happened), the counselor and I got to work. I arranged for the father to be readmitted to the hospital; the constant care he needed was simply too much for his wife to provide at that moment.

The counselor fixed it for the daughter to go stay with her married brother for a week.

Callie got a week without tentacles, a week filled with eight hours' sleep a night.

Mother and daughter are doing fine now. Both understand what set off the explosion: The mother was scared and exhausted. The daughter too was scared and exhausted, and she was twelve.

Remember:

Mistakes made with love are easy to correct.

And sometimes everything has to escalate before a family faces the fact: "Wow, we are in big trouble." Then they can accept help.

GETTING IT TOGETHER: A SUMMARY

After Diagnosis, Expect Two Phases in Your Family's Life

- The first few days to a week (the first phase), when you run on autopilot (page 36)

- The second phase:
    Less help as helpers return to their own lives (page 36)
    Everyone on an emotional roller coaster (page 37)

It's vital to prepare your children for the emotional swings and the lack of parenting that lie ahead (page 37).

Getting the Help You'll Need

- Appoint a family communicator to keep relatives informed (page 38)
- Use your answering machine and voice mail to keep callers updated and get you off the phone (page 38)
- Use the Internet (page 38)
- Accept offers of help, and tell people what you'll need (page 39)
- Arrange help for the future (page 40)

Getting Help From Your Kids

- What kinds of help? (page 42)
- How children grow under stress (page 43)

The Help You Can Expect, by Age Group

- The youngest through preschool (page 44)
    Give them little jobs they can succeed at
    Don't look for deep understanding of what's going on
- School-age Children (page 44)
    Job one: continue to succeed at school
    Divide the chores, and assign them fairly
- Teenagers (page 45)
    Job one: school performance still the priority
    Big help, big sacrifice: caring for younger siblings

A fair sharing of household chores

Caution: Don't expect them to take on the role of the sick parent

Giving Your Kids the Help *They* Need

- Infants through preschool (page 49)
  Keep the number of caretakers to an absolute minimum
  Minimize change
  Maximize security
- School-age children (page 50)
  Maintain normal activities and routines
  Provide regular updates on the sick parent
  Keep the school informed
- Teenagers (page 50)
  Encourage interaction with other teens
  Reward mature behavior with extra privileges
  Keep up normal activities and interests
  Keep the school informed

And sometimes, despite all this good advice, you'll just be overwhelmed. Some thoughts about that (page 52).

Kaitlin Plank, age fifteen, draws her warring thoughts (love/anger, happy/death), and even her maturing sensitivity (humanity/peace) when her mom was diagnosed with breast cancer.

3.

Early Warnings

Moira Is Fine

The one thing Dad was sure of: Moira was fine.

There were four children, ranging from three to twelve years old. A few weeks earlier, Mom had been diagnosed with breast cancer. The family was close and loving; Mom and Dad had explained her disease to all the kids, each on his or her level of understanding. The medical prognosis was good. And as Mom began treatment in the hospital, Moira, the eldest, pitched right in, helping Dad with all the younger kids . . . almost a surrogate Mom. No problem there; she was being marvelously mature.

But he worried about the others; how were they handling it? Could he be missing some important signs with any or all of them? So he asked me to see them.

We divided them into two groups; I spent the first hour with the nine-year-old. I was impressed; he didn't talk much, but he knew what was going on with Mom, knew the children had Dad and each other to huddle with, knew Dad and Moira could do the Mom things. He gave Moira a lot of the credit.

Before he left, he drew a lot of pictures to give Mom next time they saw her. They took the pictures home.

A day or two later, Dad brought in the three-year-old and the five-year-old. Moira came too—because, she said, the little kids might be scared. When she introduced me to them, I got the feeling Moira was checking me out. Then she asked, while I played with the children, could she just sit and draw something?

The preschoolers were a delight—outgoing and bumptious, with a lot of medical play, which showed me they pretty well understood what was happening to Mom and weren't afraid. No sign of insecurity anywhere. This father had done one heck of a job with his children!

Meanwhile, Moira had drawn a strange and lovely little picture. There were trees, flowers, a rainbow, color everywhere—and everywhere colored balloons floating up toward the sky, becoming smaller as they drifted away. I asked Moira to sit on the couch with me and tell me about her picture.

"Oh," she said, "it's just a park."

"And the balloons? Tell me about the balloons, floating away?"

"Well," she said, "that's what happens. When something's real special, or real pretty, and you love it, it goes away and never comes back." And she burst into tears.

What Moira was telling herself, me, and anyone else who looked at that drawing was this: Moira was *not* "fine." Moira was good, helpful, no trouble at all; for parents in crisis, Moira was *easy*. But she was not fine.

Those tears, unlocked for her by her own picture, were her first release. She told me she was never sure she was doing a good enough job helping Dad with the other kids; she worried constantly about that. The others, she felt, were expecting her to do all the Mom things, and she didn't always know how.

Then, as we talked further, some of the anger began to surface: It was *too much*. Too much was being expected of her by too many people; Moira wanted to do some of her own things, as well. She was, after all, twelve years old.

At length I told her, "This is really important stuff, and your dad needs to know it. If the three of us sit down together, can you tell him?" Yes, Moira thought she could.

And we did, and she did. And her father, who'd been worrying about the other children, sat there astonished at what his oldest daughter was telling him. And then he took over:

"I didn't know you felt any of this," he told her. "You are not the mom in this family; Mom is Mom, and Mom will come home in a few days; she'll be sick, but she'll be your mother and my wife. As to you, you're my little girl."

And they cuddled while he told her this.

"As to the help we need," he said, "there's plenty available," and he listed the aunts and uncles they could call on to do the "Mom things." Moira would still be needed, of course. Sometimes he'd call on her to take care of the other kids, but if she had something special on, a party to go to or just friends to be with, then that would take precedence. They'd *make* it happen.

It's a true story, and it still makes me feel good, particularly since the mother is doing fine after her breast cancer surgery. But it raises the questions we'll look at in this chapter:

- What kind of trouble may your children be having?
- How can you know? What are the signs of trouble?

Looking for the Patterns

First, let's throw out what we're *not* going to worry about. Almost never will we be concerned with one single act, one moment of time, however rotten. Terrible days are normal, as long as they don't happen every other day.

What we *are* going to look for are *continuing patterns of behavior* that tell us the children aren't handling the stress of Mom's or Dad's illness.

Any situation that interferes with your child's normal functions—school achievement, interaction with friends, eating and sleeping patterns—is abnormal. And the longer the abnormal situation continues, *the greater the potential for long-term damage.* And that's what we're really concerned with: spotting and cutting off these abnormal patterns *before* they begin to do damage.

No child can stand alone. Your children are part of a unit called family, and they will draw their strength from it as you draw yours. No child can make her own way through a family medical crisis; my own practice proves it to me every day. *The children who emerge whole and healthy are the ones whose parents recognize how much of their children's emotional survival depends on them.*

Pictures and Play: How Children Communicate

Remember how Moira gave the first indication that she was troubled—more troubled, I suspect, than even she realized? With a drawing. Children, younger children especially, aren't very good at expressing themselves verbally. They tell us their really important secrets through what they do and what they create—through play.

There's a remarkable sequence in the NBC News *Sunday Today* report on our work. A young mother entered the hospital for gynecological surgery, with every prospect of success. And she wanted to be sure her daughters—Kara, age eight, and Jean, who was four—understood: *Mom fully expected to be all right.*

I started medical play with the girls, and as Jean was placing a catheter (correctly) in a doll, I asked, "Is she going to be okay?"

Jean shook her head. "No," she said.

I said, "She's *not* going to be okay?" Jean shook her head again. At this point Kara interrupted authoritatively, "Yes she is. She's going to be okay." Jean stopped speaking . . . and a few minutes later, she picked up the doll and hurled it clear across our playroom.

You didn't need a degree in psychology; what happened was clear to anyone watching: Jean was announcing that she wasn't satisfied; she still doubted that the doll—that Mom—was going to be okay, and Kara had simply cut her off in mid-doubt.

So I let Kara play with something else while I sat down face-to-face with Jean and said, "I really do think she's going to be all right now." I repeated the message in several ways until, finally, Jean made eye contact and nodded agreement: Yes, she thought so too.

The moral is simple: Watch your kids and listen to them. Watch and listen while they play; there are messages, and the messages aren't subtle.

- Watch for signs of fear and anxiety. Look especially for forms of play that weren't there before. Children who are worried about a parent's illness, particularly where surgery is involved, may begin to mutilate things, to tear up dolls, toys, Lego structures.

- Or toys may begin to disappear; a favorite doll isn't there anymore. Why? "She doesn't like me." Such disappearances are frequently symptoms of the child's *fear of separation*—and again, the signs are not subtle.

- Watch for newly aggressive play, games of war and gangsters. A child's anger or fear may show itself in a sudden interest in death and killing. Watch how your child behaves with the family pet.

- Listen to what they tell dolls, or stuffed animals, or imaginary friends in those half-murmured conversations. In their playing, is someone sick? Is someone dying? Is someone never coming back? Listen for problems:

- "I have cancer, and now you're going to get it too!"

- "You were a bad dolly, and now I'm sick—see?"

What to do? Probably it's best not to interrupt the games that are worrying you; let the child play them out. But afterward, you can open discussions: "I noticed you had the mommy truck not come home—do you think I'm not coming home?"

You will need to continually reinforce those first key ideas from chapter 1; they'll keep coming up in a dozen different ways. Remind your children:

Nothing you did made me get this.

There is no way you can get it from me.

Directing Their Play

Children always play, and they play the themes that are important in their lives. But high levels of stress and distraction, with a noisy, confusing home environment, may limit their play—and what you can learn from it.

Since children, especially younger children, express themselves more easily in play than in conversation, you as the parent may want to step in and *direct* the play, to see a bit deeper into those remarkable little minds.

You'll need to do what we do in our playroom:

- Establish a quiet atmosphere—your living room or the child's bedroom will be fine.
- Keep the stimuli down—no TV, no other people wandering in and out.
- Have just the parent or parents present, ready to be patient and play at the child's pace and direction.

You'll want to provide toys that let your children make up stories, especially stories around the areas that concern you. In our playroom we have

- Dolls and puppets that can represent family members
- Stuffed animals, cars, trucks, boats, airplanes that can also represent the family at a little safer distance: "the Mommy bear" or "the Mommy truck" instead of "the Mommy"
- Play money, to help get at worries about family finances
- Dollhouses and building sets, that can focus on sleep problems and family security
- Medical toys and real medical equipment for directed medical play

With the kind of toys that represent your areas of concern, you can start off the playing. Say, for example, "You be the daddy doll, walking into the doctor's office. What do you think is going to happen there?"

Just at the beginning, guide the play: "And I'll be the little girl doll, sitting at home. What does she say? What's she feeling now, do you think?"

Pretty soon the child will probably take over the little drama and direct all the characters.

Medical Play

Medical play can be especially informative. You can get doctor and nurse kits at a toy store, and a lot of hospitals will lend you the kind of equipment they'll be using in the parent's treatment.

There are two ways you can use medical equipment: for education and for directed play.

Educationally, you can demonstrate for a child exactly what's going to happen to the sick parent—a catheter here because Mom can't get up to go to the bathroom; a breathing tube in the mouth; an IV line because with the tube in her mouth, Mom won't be able to eat for a while. This is good, useful information, but it's not medical *play.*

A lot of your child's interest and anxiety right now is medical, and medical play—making up stories—can bring out what's going on in her mind. As she "treats" the daddy doll, she'll display her understanding of what's wrong and what will be happening in the hospital. Knowing what she *thinks* is going on can help you guide her to a better understanding.

She'll also give you insights into her own medical worries. Children do worry about their own health, especially when there's serious illness in the family. Children play mostly out of their own medical experience, finding parallels with what's happening to the parent. Adult medical problems can stir the child's fears for her own well-being. As you watch that medical play, you can see and address your child's own worries and fears. Again, the play can help you help your child to a better understanding, even if it's just repeating the mantra, "No, sweetie, there's no way the little girl doll can catch cancer from the daddy doll."

Directed Drawing

I asked a little girl, whose father was under treatment for cancer, to draw what she would wish for if she had three wishes.

This is what she drew:

- A cigarette with the universal "no" symbol across it
- A little girl lying in bed, dreaming of skeletons and wolves
- A man and a woman shouting at each other.

When I showed the picture to her parents, they were absolutely shocked. With a single picture, their daughter had told them three things that they'd had no idea of and that they really needed to know:

- She blamed Dad's smoking habit for his cancer.
- She was having constant bad dreams.
- Their bickering was tearing her up.

Probably your younger children draw a lot of pictures without any prompting from you. And if they're like most kids, every picture quickly comes before you with, "See what I drew?" But if you want to find out what kind of pictures are going around inside your children's heads, there's one surefire way to start them drawing:

"How about making a picture for Daddy in the hospital?" That lets them do something they like to do anyway and feel good about doing it.

You can also suggest the surefire subject: "What about making Daddy a picture of all of us?" The way your child perceives his own family can tell you a great deal about his state of mind. It may surprise you. And it might convey some very important messages.

A six-year-old boy drew the picture on the opposite page, and he's sending a message just as clear as Moira's.

His father has cancer and is undergoing radiation therapy. That makes Dad irritable all the time; he can't or won't control his anger. He'd been an active man, a successful businessman, who'd enjoyed teaching his son to ride a bike, spiral a football. Now he's at home, sick—and angry.

This is a picture of trouble. The little boy sees his father's face as huge, fierce, and furious—and looking right out at the child drawing it. The boy sees himself as tiny and insignificant in relationship, and he's drawn a series of lines around himself—there's a sense, almost, of waves coming at this child, waves of rage beating him down. Or those lines may be some sort of barrier to protect himself from that rage; I don't know, and it doesn't really matter.

The father's face is drawn in great detail, but the little boy hardly

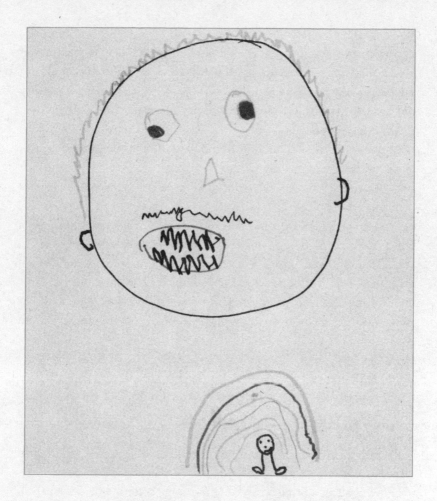

sees himself at all. The message here is simple, easy to read, and vital to deal with:

"Daddy's mad at me all the time."

Looking at this picture with me, the boy's mother understood that she must now take a stronger, more active role in the relationship, must try to break down the tensions that were coming between her husband and her son—*must protect her child from that rage.*

Suggesting Subjects

If you think your child is troubled, or upset, or confused about what's going on, you can direct his natural inclination to draw and gain important insights painlessly. The "Three Wishes" drawing is a nifty tool; it provides a nice, safe opportunity for your child to show you what's on his mind.

If your child wishes for a million dollars, a new bike (with speeds!), and a hundred more wishes, chances are that he or she is coping just fine. But you may also get something as revealing, as insightful, as that little girl's three pictures.

You don't want to get too specific, *too* directing. I wouldn't ask a child, "What would you wish for Mommy?" But it's perfectly fine to say, "There's so much going on around here, so many things we all want now. I was thinking what I'd wish for if I had three wishes. How about you? Can you draw three wishes?" (Of course, your child is probably going to insist on knowing *your* wishes too; better have them ready!)

Body Drawings

Body drawings are a wonderful tool for finding out what's hurting your child, inside or out. Either parent can play; all you need is a pencil and a handful of bright crayons.

Sketch a gingerbread-man kind of outline and say, "That's me!" or "That's Daddy!"

Now draw in a bright circle: "This orange color is where the cancer is." Or "This red spot is my heart, where it hurts sometimes because of the operation." A few more colors about you, and then it's the child's turn: "Draw you!"

Let her sketch a little gingerbread figure beside yours.

"Pick a place where *you* don't feel good. What color is the place? Why?"

"What's the quiet place inside you? What color is the quiet place?"

"What's the thinking place inside you? What color is the thinking?"

This little outline can provide you with a much fuller, vividly colored insight into how your child feels and is handling the family crisis.

Directed Play and Drawing: A Caution

All of these structured activities are really good for your children—not only do they guide you, but they give the children that indispensable sense of closeness, security, and love. So if certain things about your children's conduct concern you—anger, fear, new behaviors—you can safely direct their playing or drawing to those areas, *as long as you don't force them to confront things they're not ready to confront.*

If your five-year-old says, "I don't want to do that," or "I don't want to play that right now," or "I don't want to make a picture of witches; I want to make a picture of a police car," back away; let her have that amount of control. As long as you recognize that your child may be too threatened, for whatever reason, to push into certain areas, then this kind of directed play and directed drawing is both safe and enormously valuable for both of you.

"Be Happy, Mon"

Now let's look at another picture/message on the next page:

The artist was Kayla, age around eleven or twelve. Her mom had cancer; the prognosis was good, but the treatment was agonizingly long—Mom was somewhere around the middle of eighteen months of chemotherapy. It's a well-drawn picture yet oddly depersonalized; the child appears to be another creature, separate from herself. And there's that remarkable, courageous line in the midst of crisis:

"Don't worry be happy mon!!!"

When we talked, Kayla did not want to know *anything* about her mother's medical situation. Each time I raised it with her, she would change the subject. She didn't want to visit her mother in the hospital, didn't want to see the medical unit where her mother would be cared for.

Here, the mother and I decided, is a child trying very hard to cope *and doing it pretty well.* She's trying to keep a good attitude, to stay

positive. She's developed some skills of her own to maintain mental wellness. And part of how she copes is just to try to be happy, not to worry, *not to think about bad things*.

Her picture, and her attitude, told us very clearly: Kayla is in a state of avoidance; she is refusing to face the situation, and that's how she's coping. *And right now that's okay.*

(In the previous edition I spoke of a state of *denial*. But my own thinking has evolved as I've worked with the children, and I've come to realize they are *not* "denying" the ugly truth, not pretending it's not there; they're all too well aware of what's going on. I've learned: When you tell them, "Mommy's sick, Mommy's going to the hospital, Mommy's not getting better," *they hear you.* Somewhere the unpleasant words are sinking in—even though, next day, when a neighbor asks, "How's Mom doing?" you may be shocked that your child answers, "Fine." Your child is, for the moment, *avoiding* the truth, because she's just not yet ready to think about it. Or this may be her way of coping with something she can't do anything about.)

Scarlett's Way

In a situation like this, where Mom's medical condition is going to continue and nothing will change drastically for a while—perhaps a long while—it's all right for your children to dodge the bullet, to say, like Scarlett O'Hara, "I can't think about that right now. I'll think about that tomorrow."

If that avoidance lets your children cope, if their schoolwork keeps up, if they keep getting along with their friends, if no other signs of trouble turn up—then they are coping *successfully*, and you should probably allow them their avoidance.

What you do, as a parent, is make an offer: "Do you want me to tell you about Mom?" If the answer is no, that's fine, at least for now. *Don't impose information on a child who doesn't want it.* Let the child decide.

Only if the patient's situation takes a sharp turn, if life-or-death matters become imminent, should you begin to force your way past the child's barriers, to say, "I know you don't want to know, but there's a problem now, and you need to be prepared." Unless or until that happens, then "Don't worry be happy mon!" is perfectly all right.

You might even want to try a small dose of it yourself.

It's Your Call

Remember: You, Mom, and you, Dad, are the experts on your children. When you sense that something is different, something *is* different. And sometimes—often—all that's needed is to sit down and talk, and to help your son or daughter bring the doubt, the fear, the anger to the surface where you can look at it together.

There's a contradiction here. Your children need this extra time and attention just when you have less time and attention for them than ever. Here are a couple of suggestions for coping with the contradiction.

- Set aside a time—ten minutes at night, perhaps—to go over their day, to let them open up to you. Take the relaxed moments around bedtime and bathtime to chat, free-form.
- Every family has things it does together—take a bike ride, walk to the park, toss a football. Even amid the pressure of illness, of your own doubts and concerns, set aside time to do those things. That's where your children will talk to you—verbally, and in so many other ways.

These few special moments of attention help in two ways:

- They let you spot signs of impending trouble.
- They increase your children's sense of security at the very time they need it most. The conscious investment of just a small piece of your dwindling time can pay tremendous dividends for the health and comfort of your children for years to come.

Warning Signs That a Child Needs Help

In the next chapter, we'll talk more about what you can do, and the help you may need, to cope with signs of trouble *before* they turn into serious problems. But for now, let's look at a few specific warning flags your children may wave at you.

Early Warning #1: Sleep Disturbances

Sleep disturbances are early warnings in two senses—they can signal trouble brewing, and they're especially important in toddlers, who aren't yet verbal enough to *tell* you they're in trouble but who can *show* you.

We're not talking about the child who, in this stressful time, doesn't want to go to bed, or doesn't want to sleep alone. When a youngster is lonely, scared, or upset, looking for security, it's perfectly normal to want to sleep in Mommy's bed "just for tonight, *please?*" And, just for tonight, you may give in. Or you may compromise:

- Set up a cot for the child in your room—"Just 'til Daddy comes home, you understand?"
- Leave the child in her own room but with her door and your door open.
- Set up a night-light.

Do what feels right to counter these normal night fears.

But when the child is living in his own house, his own room, his own bed, and with a parent at hand, then *sleep disturbance* is a serious sign: You want to deal with it without delay. If your child:

- Is continually having bad dreams
- Repeatedly wakes in the night and wanders around the house
- Repeatedly wakes from nightmares she can't quite remember
- Walks in her sleep

These are all signs that your child is really stressed and isn't getting through the stress in her waking hours.

Sleep Disturbances: What Can You Do?

Your first approach should be to try to help your children work through the stress *while they are awake.* Give them options, verbal and physical. Set aside talk times and help them talk through what's bothering them, the questions and uncertainties they're carrying into bed. Look at some of the conversational ideas in the next chapter, under "How to Fish for Answers."

Encourage plenty of physical activity; help your children tire themselves out with a lot of play. Just using the body hard can flush out a host of mental poisons. You've probably done this yourself; you know how a fast game of racquetball can counter the mental miseries of the workplace. Kids' bodies work just like yours.

Keep your children's bedtime a calm time, focused on *them*. They shouldn't be going to bed while Mom is on the phone, talking to Grandma about how sick Daddy is. Get off the phone, get off the world, snuggle up for fifteen minutes and read them a story with a happy ending. A story, a tuck-in, a kiss and a cuddle can do wonders to promote a good night's sleep . . . for both of you.

Sleep Disturbances: The Danger

One vital reason to attack sleep disturbances right away is this: A child who is overtired, whose sleep is constantly disturbed, *is at great risk for other problems*. You certainly know this from your own experience: When you're overtired, even routine stresses become overwhelming. *You just can't cope*. And your overtired child will lose the ability to cope with all the other stresses—of school, of friends, of having a sick parent.

So if you've done your best to handle the sleep problem just between you and your child, and the disturbance continues, is becoming chronic, *that's a sign you need outside help*.

The place to start is with the school counselor or hospital social worker, both of whom may have suggestions to counter the sleep disturbance. But if the troubles continue, then think about getting help from a mental-health professional—a psychologist or psychiatrist. In the next chapter, we'll talk about how to find the right one.

Early Warning #2: Eating Disturbances

"I Say It's Spinach, and I Say The Hell With It."

A sharp change in your child's eating patterns can be a warning sign of other troubles, particularly in a preschooler. But let's get clear what is and isn't a change in eating patterns:

Many children are picky; almost all are intolerant of new foods. Yet frequently, when someone gets sick in the family, that's exactly when Mom decides to turn over a new leaf: "All right, from now on, *this family is going to eat healthy.* We're going to have leafy vegetables four times a day, no more fat, no more cholesterol, no more_____" (you fill in the blank from among the ten kinds of junk food your kids love most).

I remember one family in which the father became ill, and the four-year-old son basically stopped eating. His mother was frantic. But when we started talking about what she was feeding him, it turned out she'd drastically altered the family menu. Suddenly, instead of the peanut butter sandwiches that had sustained him for the past year or two, there were . . . *rice cakes!* And this young man basically folded his four-year-old arms and announced, "Uh-uh. I'm not eating that. *That's not food."*

This wasn't an eating disturbance; it was simply disturbed eating.

The fact is, with one parent seriously ill, too much has changed already in your children's lives. This is not the time to fool around with diet or any other part of the family routine that can be left alone.

Try to keep as much as possible just the way it was, because one thing—a parent's health— has changed so much.

A true eating disturbance is a change in your child's normal patterns. All children go through cycles of eating more, then eating less. But:

- If your child seems to be eating constantly, overeating, without ever getting much satisfaction from the food, or
- If the child seems to be eating very little over an extended period, picking at food, staring at it with that This-really-isn't-going to-do-it look, or avoiding mealtimes,

then you're dealing with eating disturbance, and your child's mealtime behavior is telling you something larger and deeper.

Eating problems are an indicator that your child is not handling the whole situation well. So trying to do something *about the eating* is likely to be counterproductive. Yet too often, parents who see a lot of other things spinning out of control think, "Well, this, at least, I can deal with." They turn a child's eating problem into a contest of wills, and they start to nag: bad mistake.

The first thing to do about the problem is nothing, *let it alone for a while.* Particularly if you're concerned with undereating, remember this: *No child is ever going to starve himself to death just because a parent is sick.*

When your son or daughter gets hungry enough, he or she will eat. So give it time; *most* children react to stress at first by undereating; some overeat. If they're handling the stress, they get past the eating problem.

An eating problem is a warning; it tells you something else is going on. That means you want to focus, not on the eating behavior, but on finding the underlying cause. In calm (non-mealtime) moments, start to ask some open-ended, "fishing" questions:

"I notice you're eating all the time, and you're never really hungry. Something on your mind? Let's talk."

Since eating problems are a frequent sign with children too young to verbalize their worries, you might get out some toys, play some "house" and medical games, then watch and listen for clues to what's on their minds.

Exercise is a good idea for both the overeater and the undereater: It will take their minds off their troubles and work up a real appetite.

Once again, the next chapter will offer more suggestions on ways to help your children—and how to find outside help if it's needed.

Keep in mind one final point: Children's eating, like so much else about their behavior, goes in cycles as they grow. And stress can accelerate the next cycle. So a change in pattern—from what you consider undereating, say, to what you consider overeating—if not accompanied by other signs of trouble, may simply be the next phase coming along ahead of time. Remain calm.

Early Warning #3: Fear

All kids—all people, for that matter—are afraid of something sometimes. It's a good thing we are; there's a lot of dangerous stuff out there, and some normal, healthy fear simply gives us the common sense to avoid it.

But now we're talking about the abnormal: fears that your children didn't have before, and that won't go away.

The fear can be of almost anything, or nothing; it can be closely linked to the parent's illness, or mystifyingly unrelated. I've seen:

- Fear of going to the hospital for a visit
- Fear of being left home, of *not* going to the hospital
- Fear of being with the sick parent
- Fear of *leaving* the sick parent
- Fear of a harmless neighbor
- Fear of mailmen or people in uniform
- A constant fear without any specific form

It can be almost any kind of fear. The warning sign is that your child becomes afraid of things he wasn't afraid of before, and that these new fears continue over time.

Early Warning #4: Developmental Trouble. Failure NOT Permitted

There is one very serious way your child will warn you of trouble: He or she will begin to fail.

A toddler who is toilet trained suddenly isn't toilet trained anymore. A first or second grader who was reading just fine, developing vocabulary by leaps and bounds, suddenly stops reading, stops adding new words. A daughter drops out of band practice or French club. A teenager loses interest in classes; A's and B's turn into C's, D's, and incompletes.

> ### *Loss of skills may be your child's most urgent warning to you that something is wrong.*

There's a natural tendency here, and it's a bad one—bad for you, bad for your children. It's the tendency to say, "Well, no wonder! With all that's going on, *of course* Davey or Julie is failing chemistry." It's a tendency you as the parent must fight in yourself, and must fight (and it can be a tough battle) in Davey's or Julie's teachers.

The teachers should know, of course, what's going on; to the extent you're comfortable, bring them into the loop. But as a parent, you must make it unmistakably clear to the teachers: You expect your child to continue to perform, and you expect the teachers to expect that too.

If there's trouble in school, meet with the teachers involved, *and take your son or daughter to the meetings;* make him or her a part of what's going on. Children, especially teens, can be positively paranoid if they think something that affects them is going on behind their backs.

You won't find many absolutes in this book, but here is one:

> ### **The very worst favor you can confer on your children is to allow them to fail.**

Even in the presence of grave illness—even after a death—life, growth, learning, and achievement must go on. The pattern you set now will be lifelong.

Of course, it doesn't serve any purpose to *punish* the failure; that can only alienate the child, tear the two of you apart when you most need to be together, and ensure further failure. What then?

Your most sensible course is to be frank and straightforward as to what you expect:

"Mom and I know you're hurting. There's no way around the hurt. But what's not okay is for you to let go in school. It's Mom's job to try to get well. It's your job to keep up your grades, to keep on keeping on—to keep us as proud of you as we've always been."

Remember this for the future: A lot of children experience significant failures immediately following a loss. If those failures are not addressed right away, at the time they're occurring, they can lead to a *cycle* of failure that will give your child no chance to succeed—ever.

More About School

What's happening in school—beyond that central issue of success or failure—can tell you a whole lot about what's happening in your child. In fact:

- study problems
- bad behavior
- school avoidance
- fighting with schoolmates

are all clear warning signs. Indeed, they are *diagnostic* of trouble.

Again, you want to make absolutely sure your child's school knows what's going on at home. Here's an example of why the school *must* know.

Inez was referred to me after missing three of the past four school days because of "stomach aches."

The first time, she'd persuaded the woman she was staying with, the mother of a schoolmate, that she was too sick to go; on two other days she'd gone to the school nurse with her "stomach ache," and the nurse had simply sent her home. What the nurse didn't know, and should have been told, was that Inez's father was undergoing a bone marrow transplant at a hospital four or five hours from home. Understandably, he wanted his wife with him during the frightening procedure and the recovery period—a total of four weeks. So Inez was sent to stay with a friend. She wasn't happy about it, but she seemed to accept it. But as soon as Mom went away, the little girl fell apart.

And it had happened once before. Weeks earlier, when the father went in to prepare for his bone marrow harvest, Inez had gotten so sick that Dad and Mom had had to rush straight home. Next morning they drove all the way back to the hospital; Dad was overtired and edgy—a bad way to undergo a medical procedure.

Inez's stomach aches were real—*the stomach aches are always real.* But they had nothing to do with a bug, or a virus, or eating something or not eating something else.

So we sent Mom home, all those hours over the road, to spend some time with her daughter, to talk to the friend's mother, and to explain the matter at school. I believed Inez *could* handle the separation, but she needed a lot more support than she'd been getting so far. No one had really talked to her. And I suspect that, somewhere below the level of consciousness, she thought that if *she* just got sick enough, Mom would come home.

School avoidance is most likely in kids who are already struggling in class or having problems there. In fact, if your child is a really good student and starts having some school troubles, you might let that go on a little longer than if he's a marginal student.

The good student will probably snap back; school is, after all, a pleasure and an escape from the problems at home. But the marginal student is more likely to say, "This is a miserable time in my life anyway, and school just makes me more miserable, makes me feel crummy inside." In a way, he's taking advantage—finding an excuse not to do what he doesn't want to do anyway. But it's not a conscious scheme. It's just another expression of misery.

Yet even the good student, faced with a family medical calamity, may need "permission" to enjoy school. I'm thinking of three children I saw recently: a girl fifteen, a boy eleven, and a girl nine. Their father had suffered a massive heart attack. He'd been put on a HeartMate, an electrical pump, to keep him alive until a donor heart could be found for transplant.

All three kids were really good students and involved in all kinds of extracurricular activities—soccer, gymnastics, modern dance, peewee football. Their mom and I talked to them about what was going on and how they'd be going to stay for a while with an aunt they liked. And I told them something to the effect, "Your job now is to get back to school, to do as good a job as you possibly can with your regular life and activities, and to let your mom stay at the hospital so she can give your dad the support he needs."

They were astonished. They asked me, "You mean, it's *okay* to go back to school? It's *okay* to do the things we like to do? It's okay to have fun?"

They went back the next day. Their father remains critically ill, but they needed to get back to their normal life *because that life is their support*. But first they needed permission to return to it—just as, sometimes, in the midst of all that's happening, *your* children may need permission to laugh, to play, to have fun.

And you have to tell them, that's okay.

School: The Up Side

There's a good-news side to this story: If your child is continuing to do well *in school*, then he's probably okay, no matter what bad things you are seeing *at home*.

In fact, you may be seeing your kids at their worst, what with, "You don't pay any attention to me anymore" and "Why can't my friends come over for a rock party tonight?" and the third time their room door slams hard enough to rattle the walls.

Remember this: If your kids can put together six consecutive hours each day during which they're coping, interacting with friends, getting their work done, *then they're probably okay,* no matter what kind of troublesome behavior you may be seeing at home.

Early Warning #5: Beware the Quiet Child

Remember Moira? Moira, I said, was easy. Moira was *quiet.*

More even than the child who screams, breaks things, and gets into fights, I worry about the quiet child. And the reason is that for parents distracted by illness or worse, this child *is* easy—easy to ignore. Stressed parents tend to accept gratefully when a child sort of disappears into the wallpaper. But a child who used to be lively, noisy, even troublesome—in a word, normal—who suddenly retreats into silence, is a child silently warning you of trouble to come.

If your son or daughter responds to the family crisis by going silent—by "going away"—then you should go after him or her. Find time to talk or play together and try to draw out what's going on: "I notice you get kind of quiet when you're worried. Are you worried now?"

You might present some of the possible causes and see how your child responds:

> "Are you thinking a lot about Dad?"
> "Are some of your pals kind of insensitive?"
> "Are you worried about going off to camp, about what might happen while you're away?"
> "Are you having trouble keeping up in school, with all that's going on around here?"

You may not get a response the first time you ask, or the fifth time. Kids are like that. But keep reaching out, keep following your quiet child into the silence.

The Little Girl Who Didn't Care

A young father brought his five-year-old daughter, Sara, to our program. His wife was in the hospital recuperating from a heart transplant. She was not doing well. And Sara didn't seem to care.

"She's acting like her mother doesn't even exist," he said. "She won't talk about it, won't listen when I tell her how Mom's doing. I don't know whether she's happy or sad. *She just won't address it!*"

At her kindergarten, Sara was acting hyper—starting fights, taking other kids' stuff, beginning a typical downhill spiral toward the unpleasant label of "troublemaker."

Sara and I decided it might be nice to make an audiotape for her mom. Sara sang a little song, then, as I reached for the switch, she said, "Don't turn it off." And Sara started to talk about cooking—about making chicken. Then she said, sadly, "Grandma was a good cooker."

Sara's father had told me that his mother had died a few months earlier, and that, with the sudden onset of his wife's grave illness, he hadn't had time to think about his mother's death; he couldn't even grieve. He'd "put it on hold." He'd never even talked to Sara about her grandmother's death.

Now I said to Sara, "Your daddy is sad about Grandma."

And she said, "You know who else is sad? Me."

With the tape running, Sara told me about her grandmother; she'd lived in her own apartment, and every day Sara would go over to help her.

I said, "Gee, it sounds like you helped her a lot."

"Yeah," Sara said miserably, "*until she died.*"

And it began to come out: Sara's real attitude, deep inside, was, "If I had helped Grandma more, she wouldn't have died." This child believed, below the level of thought, that she hadn't helped her grandmother enough to save her life. It's the most dramatic example I've encountered of a young child's "magical thinking"—what happens around me happens *because* of me, and I have the Power. If something goes wrong, it means I did something wrong.

Sara couldn't *begin* to cope with her mother's illness, because she had never gotten through her grandmother's death. It was all right—it was normal—for her *father* to say, "I'll grieve about my mother later, after we get through this new thing," but Sara couldn't handle it that way.

So at last they cried together about Grandma, and then they cried together about Mom.

Because only after they talked about Grandma—after Dad and I had reassured Sara that her help and love were the very best thing in his mother's last days, and that his mother had told him so—only then could Sara get past that earlier tragedy and begin to deal with her mom's illness. And within a few days, Sara began to ask the normal questions about her mother: "Where is Mommy's old heart? Why isn't the new one working right?" At school, she was the old cheerful Sara.

Because we all like happy endings, and are entitled to know about them, I'll tell you that after one terrible month, Sara's mother and her new heart decided to get along together: She wound up with an amazingly good outcome to the transplant.

Remember, as you begin to cope with this new family crisis: If your children have any unresolved *earlier* crises going around in their heads—the recent loss of a pet, a serious school problem, encounters with abuse or crime, a recent divorce—*they'll have to deal with the earlier crisis before they can handle the new one*. If they're still sad or upset about it, if they haven't talked it through, if it's still churning inside, unresolved, then when something new comes along, *they may simply shut down*. Their capacity to cope is overloaded. And before you can help them through the present, you're going to have to help them through the past.

The Warning Signs of Suicide

Up to now, we've been dealing mostly with mental, psychological, and emotional damage to children. But in fact, children are young human beings, and are capable of almost everything their elders are capable of—including, intentionally or not, hurting themselves.

Some studies in the past few years suggest that children, even very young children, *even children too young to understand what death is,* may attempt to hurt or kill themselves. Luckily, very few young children succeed, but there is some evidence that teenagers who do, tragically, manage to take their own lives have made earlier, unsuccessful tries when considerably younger.

The Three Levels of Danger

Generally, in the area of real, physical dangers, we see children operating at three levels, of increasing seriousness and, fortunately, of decreasing frequency. But let's be clear on one thing: *Every one of these levels of talk or action is to be taken very seriously indeed; the question is not whether to pay attention, but what to do.* The three levels are:

1. Talking about it
2. Taking risks
3. The real thing

Talking About It

In this fiber-optic age, in our hardwired society, there's hardly a child of six who hasn't heard about suicide, or who doesn't have *some* idea of what it means. And your children will talk about it. Sometimes it will be perfectly meaningless: "I'm flunking geometry; Oh, God, I think I'll kill myself!" "My boyfriend dumped me; there's nothing to live for."

But in your present family crisis, this kind of talk can be a real cry of despair and a plea for help. If your child is obviously depressed by what's going on around him, and you begin to hear, "I wish I wasn't alive" or "I just don't want to live anymore," *it is always serious.* That doesn't mean that the next day your child will actually make an attempt, but he's playing around with the big issues of what life is, and how one handles emotional pain: ultimate questions of being and not-being.

How Do I Deal with This?

First, *you never ignore it; you never ridicule it; you never deny children their feelings.* If the words are there, the thought is somewhere, *and attention must be paid.*

By now I hope you're coming to share my belief that communication is the key to almost everything between parent and child in times of stress, and that the parent's job is to keep doors open and keep opening doors. So when your child tells you through tears, "I wish I could die, so I'd never have to hear you and Mommy fighting anymore," you must *never* say what for many parents is the most natural thing in the world to say:

"That's the most ridiculous thing I ever heard; I don't ever want to hear you say anything like that again." Because you may get your wish; you may never hear your child say it again. But the thought behind the words is still there, festering deep inside—and you've just cut off the chance of bringing it out into daylight, looking it over, and dealing with it.

What you do is pretty simple. First, you pay full attention. Then you try to find out how serious your child may be: Is he just thinking about it? Or has he crossed the line to thinking about *how* to do it?

An unfocused, unhappy "I wish I were dead" is probably something you can deal with, talk out. But if you discover that your child has begun to think about particular methods of hurting or killing himself, *that is an absolute indication that you need professional help, on the level of a psychiatrist or a psychologist.*

The Questions to Ask

The kinds of questions you'll want to ask are open-ended, putting the ball in the child's court. Avoid questions that can be answered with a shrug or a nod, a yes or a no.

You might start along these lines: "You seem really sad these days. Tell me what you're feeling inside . . . tell me what kinds of things you're thinking about."

If the child says something like, "I don't think I want to live anymore," "Nothing's fun anymore," or "Nothing's ever going to be the same again," then you can continue probing, with more nonthreatening, open-ended questions.

"What does that mean? What do you think you might do? Are there things you can think of that would make your life happier again?"

I can't script these conversations; each answer determines the next question. The important thing is *not to put ideas into children's heads*, not to ask specific will-you-or-won't-you questions, but to help the child explore what's going on and how he might become happier.

The issue is most likely to arise with older school-age children or teenagers; they're old enough to understand the concept of death, and they've been exposed to the idea of suicide in school, on television, and probably in their own conversations. And because they have that sophistication, I think it *is* safe for parents to address the issue directly.

When a child says, sadly, "I just feel like killing myself," it's perfectly appropriate for you to take that head on, to say, "Gosh, it really makes me sad to hear you say that. Tell me what you're thinking about. Tell me whether you're thinking about how you might do that. Tell me if your friends have been talking about that. If you were going to do something like that, tell me what you might actually do."

Boys and Girls Are Different

There really aren't a whole lot of behavioral differences between preschool boys and preschool girls. But once they reach school age, they begin to diverge, and the parent has to think about them differently. Somebody once said "All girls are born actresses, but very few boys are born actors." True or not, I find that school-age and teenage girls are the ultimate dramatists. And what they dramatize most is themselves; they are constantly the stars of their own TV shows. Your daughter who decides at thirteen, "I'll never have a boyfriend; I'll just kill myself," probably will have a boyfriend and probably won't kill herself.

But *a suicide statement from a boy is probably to be taken more seriously than the same statement from his sister.* Because boys don't self-dramatize to the extent that girls do, because they tend to keep bad stuff inside them, boys are more serious when they make suicide remarks. It's very hard indeed for a boy to made a comment like that aloud, and it indicates a deep anguish within.

Handling It—Continued

If your child hasn't gone beyond that generalized, "I'm just so sad, I wish I could end all this," you can probably deal with it. And one way to do that is by laying out alternatives.

Your child can build up a terrific load of pain. But children are also better than adults at seeing options—they tend to be more optimistic than grown-ups; more of the stories they tell have happy endings.

Remind your child that this illness isn't forever. Talk about specific good times coming and what you'll do then—on the next birthday, or Saturday at Great Adventure, or next spring when school's out, or Friday night when we play Westwood High. Again, physical activity, from punching the heavy bag to riding a bike to taking karate lessons, is a good way to boil off the emotional poisons. If you can find a way, get out and do something together that's fun.

Manipulation

And keep in mind: Kids, especially kids in those middle years from about eight to eleven, are the most incredible manipulators. If they see that "I just think I'll kill myself" gets a rise out of you every time they say it, then they'll keep saying it for all it's worth.

The key to heading off that kind of manipulation is your own expert knowledge of your children. You make mood judgments all the time. If your child doesn't look terribly "down," if there's that certain glint in the eye that says "put-on," if she's sort of watching your reaction out of the corner of an eye when she says, "I just think I'll kill myself," then something *other* than a real suicide threat is going on.

A child who is really sad, really depressed, doesn't bounce back right away. So if your son says, "I just think I'll kill myself," and a few minutes later is outside playing with his best friend, he isn't telling you something serious about self-destruction. Nevertheless, *he is telling you something serious.*

These little manipulations aren't conscious on your child's part. But they *are* a cry for help. They're an attempt to gain your time and your attention, and that's what the child is telling you he needs: your time and attention, your feedback, your approval—the normal, accustomed parent/child things that may be overwhelmed by the family crisis. So even when a suicide threat is not a suicide threat, attention must be paid; it *is always* an early warning of trouble.

Making It Better

One thing you can do immediately is help your child come up with things to make him or her feel better, more positive. Ask, "Would you like to feel better? Can you and I together find ways to make you feel better? What can we do together?"

Remember, a child's nature is basically optimistic. So if you can open a door toward feeling better, your child will walk through it.

One tactic I've found effective is to focus on something, just one thing, that's been good in a terrible day:

"Hon, I've had a rotten day too, but I did have one fun thing. Coming home from the store, I met this *beautiful* Old English sheepdog. And what do you think his name was? Heathcliffe! Can you imagine? Can you think of just one really good thing that happened to you this rotten day?"

"Affect": A Key Indicator

"Affect" is a term we use to describe the way the child *appears to feel*. If your son or daughter is constantly "down"—in chronic distress, in continuing emotional pain, just doesn't "lift" very often; if the things that always used to bring pleasure no longer bring pleasure—*then you definitely need outside help.*

Risky Business

This child is past the talking stage. This child is *doing*. And what he or she is doing is taking risks:

- Darting out from between cars into traffic
- Balancing on the railing of a bridge
- Teetering along the narrow top of a high wall

The actions bring your heart into your mouth; they make you want to grab the child and shake or slap the stupidity out of him. It may not be actual suicidal behavior, but the child is pushing the envelope, seeing just how far he can go and still pull back to safety.

These actions are actually a huge, silent cry for help: "Please pay attention to me. I can't stand this. I'm on the edge; you've got to do something to help me."

Once you understand that the high-risk behavior—the car dodging, edge walking, pill tasting—is a cry for help, then you understand that *the help your child needs now is professional.* You're past the point where you can *risk* tackling the problem yourself, past the point where such first-resource people as school counselors and clergy can help. You can't take *any* risk.

When you see your child in overt acts that threaten his physical well-being or his life, it's time to bring in a psychologist or a psychiatrist.

The Real Thing

True suicide attempts by children are the rarest of all; you'll probably never deal with them. Yet they do happen—a child will cut her wrists, swallows a vial of pills, climb to the top of a bridge *with the serious intention of dying.*

Once again, in this most unlikely but most dangerous situation, the answer is *immediate* intervention by a psychiatrist or a psychologist, with no steps in between. A child who gets this far may well need to be hospitalized, to make absolutely sure there are no further attempts.

Throughout this chapter, we've looked for trouble, and maybe we've found it. So in the next chapter, let's talk about where and how to get help.

EARLY WARNINGS: A SUMMARY

We won't worry about the occasional bad day.

We will worry about continuing patterns: behavior problems that don't go away (page 60).

The goal: to identify and change stress reactions before they do damage (page 60).

Some Things You May Be Seeing or Hearing:

- Fear and anxiety (page 61)
- Toys that vanish (page 62)
- Aggressive play (page 62)

Some Ways You Can Direct Children's Play and Interpret It:

- Getting the atmosphere right (page 62)
- Some toys that can help you get information (page 63)
- What you can say and do (page 63)
- Medical play: It can tell you a lot (page 64)

Some Ways You Can Direct Their Drawing:

- Understanding what they draw: some examples (page 64)
- Subjects you can suggest (page 68)

A caution: Don't force the play or drawing if your children are reluctant (page 69).

Making Time for Your Kids When You Don't Have Time:

- Bedtime and bathtime (page 72)
- Try to keep doing the "family things" you all do together (page 72)
- Two benefits of making time: helping you and helping them (page 72)

Important *Warning Signs* That a Child Needs Help:

- Major changes or disturbances in *sleep* (page 73)
- Major changes or disturbances in *eating* (page 75)
- Appearance of *fears* that weren't there before (page 77)
- Developmental trouble: loss of skills, falling grades (page 78)

Remember: The very worst favor you can confer on your children now is to allow them to fail.

- The quiet child (page 82)

The Warning Signs of Suicide

- Three levels of danger and what you should do (page 85)

Remember: You are the expert on your children. When you sense that something is different, or something is wrong, you're probably right.

Juliet Belardo, age nine, whose dad was diagnosed with lung cancer, describes the impact of the disease, and, as "someone who knows," offers some advice to other kids facing the same kind of crisis.

4.

Help! How to Give It, Where to Get It

Ripples

Something in the last chapter has registered; a sign of trouble has clicked with you. You think your child is giving a signal and, because you're the mom or dad, you're probably right.

We're going to look at help as a widening set of ripples, starting right in the center with you and your children and working outward through the levels of help available as the problem proves increasingly tough. (In chapter 9, we'll find that the sequence of ripples is somewhat different when the parent's illness is a mental one.)

The good news is, you probably won't have to go very far out from the center: you and your kids together. Most of the time, parents tell me, forewarned *is* forearmed. When they know what problems to expect, and how to react, the little troubles don't turn into big troubles: Mom and Dad find they can get on top of the issues, get past them, and help their children get on with their lives. In about half my practice, I never even see the children; the parents themselves can handle the problems. And I'm about the third ripple.

"I Know Worse Words!"

Her name was Joanie. She was about seven years old, and she had a brain tumor. Because she'd been having chemotherapy, her eating was disrupted; for a while she lost everything she ate. But now the treatment was over; she should have been recovering. Nevertheless, Joanie still wouldn't eat, not even her very favorite food, graham crackers. And the doctors couldn't release her from the hospital until she started taking real food. Could I see her?

What I saw, tiny in the middle of a pediatric bed, was a bald, skinny, pale, depressed, just miserable little kid. She wouldn't really talk to me; she certainly wouldn't smile.

I persuaded Joanie to go to the playroom with me, and trundled her off through the hospital corridors in a wheelchair. In the playroom, the one thing—the only thing—Joanie would do was to draw; Joanie loved to make pictures.

She started to draw a dinosaur. And she began folding the paper, a sort of origami thing she'd learned in kindergarten, to make the dinosaur 3-D. We talked as she worked, and, just to lighten things, I asked what we might do to make him look "really weird." She thought about that as she drew in the face. Then Joanie said:

"There. I think it's done. Except . . . *do you want me to make snot dripping out of its nose?*"

I was astonished. Picture this tiny, skinny, sick, depressed, pale kid, looking at you out of enormous eyes and asking, most seriously, "Do you want me to make snot dripping out of its nose?"

Well, I cracked up. I started rocking back and forth with laughter, so Joanie started to laugh. She laughed, and laughed, and laughed.

I said, "Joanie, I can't believe you're using words like that!"

And Joanie grinned and said, *"I know worse words!"*

"You do, huh? Well, why don't you tell me some of the worst words you know?"

And she did. Most of them were kid words like poop and pee, but she had a few more advanced ones too. I just laughed and laughed through this proud litany, and Joanie did too. She wore herself out laughing.

As I rolled her back through the hospital lobby, Joanie started to review some of her words, and pretty loudly. I said, "Joanie, you can't use words like those in public!"

"Ya mean like *POOP*?" Joanie shrieked at the top of her lungs, as all eyes turned toward us.

"Ya mean like *PEE*?"

When we got back to the room, the first thing Joanie asked for was a graham cracker. That afternoon the doctors sent her home. One of them told me, "If she's eating graham crackers and acting happy, there's no reason to keep her here."

Sometimes, just as the *Reader's Digest* used to tell us, laughter *is* the best medicine. And sometimes tears are. What we're going to learn now is how to help your child reach inside to the laughter, or the tears—to the best medicine.

Getting Physical

As we work our way out through your children's problems, and the ripples of help available, a lot of our emphasis will be about *talking* with your kids. But let's start out with a little context—what to *do* while you're talking, or while you're not talking. And this advice applies no matter how much or how little help your children need.

Think for a moment about your own style, and your family's style. What do you *normally* do to support your child when he's stressed? A pat on the shoulder? A hug? A snuggle? A tickle? Group hug? All these and more? Right now your whole family is stressed, and you may have a tendency to withdraw, to be at arm's length from your kids. You may not think about getting physical. But in order to support and comfort your children, you've got to give them *at least* the warmth and attention—the physical love—they've grown up with until now.

So if in the middle of some of the conversations we'll be talking about, you suddenly think, "You know, a hug might be good right here," you're certainly right.

Count on it.

The Center of the Circle of Help:
You and Your Kids

How to Fish for Answers

You think your child is worried, and the worries aren't coming out. She's not asking the questions you know are inside there—about how serious your illness really is, and will we be able to see you in the hospital, and who'll take care of us, and *could you die*? And what you want to do now is get these questions on the table, so you can look at them together, get them settled, and get on with things.

What you can do is to ask some open-ended, "fishing" questions— questions that *don't* answer themselves.

For instance, I would *never* ask a child a question like, "Are you afraid Mom's going to die, yes or no?" Give a child a worst-case scenario, and she'll grab it every time. The question is there, waiting within the child, but *she* has to bring it out, as part of a range of possibilities.

Instead, you might start this way:

"What kind of questions do you have?" That's open-ended but it
    requires an answer.
"You seem a little blue. What kind of feelings are you having
    about this?"
"Are you feeling a little scared? What kinds of things are you
    afraid of?"
"What do you think could happen?"

"What do you think will probably happen?"

"What's the best thing that could happen, do you think?"

"What's the worst thing that could happen?"

The idea is to put the ball in your child's court. Not to *make* her think, because I promise you, deep inside she's already thinking, furiously. But to bring *her* ideas, hopes, fears up to the surface where you can both examine them in healthy daylight. These open, nondirected questions are the way to probe *safely*.

Going Deeper

If you want to go deeper, because some specific behavior change is warning you of trouble, then focus on the change itself, *not* what you think might be causing it:

"Hon, you say nothing's worrying you, but:

"I see you fighting a lot with your friends . . .

"You're just not sleeping very well; I think there's something on your mind . . .

"You're very quiet, and that's not like you; usually we can't shut you up . . .

"Now, you're the expert on you. Why do you think you're doing that?"

Whatever the problem behavior is, try to question the *behavior*; let the child come up with what's behind it.

Smorgasbord

Sometimes I'll offer a child some possibilities about what might be going on. I might say:

"A lot of kids ask me, 'Why does Dad have to go visit Mom every single night after work? Why can't he stay home with us?'" Or "A lot of kids worry about what's going to happen to Dad with Mom so sick; is that on your mind?"

Or "One kid worried that he'd have to quit basketball, because Mom can't drive him to practice."

Or "Kids ask me whether they'll still get their allowance, with Dad away."

What I'm trying to do is lay out a smorgasbord of the things kids might worry about, from the fairly trivial to the pretty serious, and let them pick.

You can adapt the smorgasbord technique:

"I've read where lots of kids whose parents get sick worry that . . ." and offer some likely possibilities.

If you persist, and pick the moments when your kids are open to you, they'll usually let you into their heads and talk out what's troubling them. But if not, and if the troubling behavior continues, you can begin suggesting the next level: "I understand you don't want to talk to me about it—maybe you're not even sure yourself what's bothering you. So I'd like to find someone else you can talk to."

Getting the Emotions Out

We Americans tend to treasure a Norman Rockwell view of childhood—sunlight and porch swings and no conflict worse than a schoolyard shiner. The fact is, children are not puppies; they are not warm and cuddly. They are small human beings, confused and conflicted and frequently in need.

In a family medical crisis, your children inevitably are going to lose some measure of parenting—and children respond very strongly to that particular loss. We can minimize the loss, but we can't make it not exist. So your pleasant, comfortable children may become angry, sullen, afraid, even mean. It's hard for you to accept; you don't want your children to have such ugly, negative emotions. Yet your job now is to let your children know that the anger and the fear are okay, are *right*— and to help them live and thrive beyond those emotions.

Consciously, deliberately encourage your children to be themselves, to be children. It's okay to show emotion, it's okay to cry, and it's okay to laugh. And it's okay sometimes to get angry, to slam a door, to kick a garbage can—even to scream at you. What's not okay is to keep stuff inside that needs to get outside.

One fourteen-year-old told me that when things get just too hard to bear, she slams her bedroom door a few times. "My parents used to yell at me, but now they know I *need* to do it."

She carefully took down all the pictures on the door side of her bedroom, so they won't get broken when it's time for a few therapeutic slams. We've even talked about slam calibration—what's a two-slam problem, compared to a four-slam problem?

Ways to Let Go

Slams or not, every child needs some private place in the house to retreat and let go. Prominent in our own playroom is a big punching bag, heavily scarred from all the childhood aggressions that have been taken out on its tough hide. Punching bags, store-bought or homemade, are good; so are toys kids can kick—anything that lets them get their feelings out without having to talk about them. Sometimes we suggest that the kids draw pictures of people or things they're really mad at, and paste them on the punching bag. Physicality is important with kids, who can't always express themselves in words.

When you see your child tightening up, send him out for a walk or a run or a bike ride, something to divert his attention and tire him out physically. One family I know used to tear up the Yellow Pages together; they wound up with a lot of yellow paper on the floor but in much better mental shape, and nothing got broken.

A lot of kids who seem out of control can really benefit from things like karate or *tae kwon do*—sports that emphasize control, not wildness. This focus on action is especially helpful for boys, who at any given age tend to be far more physical and far less verbal than girls of the same age. Some girls do go after our playroom punching bag, but it's the boys who really make its life miserable.

The Sound of Pumpkins

As of last Halloween, I can offer one more coping mechanism, from personal experience. There's only one problem: It's seasonal.

I'd had a really rotten week, so bad that I almost didn't answer the phone as I was leaving the office Friday night. The call was from the mother of a family I'd worked with and liked, and the news was terrible.

The young father had just had a new MRI: His cancer had returned.

After all the personal and family pain of the first siege, the doctors now wanted him to return Monday to begin a whole new course of chemotherapy.

The parents told the children—a boy twelve, a girl three. All four were devastated . . . and furious. It was so unfair!

The mother told me: "We're just so angry! It wasn't supposed to be like this . . ." And it was worse for the children—the little girl in tears; the boy shouting, "I'm not going to go through this again!"

In a way it was even worse than the first time—not just because they'd hoped it was over, but because this time all four *knew* just how rough the next few weeks and months were going to be. Finally, the mother said helplessly, "Kathleen, I think we all need to pound on something!"

I said, "Why don't you find something and do that?" It wasn't much, but it was the only help I could offer.

On Saturday afternoon, my phone rang at home. It was the mother, very excited. She said, "We found it!"

"Found what?"

"You know the jack-o'-lanterns? Do you know what it's like to hit a pumpkin with a baseball bat? It's *wonderful!*"

Late the night before, she told me, the four of them had picked up a couple of bats, gone outside, and smashed pumpkins together. They wound up with an enormous mess—and rolling with laughter.

I thought about that for a while, thought of the kind of week I'd been having. Then I dug out a bat and went outside to talk things over with my own jack-o'-lantern.

It really *is* wonderful.

Helping with Relaxation and Imagery

Relaxation techniques are a really good way to reduce stress, both for children and adults. Your public library has books and tapes that go into as much detail as you wish.

These techniques are based on one simple principle: Stress and relaxation are incompatible. *You can't be really stressed and really relaxed at the same time.* And we *can* learn how to relax. As we make ourselves relax, the stress correspondingly disappears. Unlike love and marriage in the song, you can't have one *with* the other.

It does little good to tell children "Don't be scared." Or "We don't want you to worry." It's a lot more helpful to tell them *what to do* to make themselves feel better. And while some kids think self-relaxation is stupid, most become really good at it. They come to love the feeling they get inside when their bodies go limp, loose, comfortable, *relaxed.*

There are all kinds of relaxation techniques. Let me describe one of them: progressive relaxation.

Make a fist. Clench it as tight as you possibly can. Now feel how it feels—not just in your clenched fingers, but also in your wrist, the back of your hand, the inside of your forearm, all the way up to your shoulder.

Got it? Now relax the fist. Feel how loose all those same muscles are. *Learn the difference* between how your muscles feel in a clenched fist and a relaxed hand. Whenever you're feeling stressed or tense, *make those muscles feel relaxed.*

If you're a child, and pretty good at it, then the next time you feel like yelling at Mom, you can check: Is my arm tense? Are the muscles all stiff, like when I clench my fist? If they are, then make them relax, make them feel all loose and comfortable. That will help *you* relax, put you back in control. And you'll be able to negotiate with Mom about what you want without getting into a big fight and being sent to your room.

Imagery

Relaxation imagery is another helpful technique, especially with young children. Say something like this: "Close your eyes and be at the seashore. Listen to the waves. Feel them bubble over your ankles."

It's a way of using the mind to recapture pleasant sensations, to slow the breathing, lower the heart rate, to *relax* and drive away stress.

Children's imagery tends to be a little more active than grown-ups'. You or I might remember lying on a beach, basking; your child is more likely to board Aladdin's flying carpet, go swooping up to the clouds, then down under the Golden Gate. It's not as passive, but it's just as relaxing.

There are self-teaching books and DVDs on deep relaxation; many parents get very good at it, both with their children and with themselves.

Music

For older children, there's music. A lot of teenagers tell me they use their music to get through or get around their troubles. I remember one fifteen-year-old girl in particular. Her father was awaiting a transplant, and the continuing fear and suspense were devastating. She told me, "I put on my headphones and play the music *I* want to hear, however loud I want to play it. I let the music go right through my brain, from one side to the other."

The music going through her brain blocked everything out for her, *including her thoughts.* When she doesn't want to think about what's going on—and she's entitled *not* to think about it sometimes—her music lets her not think. It's a really strong technique for older kids. So if your kids love music—any kind of music, whether you can stand it or not—encourage them. Probably you should try to steer them away from gangster rap, but let them listen to whatever works.

Laughter: The Best Medicine—Sometimes

I know a family whose oldest member lives in a senior citizens residence. One afternoon several years ago, her grandchildren came to visit. They were walking with her down the corridor toward the dining room, when an elderly gentleman passed them in the opposite direction.

Both old folks were a bit hard of hearing. So when the gentleman called out, in a friendly fashion, "Hello, are you going to lunch?" the grandmother smiled, waved, and called back cheerily, "No, I'm going to lunch!"

It's been a sure laugh line in that family ever since; any time somebody mis-hears something, or gets confused, one of the kids will pipe up, "Are you going to lunch?" and the other will call back, "No, I'm going to lunch!" Then everybody dissolves.

That kind of family in-joke is a sure tension reliever at tough moments, and the really neat part is that nobody outside the family will have the slightest idea of what you're all laughing at.

You and the kids can cheer each other up with riddles, jokes (including those dreadful knock-knock ones), anything that will break through the tension.

But remember: What you don't want to do is make jokes about your children's honest concerns.

When a child is being serious, stay serious.

When your children need information or need to share a feeling with you, never belittle that or pretend it isn't serious. It's when the *child* tries to lighten up, tries to say something funny, that you've got your signal: Now she's ready to break the tension.

A lot of my work involves cancer, and a lot of times I have to warn kids that their good-looking Mom or Dad is going to lose all her or his hair, temporarily. And it's upsetting, so I say, "It's going to be hard to see Dad without his hair, isn't it?" And the child will usually nod gloomily, and we'll talk about ways to help—maybe going out with Mom to buy Dad a couple of hats.

But usually, in a little while, I can see the child lightening up. I may ask, "How do you think your Dad will look without hair?" And the child will come up with something like, "I think he'll look kinda like a big hard-boiled egg!" And we both start to laugh.

And now you can build on that, get silly; you can suggest, "How about drawing pictures on Dad's head?" and think of what pictures might be appropriate.

And this is the pattern: Being honest with your children means exposing them to a series of new, frequently unpleasant realities. They're not going to like that, and you must respect their distress. But soon you will see them trying to find a way to cope, and that's where you can bring in humor to help them cope.

"Are you going to lunch?"

"No, I'm going to lunch!"

The Terrible, Horrible, No-Good, Very Bad Day

That's the title of one of my favorite books: *Alexander and the Terrible, Horrible, No Good, Very Bad Day* by Judith Viorst. I like it because I have those days, and so do you, and so do your kids. (Most of the pages end with, "I think I'll move to Australia.")

These are days when, from morning to night, nothing goes right, nothing can go right, nothing will ever go right again, and even the things that do go right go wrong.

When your child is having one of those, he will absolutely defy your very finest efforts at parenting: You are *not* going to make me feel better. Try all you like, you are *not* going to help me. I can't find my favorite tennis shoe; this shirt has a spot on it and I want to *wear* it today; oh God, did you buy nonfat milk again?

When those days come, for you or your child, just remember: *You can't fix it, so just let it happen.* Minimize anything that needs to be done that day. If you have plans you can postpone, postpone them. Get through the day, get everyone to bed at the end of it, and remember, if you can:

Tomorrow will be better.
Probably.

When Enough Is Enough: Talking Tough

There's a technical word in psychology: *perseverate.* I like it because it sounds a little quirky and because there's no other word exactly like it. Perseverating is a kind of circular thinking, or a downward spiral.

You begin to worry about a problem, and that makes you think how serious the problem is, and that makes you worry *a lot* more, and that makes you think how *terribly* serious it is and . . . And you're perseverating. It's pathological—worrying at the same problem again and again, *without affecting the problem at all.* It's something kids do a lot, especially in a family crisis. And sometimes when they do, it takes a verbal parental whack to snap them out of it.

Because you're a good parent, you want to solve every problem for your children. Maybe, secretly, you think you *should* solve every problem for them. But there are problems you can't solve. *Sometimes you can't make it better.*

So when your child comes at you, again and again, with the same unanswerable questions ("*When* is Mom going to be better?" "*Why* did you get a brain tumor?" "I'm so sad; *why* can't I go over to Sammy's and play Nintendo?"), when the child is becoming a total pest on one subject, you're dealing with perseveration.

Sometimes you can compromise, offer alternatives, break into the cycle. If the house rule is no friends until homework is finished, and Dad is home sick, perhaps you can modify the rule a couple of afternoons a week.

But if you've done all the compromising you reasonably can, and your son or daughter still keeps coming at you with the same refrain, then it's perfectly okay to say, "Look, this is the situation. I don't like it. You don't like it. *But I can't fix it.* And we're both going to have to live with it for a while. Now, knock it off!"

In the words of the old song: "I told ya I love ya; now get out!"

The First Ripple of Help: Family and Friends

Maybe it's not working. Maybe you're doing your level best, but you're just not getting anywhere. The warning signs—continuing patterns of troubling, abnormal behavior—keep flaring. Maybe the "fishing" expeditions I've described sound great in a book, but with your kids they produce only more tension and aggravation. Maybe your suggestions for helping them cope meet nothing but resentment and resistance. Maybe you and your kids are simply *too* close, or not quite close enough.

A Question of Gender

Brace yourself: Maybe there's a gender problem. Particularly with young teens, it's often terribly difficult talking about certain matters with the opposite sex—even parents. Right now, one parent—one gender—is out of action. So a teenage daughter may really need to talk out Mom's mastectomy, but she simply can't do it with Dad. A son may feel horribly threatened and conflicted by Dad's testicular cancer, but it's not the kind of thing you can talk to Mom about. With teenagers, where there's a sexual component to the situation, start looking around for someone of the same sex for them to talk to. Aunts and uncles are a great resource here; grandparents can be a little too inhibiting—and inhibited. The great thing about an aunt or an uncle is he or she is the same generation as Mom or Dad—it's like talking intimate stuff with Mom or Dad, only once removed.

And maybe *you're* too stressed. You're entitled—don't beat yourself up about it. It's perfectly okay—maybe even a little courageous—to look inside yourself and decide that you simply don't have the energy, the strength, or the time to handle this right now.

If that's the case, start talking to your kids about where *they'd* like to turn for help.

Children know what adults they're comfortable talking to— *they'll tell you if you ask them.* The answers may surprise you; they can range from an uncle you didn't think they liked very much to a teacher they hardly mention to the mother of a not especially close friend—or they may indicate exactly the people you'd have guessed.

In one family, the five children named five different people they'd confide in; not a bit surprising. In fact, it's probably better that way—no one aunt or high school band director should have to deal with five troubled kids!

When you go to this next level, you'll want to make sure that the adults your children are talking to know the situation, know what they're dealing with, know your take on the troubles and what you've told the children. One suggestion: Go over some of the ideas in this chapter with them.

Teens for Teens

There's one further resource for teenagers, and it's a good one: other teenagers. Teens are a clannish group; occasionally they can seem like another species. For some, at some times, grown-ups are alien, not to be trusted. A lot of teenagers have told me that the only people they can talk with freely are their friends, *because only their friends understand what they're going through.* Some teens, at some times, won't talk to their own parents; they simply don't believe their parents can understand.

There could not be a more normal, more healthy response for teenagers. So within the limits of family secrecy—of what *you're* comfortable having outside the house and in circulation—by all means encourage your teenagers to find comfort and confidants among their teenage pals.

Artie Screws Up

Artie was eleven when his mom had the heart attack. It was massive; there was an all-out rescue effort. It took the best efforts of an outstanding cardiac-care unit to save her life.

Because of some other physical problems, she couldn't go on transplant standby right away. So for five weeks, her life had been sustained by a HeartMate, an electrical assist pump.

While she was on the HeartMate, her condition improved remarkably. She could walk around the hospital, work out on the treadmill, wear her own clothes. Of course, as long as her life depended on the machine, there was no question of discharging her from the hospital.

For her two children, the situation was a classic of medical crisis: Suddenly family members came rushing in from out of town, people were coming and going at all hours, the phone never stopped, good news alternated almost hourly with bad news.

Yet Artie's own situation seemed pretty good: He and his sister went to stay with an aunt and uncle whom they liked and who liked them. There were two other children in the house, and all of them got along fine. The family was extremely supportive, and Artie and his sister adapted quickly to the rules of the new household.

Artie's dad worked nights and visited Mom in the hospital every afternoon; nevertheless, he managed to spend some time with his children almost every day.

For Artie, it seemed, no problem.

One day, three or four weeks after the mother's heart attack, Artie's dad phoned me: "We've got to talk."

Artie, normally an A and B student, had just showed up with three F's on his report card.

There had been no warning; Artie's classroom quizzes were still coming home with A's and B's. What the father learned, in a series of agonized phone calls to teachers, was that Artie had simply stopped handing in his homework.

"Sometimes he's done it, sometimes he hasn't. But even when he's done it, he hasn't turned it in."

Artie, in fact, was doing just what a lot of kids in those circumstances do. He didn't realize it, but he was calling out for attention and help, and pretty effectively too.

On the surface, when Dad talked to him every day, Artie's reaction was always, "I'm fine, I'm fine." Inside, he needed to let the world know, "This whole thing is very difficult for me. I'm not handling it well." As we've seen, when your child is *not* "fine," school is one of the first places he'll show you.

Unscrewing Artie

Because the family was paying attention, some very important things happened in a hurry.

Artie offered his family a few levers to adjust his conduct. Two things were very important to him: his baseball team and his karate lessons. In the midst of the medical crisis, the family had gone out of its way to make sure he could still have those two outlets. Now, Artie's aunt, working with his mom and dad, developed a plan. Artie agreed, and the school approved.

Every day Artie takes two homemade forms to school. On one, he writes out every homework assignment in each class. Each teacher initials his assignment, signifying that Artie has got it right.

On the second form, the teachers indicate that Artie has turned in the previous day's assignment.

Only if both sheets are filled out and presented to Artie's aunt after school is he allowed to go to baseball practice or take his karate lesson. If either sheet were not filled out, he'd have to miss baseball or karate and stay home and do the homework. I say "if," because so far Artie hasn't violated the terms of the agreement, not once. Since the new rules have been in effect, the dog has never eaten Artie's homework.

A couple of important things have happened:

First, Artie got the help, the *structure* he didn't know he needed. He would never acknowledge, or even understand, that he wasn't doing his homework because he was worried about his mom, because he was mad at the world for letting her get sick. Children like Artie don't have that kind of self-knowledge. For Artie there were just a lot of excuses, "I forgot—I left it in a book somewhere." And now there was a plan that, Artie agreed, would help him "remember" his homework. That's really all the understanding Artie needs.

Perhaps even more important to think about now was the involvement of Artie's *mother*.

Mom May Be Sick, but She's Still Mom

When Artie's dad first phoned me about those three F's, I asked whether he'd talked to his wife about them. He said, "Good idea. She really knows Artie. I'll do that right now."

Remember, this was a woman who was functioning on half a heart. Nevertheless, *she was still Artie's mom. She still intended to be fully involved in his life,* heart machine or no heart machine. And that determination was absolutely vital *for both their needs.*

Mom needed to feel competent as a parent.

Artie needed to feel protected as a kid.

She and I have talked repeatedly about Artie's school problems, about the stress he's undergoing and how he handles it. Her husband is right; she is full of remarkable insights into her son.

It is a mistake for the well parent to try to shield the sick parent from involvement with the children.

Obviously, you can't and you won't try to push parenting on a mom or dad who's just too wiped out to get involved. And you'll want to stay in close touch with the doctors as to how much is too much. Nevertheless:

- Many parents feel so much better when they can step back, at least partially, into their parenting role.

- It is vital for the children that they continue to see their sick parent as a *parent*.

The longer the child has to go without the sick parent's supervision, the less respect he will retain for the parent as parent: Mom is still Mom, and what she says goes. So:

Once you're out from under the acute crisis, once Mom or Dad is on treatment, recuperating, able to handle it, he or she needs to step back into a parenting role as quickly as possible. Because if not, the relationship with the child may *never* return to normal.

There's a remarkable little book I recommend, called *Moms Don't Get Sick*. It's co-written by Pat Brack, a mother who developed cancer, and her ten-year-old son Ben, and it recounts their experience of dealing together with her disease.

At one point, when Pat was still on chemotherapy and feeling absolutely terrible, Ben began to go wild, to break all the rules.

The defining moment came when his mother insisted he put on a pair of slippers, and Ben turned away and whispered, "Shut up!" Here is how Pat describes what happened next:

> I remember so clearly . . . my fury at Ben when he defied me and muttered, "Shut up." In that incoherent moment I realized how little discipline he'd been getting from me and how far I had let things slide. Energy born of rage and frustration took hold and I decided I would rather die instantly of overexertion than watch this once-lovable boy become an obnoxious little beast. A battle ensued. I found untapped energy enough to bounce him around the house . . .
>
> After this volcanic encounter, Ben put on his slippers and became very cheerful and loving. I think children need to feel that someone other than themselves is in control.

Even more significant is Ben's recollection of the "shut up" incident:

Well, Mom heard and totally lost her temper. She picked me up and shook me and said she'd be dipped in chocolate before anybody told her to shut up. She backed me up and held me to the wall and told me that I would do exactly what she told me to do OR ELSE!! I went and got my slippers on fast. *I felt better than I had in a long time.* I think now that I back-talked on purpose *to see if Mom was really in there.* She sure was and that made me feel warm and safe. Later we hugged and made up. It was a wonderful day.

And that's what has to happen: The sick parent must show that even though she's sick, she's still Mom, and all her expectations for her children are intact and in place.

The Second Ripple of Help: School and Community Services

Because school is where so much of the trouble shows itself, it's a natural place to start looking for solutions. I've had some wonderful help from schools, and I've also had parents tell me they *didn't* get the help they expected. Let's talk about what your child's school needs from you now, and what you should expect of the school.

Approaching the School for Help

By now, you've probably already made the school aware of what's going on at home; if not, this is the time to do it. Start with a phone call, to find out exactly whom you can consult about helping your child through a family medical crisis. Usually it will be the guidance counselor; in some schools it will be the assistant principal. Sometimes a child's homeroom teacher is assigned to be the child's liaison throughout the school day. In the lower grades, where the child has only one teacher, that teacher may be your primary contact. For simplicity's sake, I'll call whomever you're going to deal with "the counselor" from here on.

About the Counselor

In dealing with all kinds of counselors at all kinds of schools all over the Midwest, I've come to a few conclusions about them:

Guidance counselors in large, busy schools—even very good counselors—*must* focus on academic performance and behavior in school. That's what they're paid to do, and probably it's all they'll have time to do. So if school performance or acting out with schoolmates is the problem, the counselor can be your first, and often your best, resource. But he's not employed to provide general counseling for children who are stressed *outside* of school life.

In big urban schools, with underwhelming budgets and overwhelmed staffs, the counselor probably will intervene only in crisis situations—academic failure, truancy, and the like—and his or her focus will be narrow: to help with grades, period. Occasionally you'll run across the burned-out counselor who's just biding his time until retirement, and is going to be very little help indeed. The more you know about your school and its guidance counselors, the better you'll be able to judge how much help you can expect.

In smaller, more intimate settings—good suburban schools, some private institutions—you can expect a great deal more. Counselors have more time and space for each student; frequently a counselor will take a stressed child under his wing, provide supportive one-on-one guidance well outside the narrow focus on school, stay in touch with the child, maybe even notice changes before you do. The counselor will become a friend.

All this suggests that a school counselor can be a really good resource—perhaps all the help you need—or may offer very limited, restricted assistance. If that's the case, then you'll need to look a little further for help, either inside or outside the school.

Your First Meeting

First, make an appointment for a *meeting*. Even amid all the demands on your time right now, it's important for your child's welfare that this first conversation be face-to-face, not an impersonal chat over the phone.

Plan to bring your child along to that first meeting, where you'll discuss the problem that's bringing you here. It's important to include the child because:

- Just like you and me, children prefer to be talked *with* than to be talked *about*.
- You and the counselor need to hear your *child's* idea of the problem, which may be a little different from your own.
- You'll want the child's-eye view of the counselor.

At that meeting, you'll explain *your* perception of the problem—both to the counselor and to your child. Involve the child both in explaining the problem and in planning solutions. Say something like, "It worries Mom and me that you're fighting with your friends," or "You're daydreaming during exams, and your grades show it," or "You're forgetting words you already know how to spell," or "You're not turning in your homework."

Whatever the problem, you and the counselor can begin to work out a solution, *with the child involved in the planning*.

Artie's planning session, for instance, might sound like this:

"Here's what we're thinking of doing. What if we worked up a printed form that you can write down homework assignments on and have your teachers initial that you've got them right? Then another form they can initial each time you turn in your homework? And every time you give your aunt those forms, she'll let you go to baseball or to karate.

"Do you think that will work? Can you think of anything better, to get you over these homework troubles?"

Making Judgments

At any level of these ripples, the help you get will be only as good as the people who give it. In your meeting with the school counselor, or with any other resource, you'll begin, almost automatically, to make some judgments. If:

- You and/or your child don't have a good feeling about this person
- The counselor doesn't really seem interested in your child
- The counselor seems defensive, telling you this problem is not the school's responsibility
- The counselor already seems to have negative feelings about your child
- You or your child have had conflicts in the past with this individual

then you may feel the need of going to someone else in the school. In a small elementary school, where your child has just one teacher, he or she is your obvious choice. But in the upper grades, your child probably has a whole roster of teachers, and it would be pretty hard to round up all of them.

The counselor's immediate superior is probably an *assistant principal* or *dean of students*—usually a person second in command to the principal. In most schools, the principal himself is probably too busy with budgets, school boards, and teachers' unions to cope effectively with one student's problems. But I find the assistant principal can often be of great assistance.

Don't hesitate to ask around among other parents as to who has proven helpful to them in the past, and whom they'd just as soon bypass.

Making Sure It Happens

Once you've set up a plan with the school, whether it involves special supervision, tutoring, homework monitoring, whatever, you'll want to keep an eye out that it's actually happening. A lot of parents at this point will trust the school personnel to implement the plan; that's probably naïve.

Never assume that, just because you've set up a plan with a counselor or assistant principal, all your child's teachers have been properly notified and are on board. One counselor might send a detailed, written explanation of Artie's homework plan to every one of his teachers, asking for an acknowledgment by return e-mail. Another might simply mumble in a faculty meeting, "We're putting a homework check on Artie."

If you can find the time, try to confirm the plan by phone with each of your child's teachers. Have they seen it? Is it okay with them? Any additional ideas? There is nothing worse for your child than to agree to some kind of behavioral plan, only to find that one of the people who's supposed to be helping hasn't a clue as to what's going on. It's simply devastating to a child who's already on shaky ground.

Teacher Conflicts

What if your child has a teacher he *really* doesn't like, doesn't get along with?

Under ordinary circumstances, you might keep hands off. After all, part of a child's education is learning to coexist with people—including teachers—whom he doesn't like very much. But now the circumstances are not ordinary; your child is dealing with the enormous stress of a parent's illness.

Academic problems suggest that the child is already having trouble maintaining concentration, and it's a lot harder to concentrate on someone you don't want to listen to in the first place.

It's rare that a teacher conflict is so extreme that it becomes part of your child's problems, but it *does* happen.

If your child has a long-standing conflict with a teacher (which may not be either's fault), and his school performance is suffering, then you may want to talk about switching your child to a different class. Remember, because the parent's medical situation creates such extreme stress for the child, we try to reduce any other stresses we can.

Finally, if the school doesn't seem to be helping your child—if the plan isn't working and no one at the school seems able to come up with something better—then you're going to have to start looking beyond the school, to professional tutoring or counseling, or even therapy.

Community Resources

A good place to start looking is right at the hospital. Whatever hospital you're involved with, it will certainly have a staff of social service workers and mental-health specialists on tap, who can direct you toward the services you need—anything from community support groups to psychotherapists.

If you're closely involved with your church or synagogue, ask your minister or rabbi whether he or she can recommend therapists or counselors.

There's another resource not many people think of, and it's right there by your phone: the local government section of your white pages or blue pages. Running down the list of community services in my phone book, I find such titles as

Children, Office for
Family Guidance
Mental Health
Social Services

Simply call one that sounds like what you're looking for; if it isn't exactly the right office, it can direct you onward to the service you need.

More and more communities have been setting up "information lines" to steer people toward the public services that can help them (the one in Cleveland is First Call for Help). Dial the number, and you'll talk with a real live person; explain your problem, and he or she will direct you to the agencies that can help. Private organizations like

United Way are setting up these help lines; check for one in your own community.

Religious Resources

Your family's place of worship can open new avenues of help. There are youth and sports group leaders your children may like and trust, who can talk to them on the basis of considerable experience with kids in and out of trouble.

Priests, ministers, rabbis—your clerics can often be a great source of strength for a family in crisis. But unless they have special training in handling youngsters—and you're entitled to ask whether they do—they may *not* be the best resource for helping your troubled children.

Some may be awkward with children. Lacking special training, they may not know how to talk to a four-year-old, versus a seven-year-old, versus an eleven-year-old, versus a teenager, about what's troubling them. Many clergy will see their own roles as specifically dealing with the *spiritual* aspect of life's crises, not the behavioral or emotional aspects.

The clergymen and -women of my experience are often very good at talking with children about the deep stuff—about the meaning of life, and why people have to die, and why life sometimes seems so unfair. But a child stressed by a parent's illness probably isn't worried about those things; she's upset about separation, she's dealing with anger, with a loss of parenting, with general fear of the unknown. Helping in those psychological situations requires special training. In *most* cases, I think clergy are more a spiritual resource for the family than a ready source of help for troubled youngsters.

The Third Ripple of Help: Therapy

The ultimate layer of help is one you probably won't ever have to worry about. Most children will by this point have responded and be back on track toward normal—toward reasonable eating, comfortable sleep, good grades—toward reversing whatever behavior brought you to this chapter.

But if the answer to "What works?" is still "None of the above," and in the specific case of risky behavior, you may have to start thinking about getting your child together with a psychologist or a psychiatrist. There's a lot of help available for finding one: your hospital counselor or social worker, your pediatrician, your school guidance counselor, the community service agencies you may already be in touch with.

If you do decide on psychotherapy, your child MUST understand: *This is not some kind of punishment.* Explain to her: You're stuck in this miserable situation, you're not happy, you're not *yourself,* and this doctor is going to try to help us fix all that.

In most communities you can find psychotherapists with special qualifications for working with children whose parents are very sick. One word of caution, however:

Nowadays many counselors and therapists are oriented to *family therapy*—their doctrine is to work with the entire family as a unit. But in the situations we're talking about, it can be very rewarding for the child to see someone all alone, one-on-one. The problem you're dealing with is not the stress on the family but the stress on this child. And family counseling is one more demand on *your* time that you may not be able to handle right now

Making Judgments

Once you go outside the circle of family and friends—once you begin looking for professional help, whether from a community guidance counselor or a psychotherapist—you're going to have to make certain judgments. The central one: *Will this person help?*

To a great extent, it's going to be a matter of gut instinct—whether you *feel* this person is right, or wrong, for *your* child. But a few guidelines may help:

The First Meeting

- Your child should be there. The child's judgment of this new person will be at least as important as yours. More important—particularly if we're dealing with a teen—he won't get the idea that something is going on behind his back. Help stamp out paranoia.
- The counselor or doctor should address your child by name. It's simple courtesy, and it demonstrates real interest.
- You should never have the feeling that the therapist is talking *past* your child, talking to you as if young Danny weren't there. As an adult, I find that offensive; to a child, it's a devastating put-down. Either he should be talking *to* young Danny, or looking over at him to make sure he feels he is part of the conversation. (That goes for you too, Mom or Dad—you never want to talk about your child as if he weren't there. *He's there*—and all ears!)
- The therapist should use your child's name frequently; there should be a minimum of "hims" and "hers"—not "What about his eating disturbs you?" but "What about *Dan's* eating disturbs you?" Nobody wants to be a pronoun.
- The therapist should seek out your child's opinions. In my own practice, whenever the parent tells me of a problem—"I'm worried about Dan's schoolwork"—I'll usually turn right to Dan and say, "How about you—do *you* think you're having a problem at school?" The therapist should *want* to hear from your child—more, perhaps, than from you.
- You'll want to sense a rapport between the counselor and the child, a feeling that *both* are interested and will get along with each other. Above all, if after the get-acquainted session your son or daughter announces, "I *hate* her," then it doesn't matter if the counselor is Mother Teresa or Dr. Spock—look further.

Confidentiality

There are certain things which, by law, your child's therapist *must* tell you, and must also report to the authorities. Among them: if your child is engaging in self-destructive behavior, if she's contemplating suicide, if she reports abuse.

Now, beyond that mandated reporting, the law *entitles* you to know everything your minor child tells her therapist. But if the therapy is to succeed, I'd urge you to waive that right and to do it there in the therapist's office, with your child watching and listening. Unless the child—particularly the late-school-age or teenage child—is absolutely confident she can talk freely to her therapist, and what she says *won't* get back to you, Mom, or you, Dad, then the therapy is unlikely to succeed. If the parent doesn't agree, if you say, "Well, I really kind of want to know what's on Janie's mind," Janie isn't going to open up and reveal the really important information.

"In Treatment"

You may have seen the remarkably true-to-reality television series *In Treatment*, basically a series of half-hour sessions between Paul, a skilled therapist, and an interesting mix of patients. Each patient returns on the same night every week, so you, the viewer, experience a realistic series of therapy sessions.

If you've seen it, you'll remember that two of Paul's early patients were children—a combative fifteen-year-old girl refusing treatment for cancer, and an eleven-year-old African-American boy with a heavy load of personal problems. In both cases, the outcome of the treatment was pretty good, and in both cases the parents agreed to respect child-therapist confidentiality. As you watched what unfolded in the therapy sessions, you could not help but realize that these children would never have opened up, never have given Paul (and themselves) entrée into their deepest troubles, if they thought their words would get back to their parents.

Illegal?

The therapist may even conceal from you, at his discretion, some illegal activities. It's a judgment call. I'm not a psychotherapist, of course, but in my own practice, if a child tells me she tried a puff of pot at a party last weekend, I'm probably not going to push it. If she tells me she's smoking a joint every afternoon, because it's the only way she can keep from hitting her little brother, then I'll say, "Look, you and I really need to find a way to talk to Mom about this, because you need more help than I can give you. I can't just talk to you about it; you need a therapist who specializes in youth and drugs, because you're doing drugs."

But I will *always* tell the child before I tell the parents. Even if she's pissed at me, even if she says, "I'll never talk to you again," I tell the child before I talk to the parents. Similarly, before I report abuse to the authorities (as I must, under the law), I'll first tell the parents what I'm about to do. The dad, the mom, may be furious, but I tell them in advance: "I have to report this. You smacked your child, you left big bruises on his backside. I think you did it because you're exhausted, and frustrated, and don't know which way to turn. I know you don't want to hurt your child, and we're going to get you some help. That's what the county services do; they'll help you figure out how to control your anger."

The parents may hate me for it, but I tell them what I'm going to do, and then I do it.

Results

Once you've taken on professional help, you judge its quality by what you see in your child. If he's going to a series of sessions, does he go happily? Does he look forward to the time he'll spend with his new friend? Does he talk about the sessions (especially with younger kids; teenagers may not say word one about what's going on)?

You must feel that this professional is keeping you well informed, both of progress and lack of progress. Probably you don't *want* to be involved on a session-by-session basis, but be sure you are comfortable with the level of involvement . . . with what you know and when you know it.

After that, it's a matter of results, over time. Is the eating or sleeping or performance problem that brought you into this beginning to go away? Probably the answer will be yes. If not, then talk to the therapist about why things aren't working out. And get answers that satisfy *you*.

HELP! A SUMMARY

You've identified a problem or a pattern of negative behavior in your child. We'll start at the center: you and your child together, then look at the widening circles of help available:

At the Center: You and Your Child

- How to "fish" for answers to your questions (page 98)
    Questions *not* to ask
    The right kind of questions
    Questions about specific problems that worry you
- What to do when your kids lose some of your parenting (page 100)
    Help them bring out their emotions
    Encourage physical activity
    Encourage *disciplined* sports
- Teaching your children how to relax mind and body (page 103)
- Laughter as medicine (page 105)
    When to laugh, when to be serious: Let the child be your guide (page 105)
- What to do when you *can't* make it better for them (page 106)
- When to get tough (page 107)

The First Circle of Outside Help: Family and Friends

- When your kids can't talk to you: gender problems (page 108)
- When you're too stressed to help them (page 108)
- Whom can they turn to? Ask them! (page 109)
- A major resource: teens for teens (page 109)
- This is important: Keep the sick parent involved (page 112)

The Second Circle of Outside Help: School and Community

- How to approach the school for help (page 114)
- Some guidance about guidance counselors (page 115)
      First meeting: What to do, what to look for (page 116)
      Ways you can judge the counselor (page 117)
      What if you're not satisfied? (page 117)
- Include your child in any school planning (page 116)
- Trust but verify: Make sure the plan happens (page 117)
- What if your child has a teacher conflict? (page 118)
- Community resources: Where you can find them (page 119)
- Religious resources: some thoughts (page 120)

The Final Circle of Outside Help: Therapy
If it's needed, it will usually be short-term. We're talking about a problem arising because of the parent's medical crisis, not something more deep-rooted.

- Some ideas on how to find the therapy your child may need (page 120)
- Judging the therapist and the therapy: some guidelines (page 121)
- About confidentiality between therapist and child (page 123)
- Some thoughts about results (page 124)

Nickie Schmauch, age eleven, whose father was diagnosed with leukemia and her mother with breast cancer, shows how easily children can go online for information—sometimes not very good information.

5.

The Wonderful, Terrible Internet

Think about a bright twelve- or fourteen- or sixteen-year-old. One night she hears, or overhears, that her dad has something called a "glioma." What will she do?

There's a chance she'll do nothing. Some children, particularly younger ones, don't want to know the details of a bad thing. But there's quite a good chance that she'll head straight for the computer and Google "glioma."

The first thing she'll learn is that she's called up a dozen or so of *approximately 1,650,000 entries.*

And some of those first entries will be simply terrifying:

". . . very poor prognosis . . . worst prognosis of any central nervous system malignancy . . ."

Then, just as a bonus, this opening Web page features a genuinely horrifying medical *photograph* of a massive glioma.

The Internet is a new world for the sick parent, the well parent, and all the family and friends trying to help. It is a world of great danger for children, and of great opportunity. *We must get control of this universal new medium, this new playground for young minds,* or its massive, random founts of information can undo everything we're trying to do for the children.

Even the good, reliable information about a disease can overwhelm an unprepared child. But remember one thing:

> *The Internet is the greatest source of information in human history. It is also the greatest source of MIS-information in human history.*

Anyone can post anything—anything at all—on the Internet, and it will pop up somewhere on your home screen.

We're going to look at two aspects of the Internet:

- The Web as a source of information: the Google effect.
- Social networking sites, such as Facebook, where preteens and teens spend a lot of their lives these days, and how they interact with their myriad "friends."

In both cases, we're going to find ways to make the Internet itself a "friend" of the children, so it can help them and us through this family crisis.

The Wonderful, Terrible Internet

I began with the example of glioma because that was the diagnosis that confronted Stephen and his young family. Stephen was the thirty-something father of three girls: Liz, sixteen; Ellie, fifteen; and Jan, twelve. What I could see from our very first encounter was that unique father-daughter relationship which, when it's there, is like nothing else in the world.

Quite simply, all three girls adored him, and he them.

The other thing I noticed, right from the start, was this family's blazing determination to conquer that tumor. Stephen and his wife, Joan, embodied the attitude: "This thing can be beaten, others have beaten it, and we are going to beat it." I've seldom seen anyone diagnosed with a serious, usually fatal disease sound so positive. They amazed me.

The two younger girls reflected that optimism, but Liz, at that first meeting, appeared quiet, withdrawn.

As the days and weeks passed, Liz became still quieter, pulling away even further from family and friends. Stephen and Joan, still determinedly upbeat about the future, grew seriously concerned about her. They asked me to help them find out what was going on.

Both parents had asked her repeatedly what was wrong, but neither asked the key question: *What do you know?*

So in a private meeting, I asked Liz point-blank: What do you know about your dad's illness? I'll never forget her answer:

"I know a lot more than they think I do!"

Liz confessed that at the first diagnosis, she had gone online, by herself, and Googled "glioma." I asked her what she had learned.

Liz replied, "He's going to die, isn't he?"—and burst into tears.

On the Web, All Alone . . .

Liz had found what we found at the beginning of this chapter: glioma is a very bad tumor indeed, offering very little hope of survival. What Liz learned was so at odds with her parents', and her sisters', determinedly cheerful outlook that she simply couldn't talk to them or anyone about what she now knew.

Fortunately, Liz and I were meeting one-on-one without her parents, and so she could finally let it out—she could finally cry. She told me she sometimes cried in private, all alone, but could never let the others see her cry. Because if she did, they would see that she was afraid, and they were all trying so hard not to be afraid.

Liz couldn't even talk to her sisters, who hadn't gone online: She felt she had to protect them from her secret knowledge.

I praised Liz for her courage in telling me what she'd learned, but I also told her it was really important that she let her parents know what she knew. She simply couldn't keep carrying this thing all by herself. Liz really resisted talking to her parents, so I gave her some time. I told her that as long as she would talk to me, I'd carry the secret with her for a while longer. And that compromise worked for her.

Even though she shared her terrible knowledge only with me, Liz began to brighten—her parents told me she seemed happier, though they, of course, had no idea why.

After four or five months, her father's condition began to deteriorate seriously; there was more surgery, a series of seizures. Everyone could now see that he was losing his courageous battle. Finally Liz agreed to tell her parents about her lonely research, but she still absolutely refused to let her sisters in on what she knew. I pointed out that by now the other girls surely realized things were getting worse, not better, but Liz, an enormously protective older sister, wouldn't accept that. She would talk to Mom and Dad, but not to the other girls.

It's Out There. . . .

Have you ever watched the old *X-Files* on television? Early in each strange story, the camera tilts up to a gray, overcast sky and the portentous words: "The Truth Is Out There."

At some point in even the most courageous fight against a disease, the truth is out there, and we must face it. That's what happened when Liz finally told her parents what she knew. Stephen, already racked by the effects of the tumor, was just so sad. He cried and told his daughter, "I'm so sorry you carried this all by yourself and didn't tell us, because we would have tried to help you." He went on with ideas like, "You know I'm still fighting, and still think there's a chance I can beat this." And Liz said, "I know that, Dad, and I really want you to. But I also know there's a chance you might not."

At this point I told Joan, it's time to tell the other two girls the whole truth. What they were seeing every day simply didn't fit anymore with, "I'm going to lick this thing." It was time to begin getting ready for what was probably going to happen. And all five had a series of family meetings and talked about the truth that was probably out there.

Stephen died several years ago, and the girls mourned for quite a while. Liz, who was probably closest to her dad, seemed to grieve the longest. But for all three it was a healthy, cleansing grief, and today they seem undamaged by their family's tragedy. Nobody quit school, nobody got pregnant, nobody got involved with boys her mom hated. Nowadays, when I see them at our holiday parties, they seem healthy. They seem sad sometimes, but they seem to be making it as a family.

Managing the Web

So: What do we do about this two-edged sword, the Internet? The first thing I do with a new client family is ask (as I'll now ask you): "Has your child gone online?" If they say no, I pursue it: "Are you *sure?*" Sometimes they're not.

I tell them that there's a lot of really frightening information out there in cyberspace, some of it accurate, a lot of it not. For one thing, there are a lot of bloggers, a lot of personal stories, and it's usually people in the most desperate (not necessarily typical) situations who are driven to put their own extreme stories online. And a teenager who goes online to look up Mom's disease is likely to skip the more scientific-looking (and more accurate) websites and go for the stories—in many cases, far-out horror stories that don't actually represent the average family's situation.

What I *don't* suggest is asking your child directly: Have you gone online? Children, particularly younger ones, may not even have thought of using the computer to research the disease; you don't want to plant that idea. Older teens may be deliberately avoiding getting more information than they think they can handle; once again, you don't want to drive them toward the Web. I ask children more open-ended, noncommittal questions:

"What do you know about your dad's illness?"

"Where did you get that information?"

"Do you have any plans to get more information, and where will you get it?"

"Is there any way we can help you get the information you need?"

But if a youngster says, "I've been thinking of going online," I'll offer to fire up the computer right then and there, and show her websites I think will be both accurate and useful. And that's what I suggest you do; at the end of this chapter you'll find a list of websites that can give your children correct, age-appropriate information on a variety of illnesses. Each also provides hyperlinks to other good, trustworthy sites. Your medical professional can help you find safe, accurate sites for specific diseases; be sure to let him or her know that your children will be looking at the site.

That way, instead of typing in "breast cancer" and coming up with several million sites—a lot of them dangerously overhyped or inaccurate—your son or daughter will go to the American Cancer Society website and research breast cancer with people who know what they're talking about. I'd also suggest you stay with your children, so you know what they're learning. You might even learn something worthwhile too.

Those Not-So-Personal "Personal Sites"

My sister Debbie is a tough cookie. She needs to be; she's raising two teenagers. A while ago, when they wanted their own pages on Facebook, Debbie told them this:

"You may set up the pages, but be sure you understand: At least once a week, I'm going to look up your Facebook page. You won't know when, but it's going to happen. And if I find anything I don't like, we're shutting it down."

Not only were her kids okay with this, I think they were quietly relieved to know that a responsible adult would be monitoring their sites. Because, as we'll see, sometimes what a teen posts on Facebook is really a cry for help.

Social-networking sites like Facebook are another two-edged sword of this new electronic age. Used under continuing adult supervision, they can really help youngsters stressed by a parent's grave illness. But unsupervised postings by unsupervised 'tweens and teens can result in great emotional and even economic harm to families. A little later, I'll tell you two stories of how adult monitoring of personal websites headed off serious harm to their young authors.

Nothing Personal

Let me start by giving you my orientation here: *There is nothing personal about a personal website.* Too often, parents think their child's Facebook page is like a diary or a journal—something personal and private to their child. And they want to respect that privacy. But a "personal" website is a *public* journal; your child is putting it up for all the world (or at least, all the world she invites in) to see. And you have not only every right but a serious, ongoing *responsibility* to monitor what your son or daughter is telling that world.

(A lot of youngsters tell me they're pretty sure their parents aren't carrying out that promise to review their Web pages, and I'm afraid they're right. Personally, I can no more imagine not monitoring a child's website than not monitoring homework or report cards. In the grip of a family crisis, it is easy to let the teen's Web page slide from week to week. But the family crisis is the reason for *more serious* monitoring, not less.)

Personal Sites: The Good Stuff

A page on Facebook or some similar site can really help your child decompress from the ongoing strain of a family medical crisis. It's her chance to level with the world: not "here is what I should be feeling" but "here is what I am feeling." And she'll be talking to peers who can understand, sympathize, and, yes, offer support no parent or sibling can.

You've probably already given your teens the general ground rules for safety on the Web: No conversations with anyone you don't know; no revealing information about yourself or us; no home address, etc. But now there's a major illness, a family crisis added to the picture, and you'll need some special ground rules—which will depend on what you, the parents, are willing to let your children tell the world.

You need to have a new conversation about what can and can't go on the website. And in setting these rules, be aware: What starts on the Web doesn't necessarily stay on the Web. Teens talk to other teens, who talk to parents; the Web may begin to leak to employers, to insurers, to local, state, or federal agencies. Set the boundaries you and your family are comfortable with. Tell your teens: You can say Dad has a serious illness, but *no details*. If your friends want to know more, what will you tell them? Think all of these consequences through *before* your teen touches a keyboard.

But if you're okay with your child telling this electronic world about Dad's illness, it can be extremely positive: "OMG, this sucks! I never get out of the house anymore; I never see anybody; I never have any fun."

This kind of heartfelt (if perhaps self-dramatizing) outpouring to friends can be a real catharsis for your teen or preteen; it can also give you a special insight into what's happening behind those young eyes. And if your child is sure that you're really reading her posts, there may be messages there for you.

What's on Those Sites

When I know any young client of ours has a website, I always ask permission to read it, and he or she usually grants it without hesitation. As I've followed those sites, I've found that most of those virtual "friends" out in cyberspace are supportive; they really do want to help. I'm reading things like, "Oh, that's horrible. I didn't know that was going on with you. What a rotten time. *What can I do?*"

Another potential benefit for your children is the virtual support group. If the illness afflicting your family is a fairly common one, and if you live in or near a city, you can probably find face-to-face support groups for your teens—a physical get-together with other teens facing the same family crisis. At The Gathering Place, we have several groups going at any time.

This kind of let-it-all-hang-out chat with other youngsters who are dealing with a similar trauma can be enormously helpful. But if your medical situation is more rare, or you live far from support centers, that kind of help for your children may be hard, even impossible, to find. That's where the Web comes in; because it is indeed a worldwide phenomenon, the kids your kids need to talk to may be anywhere in the world.

The sites are interactive; your children can have chat room meetings with other youngsters in the same situation who live hundreds or thousands of miles away. They may learn from each other, support each other. I say "may," because you never know for sure whether an electronic encounter with someone else who's been through the same trials will be helpful or not. But it's worth a try—and here again, the parent or helping adult should go along, and determine whether the cyber-group is a good idea for *your* child.

At the end of this chapter, you'll find guideposts to these virtual support groups.

Susan and Val: Two Calls for Help

Let me give you a couple of examples of why I believe it is so important that at least one responsible adult be monitoring your tweens' and teens' personal websites:

Susan: "I'm Trying Something . . ."

Susan was twelve; her mother had cancer and wasn't doing all that well. Susan set up a Facebook page and said it was okay for me to read it. I checked it a couple of times; what I saw was mostly just twelve-year-old-girl stuff, so I stopped looking. Then one day Susan e-mailed me urgently: "Mom is worse, Dad is being impossible, I need a lot of help *right now.*"

I e-mailed back a time and date for us to meet, a couple of days later, then I thought I'd check her Facebook page for a clue to the problem. What I found was beyond disturbing. The tone had darkened: "Mom is getting really sick. It's hard to concentrate at school. Teachers don't understand when I don't do my homework, they don't realize that at home I have to be so quiet because Dad is always in a bad mood. . . ." She went on about her mother's deterioration for quite a while, and then she wrote something that was a huge red flag: This is a close paraphrase:

"I wish I could find something to help take the pressure off. *I'm trying something one of my friends said: it's not working very well for me. It hurts.*"

I wasn't sure what that meant, but I could make a guess: Susan was cutting herself.

Cutting

It's a phenomenon of preteens and teens; both genders do it, but most who try it are girls. They experiment, cutting themselves with a razor or other sharp object, in some location where parents and other adults can't see it but they can. The inside of an arm is frequently the place; long sleeves can conceal the cuts from parents, but the child can look at the scars and remember the act of cutting.

These children don't seem to be "punishing" themselves; rather, they appear to be deflecting some emotional pain they find intolerable by inflicting physical pain. When you stub your toe, you stop thinking about unpaid bills, at least for a moment. And when a child cuts herself, it leaves a mark she can look at and remember that physical pain.

Coincidentally, Susan's aunt Julie, who'd taken over most of the responsibility for her, called me the next day: One of Susan's girlfriends had told Julie that Susan was experimenting with cutting.

I told Julie I'd need to see both of them right away, but I'd have to talk to Susan alone first. When Susan and I sat down, I asked her point-blank: What is that Facebook page about? And she admitted—

she seemed relieved to admit—that she had tried cutting herself, twice. She didn't like it; it didn't make her feel better. And she showed me a couple of small scratches on her arm. They were minor, and Susan was clearly having second thoughts; she was not yet on the way to serious self-mutilation. So we made a pact: You won't do this again. If you try again, we'll have to get you some professional help, but I have your promise: This is over. We'll have to tell your dad in any case. And I have news for you: Aunt Julie already knows.

Susan was shocked that her pal, whom she'd sworn to secrecy, would tell her aunt. But Susan was clearly reaching out for help: by telling her friend, but above all, with that Facebook posting.

Julie was marvelous. She had a teenage daughter of her own, who had tried cutting several years earlier, so she could understand Susan's despair. She didn't lecture her niece, didn't scold, didn't threaten, she simply said, "You can't do this. I can't let you hurt yourself. I know you're really upset, I know you're really hurting inside. What can we do to help?" And that was the end of it.

Susan's mother has since died, and Julie is a surrogate mother to her. They are making it.

But the beginning of the end was Susan's Facebook entry: It was a cry for help.

Val: Dangerous Ideas

Val was also calling for help, but more insistently. She was sixteen and terribly sad; her mom had recently died of cancer. Val set up a Facebook page and did more than give me permission to read it; she was oddly insistent. Each time she came in, she would ask, "Have you read my Facebook?" So I started going over it pretty carefully.

Val was coming in for sessions every other week, and that seemed to be enough for her, but then, right around Christmas—which, depending on what's happening in our lives, can be the happiest or saddest of holidays—the tone of Val's entry changed.

It read like a stream of consciousness—Everyone is so excited about the holiday . . . everyone is smiling, they're thinking what a good time they're going to have . . . everybody's so happy and I'm so sad . . . Christmas means nothing to me anymore. . . .

And then Val wrote: Sometimes I wish I wasn't even alive . . . I wonder whether it's really true that when you die you get reunited with people who've already died . . . I'd really like to see my mom again . . .

Suicidal Ideation

It's called "suicidal ideation"—the child's mind beginning to play with the idea of self-destruction. It can show up in children much younger than most of us realize—and it must be addressed *immediately*.

I called Val and her father in at once. She was pretty mad at me for reading her Facebook page, even though she had kept after me to look at it. But I told her: This has gone past privacy. Her dad and I agreed that she needed a higher level of help than either he or I could provide, and we scheduled her with a therapist. *Talk of suicide must always be taken with utter seriousness.* Far better to overreact a dozen times than to underreact just once.

Val stayed mad at me for a while, but she kept coming to our sessions. Somewhere inside her, with the help of therapy, Val decided that living is better than dying.

When teens and 'tweens put ideas like this onto a personal website, *it is always a cry for help.* These sites are a marvelous new tool for understanding and helping children, a tool that just a few years ago didn't even exist.

But we have to look.

Texting: Fastest Thumbs in Cleveland

There is one more ocean, in our children's new electronic world, which we'd be well-advised to learn to sail: texting.

It certainly didn't come naturally to me, firmly rooted as I am in a twentieth-century world of dumb, corded phones and, yes, even snail mail. But to stay in touch with my young clients, I've had to become adept at texting—I've developed two of the fastest thumbs in Cleveland. This is the natural, preferred form of communication among preteens and teens: They text as naturally as they talk, and if you, the concerned adult, can master this skill, you'll have a brand-new entrée into your children's world.

My day, and my little screen, are filled with notes like these: "Having real, real bad day; cn I c u 4 sted 4-30?" "Pls tell Dad 2 liten up, pls?"

A lot of them are pretty cryptic; sometimes something utterly weird pops up and I haven't a clue. But it's how our kids will tell us about the stresses in their lives, and we can help if we learn to text. If I get, "havng crappy day, don't think I cn pass math final," I'll text back, "Cmon, u kno yr ready 4 it; take deep brth & head on in there!"

It takes a couple of minutes of my time, and it really seems to help. Once they've put their miseries into text and sent them on to me, it seems somehow to lighten their load—they've passed their angst on to somebody else.

And it gives the parent or concerned adult a new way to send off those little love taps we spoke about earlier: "U rlly looked great going out the door this morning!" "I'm home from the dr. she sez everything's looking good!"

Turn 'em Off

But of course, as the author of Ecclesiastes might have written if he'd known about BlackBerrys, there is a time to text and a time to refrain from texting. When the family is meeting to discuss Mom's prognosis or Dad's upcoming course of treatment, every little pocket wonder in the house must be switched off. Not to "vibrate": *Off.* At these fraught moments, young Master Bruce must not be wondering whether that could be girlfriend Darlene jiggling in his pocket. Each member of the family must focus on the family to the exclusion of everything else. You might even want to banish everybody's handheld to another room. There will, of course, be anguished outcries.

Hang tough.

This cyberworld isn't yet a natural environment for some of us who are older. But it is where our children now live and grow up; as natural a landscape for them as their own bedrooms. And so we must learn to live there too.

Reliable Internet Websites for You and Your Children

For sites related to **cancer**, go to The Gathering Place website: touched-bycancer.org. Click on Cancer Resources for a list of websites we have found to be helpful

The following are reliable, user-friendly general sites, with strong search engines, to guide you to information concerning your own family's particular medical situation. Please be aware that these sites are available at this writing; they do change and evolve over time:

web.MD.com
healthcentral.com
wrongdiagnosis.com
medicineonline.com
health.discovery.com
health.nih.gov
emedicine.com
health.yahoo.net

For Jeremy Butcher, thirteen, one of the worst parts of having a dad with cancer was going to visit him in the "hospitable." Jeremy hated the smells, the sounds, and, most of all, the sight of his dad lying in bed, weak and vulnerable. Drawing the scene helped Jeremy bring out and cope with his reactions.

6.

Preparing Children for Hospital Visits

Two Kinds of Visits

Take a moment to look at the picture on the next page. I love it!

The artist was a nine-year-old girl who went to see her dad in the intensive-care unit, then drew what she'd seen. The drawing is just about textbook-accurate; every piece of medical equipment hooked up to her dad is correctly drawn and in the right place. We even get to see half of the patient next door—the artist knew she wasn't supposed to look at him, but she couldn't resist a peek.

What this picture tells me is that this little girl isn't scared, not one bit. She's taking in everything she sees and handling it with a good reporter's eye for accuracy. She shows us that she understands what's happening to her father and that all that scary stuff is really good stuff because it's there to help him. Because she understands, she's handling her feelings. Instead of being frightened, she's *interested*.

I'm showing it to you for the same reason I show it to parents who consult me—to demonstrate that *you don't have to protect your children from medical experiences. You just have to prepare them.*

In this chapter we'll talk about two different kinds of hospital visits children make.

First, there are visits to parents in intensive care, where the medical situation is never less than serious and ranges on up to life-threatening. Second, visits to parents in non-life-threatening situations: a trauma unit after a car accident, the dialysis unit for kidney work.

It's all the same hospital, but for young visitors, the two situations must be handled entirely differently.

Preparing for Critical-Care
and Intensive-Care Visits

A seriously ill parent in a hospital critical-care unit can be a frightening sight, and we must start off understanding that. All the masks are gone, even those minimal little cosmetic aids with which we face our loved ones daily—a shave, combed hair, shaped eyebrows, dentures. What remains is a pallid husk, hooked up to a terrifying array of catheters, drips, and monitors. How can we even think of inflicting such a sight on a child?

The answer is, once again, that your child is *entitled.* The more menacing the situation, the more important for your child's future well-being that he have this opportunity—perhaps this final opportunity—to visit, *if he wants to.* That's still Dad or Mom on the other end of all that hardware, and most children will want to go. (Some won't, and that's okay. It's a decision best left to the child.) And I can assure you, most children who want to visit can handle the visit just fine—we simply have to prepare for it.

Reacting Where It's Safe

The first consideration: If the child is going to react badly, you want him or her to react someplace safe—*not* in the hospital's intensive-care unit. I've been called, more times than I like to remember, to deal with a little boy or girl who's run screaming from the first, unexpected sight of Dad or Mom.

And yet children, especially school-age children, are very curious about medical stuff and absolutely fascinated with bodies—their own and other people's.

So the answer is to prepare the child for exactly what he's going to see, to let him go through all the yecchs and "Oh, gross"es safe at home—and to brace yourself for some pretty unsentimental reactions: "What did they do with Dad's old liver? Is it in a jar somewhere? *Can we see?*" School-age kids are *fascinated* with mutilation!

Dress Rehearsal

Sit down with your children in advance. Explain exactly what Mom or Dad looks like today; you might even sketch that there's an IV drip here because Mom or Dad can't eat yet, a huge bandage covering where the doctors went in to take out the tumor, a breathing tube into the mouth. Let them know just what they're going to see *before* they walk in on it.

If the parent is very sick, taking a digital picture to show the children can be a terrific help—just be sure the hospital staff says it's okay and won't compromise the patient's medical situation. Go over the picture with the children, explaining exactly what's going on and what each piece of equipment is for. Stress that the equipment doesn't hurt—it is helping Mom or Dad.

You can help prepare young children with a doll: "The doctors had to cut Dad's hair, so they could get to the tumor in his head. Shall we cut Raggedy Andy's hair and see what he looks like?" Tape lengths of tubing or fishing line to a doll to show where catheters are going and what they're for.

Keep in mind: The older the child, the more preparation he or she may need before going to see a parent whose appearance is dramatically altered. "Mom really looks different now, because of the surgery. Just remember that she's still Mom, and she still loves you. Everything else is just the surface."

Preparing for the Emotions

It's important to prepare children not just for what they'll see but also for what they'll *feel* when they visit a parent in intensive care, especially a parent they haven't seen for a while. What they'll see may frighten them, may make them feel like crying. And all those feelings are *okay*.

Looking Scary

When we get very ill, we don't look much like those very ill people in the movies and on TV—fetchingly pale, with just a little hint of pain at the corner of a clear blue eye. We look *scary*.

The patient in renal failure is frighteningly swollen. The body that is rejecting a bone marrow graft may break out in unsightly rashes. And even though the child may be forewarned, the reality can overcome his preparation

The problem is more severe with an unresponsive or unconscious parent. The parent who is in command, who can say, "Well, hi," as you walk into the room, can engage the child's interests and demonstrate that Mom or Dad is still "in there," despite appearances. But a parent whose appearance is seriously altered, and particularly one who can't respond, may trigger an overwhelming wave of fear or grief, even in a child who's been well prepared. So part of that preparation should be:

"Now, when you see Mom, it may be hard for you to handle. You may just want to cry, you may want to leave the room. However you feel, *that's okay, sweetie.* Don't be afraid, don't be ashamed. If you want to cry, I'm here to hold you. If you want to leave the room for a while, that's what we'll do. Mom will understand and I'll understand."

(And you want to be sure that the sick parent *does* understand. Warning *her* how her child may react—explaining the content of this section—is a crucial part of preparing for the child's visit.)

If, after this kind of preparation, your child decides that, well, maybe I don't want to do this right now, that's fine. But if, as is more likely, she still wants to visit Mom, then you've done it right—you've given her the preparation she needs, not only for what she's going to see but also for what she's going to feel.

The Visit Itself

In planning the visit itself—and a child's visit to a critical-care unit *needs* to be planned—keep three points in mind:

1. **It should be the *child's* visit, planned around him or her. If you, Mom, want to get and give the comfort of just holding your husband's hand silently for half an hour, do that another time. Don't plan on leaving the room to talk with a**

doctor or a nurse or a social worker. Your child's visit is for your child. You're there for support.

2. Plan the specifics of the visit—and *make sure in advance that what you want for the children is okay with the medical staff.* That may mean conferring with the doctor; more often you'll talk to the head nurse, who is in continuous contact with the patient and sympathetic to family needs. Most children like to meet the doctors and nurses who are caring for their mom or dad.

   Then explain to your children exactly what's going to happen and what they may do:

   "It's okay to touch Daddy; you can go over and squeeze his hand. He'll like that."

   "Now, he has a tube in his mouth, so he can't talk to you. But I know he'll want to listen; he'd love to hear about you guys winning the ball game yesterday."

   "And if you want me to, I'll pick you up and you can give Daddy a kiss too, even though he may not be able to kiss you back. Okay?"

   Don't go into the unit with any specific expectations; it's okay for the children to kiss the sick parent, but it's also okay for them *not* to. You make the suggestions; let them decide.

   If you're bringing more than one child, plan in advance, with the kids and with the medical staff, whether they'll go in together or one at a time. The doctors and nurses may prefer that only one child is in the room at a time. But if they okay a group visit, decide what your kids need: the moral support of a group visit, or the quiet reassurance of one-at-a-time.

3. Plan a brief visit—and, odd as it may seem, the *older* the child, the *shorter* the visit. Here's why:

   Very young children, who don't fully understand what's

going on, will be okay playing with their toys for a while around the foot of Dad's bed. But once the older child has had his visit with Daddy, his imagination will begin to wander—that array of tubes and beeping monitors is going to start overwhelming him, terrifying him with the menace of the unknown.

So: Plan to fill the time and then leave; don't give your kids empty minutes to start imagining bad stuff.

A Visit to Mom

Every rule, of course, creates its own exceptions. This is the story of a visit that broke the keep-it-short rule, a visit that went on and on—and why that was a good thing.

She was in severe respiratory difficulty. She'd been in the intensive-care unit for three weeks, unable to breathe on her own. A tracheal tube kept her alive, but she'd contracted pneumonia, then a series of infections. She was slipping in and out of consciousness; it wasn't clear at this point whether she would recover, remain at some midpoint neither sick nor well, or finally succumb as one infection followed another.

She had three sons: Curtis was three, Johnny was seven, and Billy was nine. As is so often the case, each had his own needs and his own issues to resolve.

The big problem was Johnny.

Little Curtis seemed really comfortable at the hospital, as many young children are. He wasn't afraid of the daunting apparatus surrounding his mom, nor of his mom's medical condition. For one thing, she'd been sick for most of his short life; this wasn't a big change. For another, he'd been staying with his mom's parents, and Grandma had been bringing him in regularly to visit.

But the older boys had been staying with Dad, and this was their first visit to Mom in the ICU. Their father really hadn't grasped how vital it was, not only for the boys to see her, but also, and perhaps even more important, for Mom to see her boys.

Dad and the older boys arrived late; we had only a short time to tell the boys what to expect. And Dad had an appointment afterward, so the visit was getting seriously squeezed.

It immediately became obvious that Johnny was terrified of the ICU. He arrived scared; people in the family had told him, "Mommy's going to die." He hung back, standing far away from the bed, wanting nothing to do with this frightening-looking creature with all the tubing—a creature who hardly resembled his mom at all.

After three weeks, Mom desperately needed contact—close, physical contact—with both her older boys. But Johnny hid around a corner in the entrance hall, occasionally peeking around at his mom for an instant, then pulling back out of sight.

Billy, the nine-year-old, did better. He was, of course, more mature and more verbal then Johnny. Billy walked in and said "Hi" to his mom. Initially he was a bit scared; that's typical. But soon he relaxed, reached out, touched Mom, and started talking to her.

(You'll know when a child begins to relax and get more comfortable. He'll start to look around, take things in. Finally, he'll begin to ask questions. That's when the crunch is over.)

After a few minutes, with Johnny still hiding around the corner, his dad decided enough was enough, and reached out to pull him into the room. I said, "No, don't do that." This was a time for patience. The important thing was that Johnny was *not* saying, "I want to go now." When a child insists on leaving, it's best to leave and try again another time. But when the child is willing to stick around, that's important, and you can work with it if you let him take it at his own speed. Johnny was obviously being pulled between his mom and his fears, and he needed time to decide which way he would go.

Billy Psychs His Brother

At this point something very good happened: Billy went over to talk to his younger brother. "Mom and I are having fun together!" He even played a little childhood psychology on Johnny: "I'm going to get something you're not. Mom's giving me part of her lunch!"

Now Dad recognized that what was happening with Johnny was a lot more important than any appointment; everybody stayed.

After a while, I got Johnny talking, about what he was seeing around the corner, about what was scary. And finally Johnny said, "Well, I'll come in, but *just once, just for a minute!*" I said that would be just fine.

The more we empowered him, the more we let him make his own decisions, the more things he said he would try. First he started around the corner, and ducked back again. But then he came out, tiptoed into the room, and whispered, "I love you, Mommy." He backed up then, but not quite to the corner. And now he couldn't help noticing: His older brother was holding Mom's hand; the nurse at bedside was chatting Billy up. Billy was making himself at home, was getting a lot of neat attention. Johnny was starting to feel a little left out.

As Far as He'd Go

Johnny had made a picture for Mom. Now suddenly he walked forward, right up to her bedside, and put the picture down on the blanket, then backed away a step. *And that was as close as Johnny came, on this visit.* Mom obviously wanted, needed, to reach out and hold him, but that would have scared him away again. I assured her, "By the next visit, Johnny will be a lot more comfortable."

And he was. The next time he let his mother take his hand. He was still passive, still staring fixedly, unwilling to acknowledge the environment of the ICU. But on the third visit Johnny strolled into the room, walked straight over to his mother, took her hand, and began to look around.

From what I could find out, he suffered no ill effects—no bad dreams, no eating problems, none of the warning signs of trouble. Time and patience had taken care of Johnny, and they took care of his mom too— eventually she was transferred to a rehabilitation hospital to begin the long, difficult road to recovery. Her life was no longer in danger.

After the Visit

Despite your best efforts at preparation, the sight of a parent in intensive care can be a severe shock to any child. A father whose face seems swollen to twice its size after brain surgery, a mother gray and wan and shrunken, can simply overwhelm the child's preparation and her defenses.

If you know the parent in intensive care looks very different from when the children last saw him, it's a good idea to bring along a favorite picture, from the good times. Then, if you see the child badly upset after the visit, sit down with her there in the hospital lounge and tell her the truth about the future:

"You know, after a while, Daddy is going to be back just the way he was. Remember how he looked before all this? I have a picture here; let's look at it and remember things . . ."

What If Your Child Doesn't Want to Go to the Hospital?

If your child does decide, no, I'm not going to see Dad in the hospital, then it's important for you to offer alternatives. Because pretty certainly, if the child is past toddlerhood, he's thinking, somewhere inside, "I *should* go." What's important now is to head off any guilt—which is likely to make an even worse mess later on.

Frequently I'll suggest that the child draw a special picture, which I can take to the parent. I promise that I'll tape it to the wall where Dad can see it. Or I'll ask, "Would you like to take a walk with me outside, and pick a flower I can take to Dad?"

Another possibility for an older child, if the sick parent is mentally alert, is to write a letter or a special poem.

Here is a poem written by a nine-year-old named Robbie, for his mother, who was coming home from the hospital. Her condition was terminal.

Your sons and your spouse
Love and care for you
Every day as you go through the Valley of Shadows;

There's a ruler over all:
He's the creator of the world;
He made you and me walk together.

Together we'll be for eternity;
Even though we may split apart,
We'll always be together through the heart.

Come home now, and stay in God's care.

Preparing for Non-Critical-Care Visits

Being treated in the non-critical-care units is serious enough, painful perhaps, unpleasant certainly—but *the parent's life is not threatened.* And for children visiting parents in these non-critical units, it's an entirely different situation from the intensive-care areas.

- Visits can be longer—a lot longer. They can, in fact, become family occasions, a bit of home away from home for everyone.
- Almost certainly, the patient will be able to talk with the children, to keep up conversations, perhaps even play games. Of course, if there's been a serious (if temporary) change in appearance, you might want to do an abbreviated version of the advance preparation we talked about in "Dress Rehearsal" (page 148). But unless there's an initial shock of appearance, you can probably leave it to the patient to explain any medical equipment that may be hooked up.
- You can suggest that your children bring along homework to do, or a backgammon set or a deck of cards—even an electronic game if the hospital permits. The sick parent may be delighted to have her

kids there, but she certainly doesn't want to spend the whole time entertaining them. And for a kid, talking to somebody sick—even somebody sick whom you love—can get pretty boring. So make sure the visiting children have plenty to occupy their time.

I've had families set up picnics right beside Mom's bed (let the kids plan the menu). I've known some to bring in pizzas!

- Holidays and birthdays can be celebrated right at bedside; again, the kids can plan the mini-party.

Kids to the Rescue

Just because the situation isn't life-threatening doesn't mean that children's visits aren't important. They can be absolutely crucial, both for the children and for a sick mom or dad.

He was young and good-looking, he was successful, he had a pretty wife and two super kids—and now he might be about to lose his leg.

He'd been in a car crash, been taken first to a local hospital. When the badly mangled leg failed to respond, he was medevaced to the Cleveland Clinic trauma unit.

Now he hadn't seen his eight-year-old daughter and six-year-old son in two weeks. *And he didn't seem to want to.*

The children, staying with an aunt back home, were growing concerned, starting to feel cut off. Yet their mother told a nurse she was worried about having them visit. Her husband was depressed, in great fear of losing his leg. He didn't want his children to see him like this.

I went to talk with him, and he told me, "I'm trying to keep a good attitude, I really am. But *what's my life going to be like if I lose my leg?* My kids will be embarrassed by me. How can I teach my boy to play football? How can I do any of the things that I assumed were part of my life?"

He saw the loss of the leg as so *huge*. He truly feared that his children would reject him, be grossed out by a one-legged father. I suspect he had some of the same fears about his beautiful young wife, even though she'd been demonstrating right along that there wouldn't be a problem. I thought he was missing a point: His wife and children didn't love his leg; they loved *him*.

I talked with his kids on the phone. They seemed to have a good grasp of what was happening. They didn't appear to be afraid, although they expressed a lot of anger at the driver of the other car.

The mother told me she was terribly worried. She thought it would be good for her husband to have the children come, but he was *so* depressed. What if he snaps at them? What if he ignores them? What if he makes them feel rejected?

The Toss-up

It was a toss-up. The children were eager to see their dad, but they seemed to be okay; they were showing no warning signs of trouble to come. Nevertheless, my suggestion was that they come and come now— not so much for them, but for him. He needed to see his children, and to see whether or not they would reject him. So his wife and I pushed the visit, and finally, reluctantly, he agreed.

She and I briefed the children carefully. We explained about what they would see: The leg was open, badly infected. We warned them about the odor; it wasn't overwhelming, but it was definitely there.

But what we really emphasized was how Dad was feeling emotionally. He was scared of the operation that might take away his leg. We made sure they understood that that was a real possibility, even though the doctors were doing everything they could to avoid amputation.

"Your dad's pretty discouraged now. He's been through a lot of pain, had to switch hospitals, been far away from you guys. He's feeling down, and Mom thinks you can help cheer him up."

That was the idea that caught their imagination: *You can help your dad.* They arrived at the hospital almost with a sense of mission.

When they came in the room, they were fine; they weren't afraid of anything they saw. And you could watch them take on this adult role. These were good kids of good parents; Mom and Dad had given them the strength to handle this situation long before it arose. I believe what happened next made a great difference in their dad's orientation, and in his recovery.

They started right off, telling him about what was going on in their lives, and what they wanted him to get back to. He responded slowly, rather hesitantly to this cheerful chatter.

Finally the children said very clearly: "We really miss you. We want you home. No matter what happens, Daddy, if they can fix your leg or if they have to take it away, we still want you home. We'll do everything we used to do. It'll be a little different, but it'll be okay."

The young father had been terribly depressed, yet since the accident he had never cried. Now, listening to his children, he cried—a warm, relieving kind of crying. He reached out both arms and cradled them. Behind them, his wife was crying too. Amid the tears, you watched this family come together again.

Finally he could talk, could express his feelings:

"I've been really scared. And I really missed you guys."

When I visited again, later in the day, I found him playing checkers with his daughter. A very ordinary bedside scene.

The young man did not lose his leg; the surgeons were able to restore circulation and he is now in long-term rehabilitation. Chances are he'll wind up with a pretty good leg.

What If the Parent Doesn't Want a Visit?

What we saw in the last section is not unusual. Quite frequently a parent doesn't want a visit, feels just too depressed, doesn't want his children to see him "like this." Certainly we must respect that. But we must also realize there may be another need here: the children's need to see him, to be sure he's still Dad, perhaps even be sure he's still alive.

If in time the hospitalized parent will look better, feel better, be more like himself, and you can safely postpone the visit 'til then, that's perfectly fine. But if improvement isn't likely within a reasonable time frame, or a child is wild with anxiety, then you need to start some negotiations.

Just as you don't force a child to visit the parent against her will, you don't compel a parent to accept a visit he's adamantly against. Suggest that a short visit—five minutes only—would be good for both of you, and won't upset the child. Remind him: We've been working with Carly; she knows what to expect, and she's ready for what she'll see. *And she really needs to see that you're still here.*

In the next section, and later, in chapter 10, we'll talk about final visits and what children are entitled to in a parent's last hours. But for now, if the patient doesn't want the kids to visit, let it go for a while, or give a gentle push.

When It's Better Not to Go

There are situations when it's just as well for the child *not* to visit the hospital.

If the parent's appearance is really pretty bad—especially if the parent can't respond—and *if the child is handling the situation fairly well,* then you may decide to discourage a visit, or at least postpone it. Seeing a parent who looks dreadful, who may be unconscious or comatose—it will be very hard to make such a visit valuable for a child. Unless the situation is about to change dramatically—unless this may be the *last* visit—it's probably just as well for the child not to see the ill parent right now.

But if the child is *not* handling the situation well, if she's becoming suspicious, wondering what you might be keeping from her, *wondering whether Dad is even still alive,* then, with a lot of preparation, you should take her to see for herself.

Usually, as you've seen, I encourage children to go to the hospital—especially if the parent is in a life-threatening situation. Be sure to check with the hospital in advance. Most will bend visitation rules regarding children when there might be no other chances to see a gravely ill parent . . . or when, as not infrequently happens, a child needs to see for herself that the parent really is still alive.

A Family's Decision

The decision isn't always simple, and the first instinct isn't always the best. Let me leave you with a story of a family that really needed to see a beloved, and very sick, father—and why, in the end, they agreed not to.

I've mentioned this family before: a girl fifteen, a boy eleven, a girl nine, whose father suffered a massive heart attack and was put on an artificial pump—the only way to keep him alive until a donor heart became available.

The mother had been honest with the children, up to a point. She told them at once that their father had suffered a heart attack, that he was in the cardiac-care unit, and that he was being sustained by a machine called a HeartMate. But the children were so upset that she stopped there. She decided that the wrenching part about the need for a heart transplant could keep for another couple of days. She'd tell them the rest Monday, before school.

On Sunday the mother and children went to church. And the priest asked the congregation to pray for a fellow parishioner who was gravely ill, and *awaiting a heart transplant.*

It was nothing but a series of failures of communication; the priest had no idea that the children didn't know about the transplant part. But the children were furious at their mother: "You didn't tell us about a heart transplant!"

Distrust

When she came to see me Tuesday, the mother said glumly, "My kids think I'm lying to them now."

By the time I talked with the children, they'd pretty well accepted that their mother hadn't deceived them, that she really did intend to tell them about the transplant, but events got ahead of her. But there it was: the beginning of distrust.

At this point, all three children wanted to visit their dad. In the back of their minds, I think, they wanted to make sure that he really was still alive. And when it will help the children, I can usually talk the nurses into bending the rules. But:

In this case the father's condition was extremely precarious. His doctors didn't want him stimulated in any way. They wanted not even the slightest change in blood pressure, in breathing rate. They wanted him no more alert than the twilight sleep state they were holding him in with medication. Too, with his chest open for the HeartMate connection, there was a serious risk of infection—a risk heightened by every person who might come near him.

So in this case, the medical risk to the father had to outweigh the psychological risk to the children of *not* seeing him. For one thing, the gravest risk of all to the children would be if they *did* see him, and something went wrong after their visit.

Telling Them

I told them all that, told them that even the germs that couldn't make them sick might make him sick. I told them that the spiritual part within his sleeping body might sense that they were there, might try to wake up a little to respond to them, look at them, smile at them. Just the pleasure of hearing their voices might make him try to wake up.

And I explained that the doctors didn't want him waking up even the slightest bit; they wanted him to stay fast asleep under medication, so he wouldn't strain the little bit of heart muscle he had left.

All three understood and agreed that it would be better *not* to see him. Most important, at the end of the explanation, all three *knew* their father was still alive.

The Question

And so we talked some more, and finally the nine-year-old asked the question that *had* to be answered: "Could he die?" Mom's reply was, "We just have to pray." But, as you understand by now, that was not an answer; the question remained open. And so when, at the end of our session, I said, "Do you have any other questions?" the youngest daughter asked again, "Could he die from this?"

That is a question I always try to have children answer from within themselves. So I asked, "What do *you* think?"

"Yes," she said after a moment. "I think he could die from this." The other two both nodded.

Now we all knew.

PREPARING CHILDREN FOR HOSPITAL VISITS: A SUMMARY

A general rule. If the child wants to visit a sick parent, and the hospital staff says okay, it's usually good for both the child and the parent. Here's a quick list of considerations to help you decide whether the child should visit:

- Does the child want to go?
- Does the sick parent want a visit?
- Can the sick parent tolerate a visit medically? (The doctor or nurse must decide.)
- Will the hospital permit a visit by a minor child? (Check the regulations, then talk to the staff about special arrangements.)

Two Kinds of Visits: They're Very Different (page 145)

- Critical-care units
- Non-critical-care units

Preparing Children to Visit Critical-Care Units (page 147)

- Why should they visit? (page 148)
- Prepare them at home for what they'll see (page 148)

How to use drawings and photographs (page 148)
What to tell them (page 148)
Preparing for their emotions (page 148)
The visit itself: remember three key points (page 149)
>   It's the *child's* visit
>   You should plan what will happen
>   Keep the visit *brief*

- After the visit: dealing with a shock (page 154)
- If the child decides *not* to visit (page 154)
  >   Handling the guilt
  >   Sending a token: flowers, pictures, poems

Preparing Children to Visit Non-Critical-Care Areas (page 155)

- A different set of rules
- Things to do at bedside

Two Memories

- Kids to the rescue (page 156)
- When it was better not to go (page 159)

To Make the Visit a Good One:

- Prepare your child thoroughly for what she'll experience
- Give her specific jobs or activities to do during the visit (decorating a wall, telling the sick parent something that happened)
- Explain the kind of emotions—fear, sorrow—people may have when they visit in the hospital

Even though Meaghan Callahan Diffenderfer, age eight, drew "Some people know people who get better" while her dad was very ill, her picture is about hope—children's default setting. A smiling girl, under blue skies, says, "This is better."

7.

Coming Home

"Can You Stop by My Office for a Few Minutes?"

Whenever one of our patients is about to be sent home after treatment, I like to spend an hour or so with the well parent to talk about what's likely to happen now, and especially how the children may be affected. If you could actually come to my office, we'd probably chat along these lines:

> I just heard the good news—your wife has finished her treatment and will be coming home in a day or two. That's marvelous!
>
> Your kids have been real good about all this. They've visited Mom in the hospital, and all of them have been handling their lives very well—they're in school and doing fine. But now things are going to change for them again, and it's probably not going to be the change they expect.
>
> Most kids, and especially the little ones, expect that as soon as Mom comes home, she'll be just fine, ready to start up all the Mom things right away. You know the reality.
>
> She's feeling the effects of her treatment; she's lost her hair,

she's losing weight, her energy level right now is zilch and it's not going to improve very much for a while.

So even before she comes home, it's really important that your children understand she's not going to be 100 percent the mom they remember. I'd suggest that, *before you bring her home,* you sit down with the children and explain how she's going to feel. Have her explain too, next time they come to visit. In fact, this would be a very good time to start having *family meetings.*

Regular Family Meetings

You might make a plan for sitting down, all together as a family, perhaps once a week, perhaps even more often. Set a regular time and place. Get everyone together—including your wife if she feels up to it— and update the children on any changes that are going on.

You'll want to tailor the length of the meetings, and how much information you try to get across, to the kids themselves. A two-hour family meeting might be okay for teenagers; it's far too long for young children. You know about how much they can absorb at any one time.

The First Meeting

Talk about what it will be like when Mom comes home:

- How she'll feel.
- Will she sleep in her regular room, or some special place?
- Will any medical equipment come home with her? When is it coming? What does it look like? What will it do for her?
- Any questions?

You'll find your children will handle things a lot better if you give them a little time to prepare for what's going to happen.

Especially, let your children know what to expect in terms of how Mom will feel and what her abilities and limitations will be in the first few days and weeks. Prepare them for the fact that Mom will be going through a big adjustment. Make it concrete for them. Say, for example:

"Remember how it felt when you had the flu? Everything's normal, then suddenly you're real sick. You go to bed, and for three or four days you feel totally rotten, then you get a little better. So you try to get back into normal life, but everything feels weird. You feel out-of-body, out of sync, not even sure where everything is in your own house?

"Well, Mom's been in the hospital for *three weeks,* going through some pretty rough treatment, so being back home is going to be really strange to her for a while. She's going to be disoriented, and she may seem a little weird.

"And . . . Mom's looking at her life a lot differently now. She's asking herself a lot of questions about values, about what things mean. *She's not going to be the same . . .*"

Your children need information about all those things, so they're prepared, so they understand *why Mom is still a little different,* and it will take a while for things to get back to as normal as they will get. And how normal will that be?

What to Expect Now

If the doctors tell you to expect complete recovery, reassure your children that things *will* get back to normal and give them the time frame. Mom will be all better, but it's going to take a while—by Christmas—by next summer—maybe even a year.

If things will always be different, then the children need to begin to understand what the differences will be. And coming to that understanding is a *process.* You don't achieve it in one meeting. You get there slowly, over time. (We'll talk about that in the chapter on chronic illness.)

If recovery will be slow, and especially if the disease is likely to recur, the children *must* be forewarned. Because if they expect the disease never to come back, and it does, this will be a huge disappointment, with serious consequences for them. It may be worse than the first time, because now they know exactly what to expect. They may even blame Mom for getting sick again. So right now is the time to give them all the bad news, along with the good.

Getting Ready for the Homecoming

The kids can help you get ready for Mom's homecoming and help prepare themselves at the same time. They already know she's lost her hair because of the chemotherapy, so take them shopping Saturday. Let them pick out half a dozen gorgeous head scarves. For a while, at least, she's not going to be able to pull tops over her head, or button anything in back, so have the kids select some pretty blouses that button in front. (For ideas on how the children can help out once mom is home, go back to chapter 2.)

No Big Deal, Please

For the sake of everybody—your wife, your kids, yourself—I'd suggest you keep the homecoming very low key. Resist the tendency to have a big party. Lots of family and friends are going to want to celebrate her return, especially with a good prognosis. But:

> *Your children really need private time with their parents in your own environment.*

It's fine for people to drop by, fine for friends to help you out, but *don't do it as a huge celebration.* Give yourselves a little time. Understand that your children need privacy too. If people start trooping incessantly through your home to see your wife, the children are going to feel intruded upon.

In any case, they may need some understanding—permission to go to friends' houses, permission to go to their rooms and keep the doors closed for a while. *Every child in every family needs a private space where he or she can be alone and know the space won't be violated.*

This is especially true for your older kids—the teens—they are really going to need their privacy now. No kid wants home to be Grand Central Station, and a lot of youngsters in this situation tell me that's exactly how they feel—a house full of people hanging around trying to be helpful.

Remember those invaluable crowd-control devices from chapter 2: your home phone or cell phone answering systems, your personal site on the Internet. Bring them back now. Let the phones take the calls: "Hi. This is an update. Wendy is doing fine. The doctors say she'll be up in a few days. We're just going to be a nuclear family tonight, so thanks for the call and please leave a message, because Wendy and I both want to get back to you."

A personal website can be even more rewarding. Because it's interactive, it can give friends and family continuous updates and messages from Wendy herself, and allows all those folks to leave their love and good thoughts for Wendy.

Let Mom (or Dad) Be Mom (or Dad)

There'll be a tendency now, both for spouse and helpers, to do everything, to "protect" the newly arrived, perhaps very weak patient, from any parental task or responsibility. Resist this one too.

It is extremely important to let the recovering parent step back into whatever role she chooses, to whatever extent she chooses, *as soon as she chooses.* She's the mom, and she's going to want to be the mom again. Maybe she can't do much. But if she wants to pack the kids' lunches, because she knows what they like, step back and let her pack lunches. Many returning moms tell me, "Yeah, I'm tired, yeah I don't feel so good, yeah, I'll take a nap afterward, *but I want to braid her hair.*"

And prepare to be flexible. Just because Mom feels strong enough to make the lunches on Monday and Tuesday does *not* mean she'll be up to the chore on Wednesday. Perhaps the first time Dad tried to make lunch, she snapped, "I'm home now. I can do that!" It doesn't mean she won't ask for or need help down the road. Recovery is an up-and-down process; welcome the ups and swing with the downs.

Letting Teachers and Schools Know

One more thing you'll need to do is go to your children's schools and tell their teachers Mom is coming home or is already home. (If your wife feels well enough, she may want to make the contacts by phone. But one of you should do it, and soon.)

The teachers should understand that things will probably be a little different. Mom's home, but she's still going to be on the kids' minds. Basically, give the teachers the same kind of information you did when your wife was first diagnosed. Most important, explain that while any help or comfort—from teachers or friends—will be appreciated, *there must be no compromise on what is expected of your children by the school.*

You will accept no easing up on academic demands, no "compassionate grading," above all, *no permission to fail.* All your children's teachers must understand: You and your wife will accept no compromise on achievement, and if there's a problem, you want to be notified immediately.

Let the teachers know that you'll keep them up to date, and then do that from time to time. Teachers are going to be some of your best resources and most helpful allies through these weeks or months or years of stress on your children.

Making Sure

And, in the nicest way possible, of course, you're going to have to keep after those teachers. In my years at The Gathering Place, I have seen so many parents carefully, dutifully brief their children's teachers: "Here's what's going on with Janie, here's what's happening in our family, I need to know if my children's behavior or school performance changes—"

And then nothing. The teachers never report that Janie isn't bringing in her homework, that she's failing the math quizzes. I see these careful parents growing so frustrated.

Part of the problem may simply be the increasing pressure on teachers as class sizes inexorably grow and school budgets shrink. A teacher with thirty-five or forty students per class can't possibly give each one (and her parents) as much attention as if there were twenty or twenty-five.

Another part may be teachers good-heartedly trying to shield you from worry. And part may be the assumption that you'll see her report card at mid-semester. But mid-semester may be four or five weeks from now, too late to pull your child off the failure track before the term ends.

So you're going to have to keep reminding the teachers over a period of time: You want to know what's happening with your child *as it's happening.* Here's a useful shortcut:

The first time you talk to a teacher, give him your e-mail address and ask him to use it anytime a problem arises: If Janie's struggling with spelling, if she's talking back, behaving badly in class, anytime any bad thing shows up, behaviorally or academically, just e-mail me.

That way an overwhelmed teacher doesn't have to try getting you on the phone. After school, when he's doing his e-mails anyway, he can simply add a note to you: Here's what I'm seeing with Janie; you asked me to let you know. (If you receive such an e-mail, it's a good idea to hit Reply, acknowledge receipt, and say thanks. It's the courteous thing to do, and it will encourage future contacts.)

Continuing the Family Meetings

Some families have meetings only around new medical crises. That's okay, but I strongly recommend *regular* meetings that don't carry an aura of emergency. Periodic, scheduled meetings assure your kids that they're in the loop, being briefed regularly and openly. When the patient is up to it, meetings let the children hear from both parents together, so they aren't tempted to manipulate one of you against the other.

But on a more basic level, family meetings make *all* your children, even the little ones, feel more mature and responsible. They see that you consider their input important. They know that grown-ups, that Dad and Mom, have regularly gone off to important meetings. Now there's a family meeting: *It must be important.*

Spell Out What's Expected of Everyone

A lot has probably changed while Mom was away, so in the first couple of meetings, you need to remind the kids of what you and your wife expect: who does what chores; bedtimes; behavior; house rules. Address the situation very honestly: We know Grandma didn't make you clean your rooms, but Mom's home now, and we want to get back to the way things were.

You and your wife have to confer about the rules, think about which ones you might want to modify, make a plan. Remember: *Your children will do best if they have the security of getting things back to normal routine as much as possible, as soon as possible.*

Schedule Private Time

Meetings or no, each child is going to need some private time with you, and some private time with Mom. It's really important that you and your wife build that into your days; you're going to be pulled in a million directions now, *but the kids still need some time with each of you.*

Watch for ways you can incorporate that private time into the routine. If your teenage son has the job of washing the car each Saturday, you can go out there with him, catch up with what's going on at school and with his girlfriend (unless he just *hates* washing the car, then it's a good time for you *not* to be around!).

Family meetings are for information and reassurance; your kids won't share their feelings then. It's going to be in private, one-on-one, that they'll share. You know what times they're most communicative. One may tend to confide at night, just before going to sleep; another gets very thoughtful in the morning, over cereal. So try to zero in on those times, and find a moment to say, "I just wanted to see how you're doing. Got any questions about Mom? How are things going? Are you getting back to normal at school? Got any plans for the weekend? How was the Brownies meeting?"

Just chat with them about their feelings and activities—touch base with them. *They'll really need that from you.* They'll need some private time with Mom too; you and she together have to balance that need against not wearing her out.

Each child needs to find a time alone with her, when they're not competing for her attention. Especially your quieter kids, who are likely to be less assertive, to stand back and wait for someone to invite them.

When you see your children doing that, you need to open that door, to say, "I have to work in the garage for a bit; can you sit with Mom? I think she'd enjoy the company." You need to help it happen. And of course, you need to be sure Mom is up to it. The two of you should do a little plotting together.

Watching for Signs of Trouble—Again

Both of you must *watch for behavior changes in your children*—those signs of trouble we talked about at the beginning of all this. (See chapter 3, "Early Warnings.")

Trust your gut. If you think one of the children looks worried or distracted; if she's angry at everything when there's nothing to be angry at—you may not be able to figure out what's wrong, *but chances are something is wrong.* Try to find a way to get at it. But *don't try during the time your child is really upset.* Wait until a quiet time, when she is open to you.

Dads' Laps and Moms' Laps

Remember, we're talking about behavior that continues over time. There will be moments when your children appear sad; children's emotions go on incredible roller-coaster rides.

Being sad for a short period of time is perfectly okay. At some point, you're going to come into a room and see your child wipe away tears real quick, and say everything's fine. And you know he was just crying. Go put an arm around him, give him a hug or a squeeze or a pat on the backside, whatever is comfortable for both of you, and say, "If you want to talk about it, I'm here, but if you just want a hug, I'm here for that too."

The kids don't really have to understand; they'll just have these down moments. They don't even need to talk—just to know you're there for them, and you'll do whatever is needed to try to make them feel secure.

I like to remember a lovely line in a lovely book called *A Taste of Blackberries* by Doris B. Smith: A little boy says:

"I forgot that dads' laps could be as good as moms' laps."

COMING HOME: A SUMMARY

Warning: Hopes May Be Too High (page 165)

- Make sure the children know: the parent *isn't* "all better"
- Everything will *not* be back to normal immediately
- There may be changes in the home: new equipment, furniture, or rooms rearranged

Suggestion: Start Having Regular Family Meetings (page 166)

- Your First Family Meeting
- Tell your children what to expect:
    If full recovery is likely
    If full recovery isn't going to happen

Making Plans for the Homecoming (page 168)

- Get the kids involved: planning, shopping
- *No* big parties, please
- Make sure the children, especially the older ones, know they can go to a private place if they get overwhelmed
- A helper in the chaos: your answering machine

Bring Teachers and Schools into the Picture (page 170)

- What to tell them now
- Once again: *No compromise on your children's performance*

A Good Idea: Keep up the Regular Family Meetings (page 171)

Another Good Idea: Reestablish Your Family Rules (page 172)

Important: Make Private Time for Your Children and for Each Other (page 172)

Watch for Signs of Trouble—Again (page 173)

This is how Jasmine Hanna Funk, age nine, remembers her dad's long, losing battle with cancer:

"It's like you go one step at a time. First you find out about the person being sick; it's like you've got chains wrapped around your whole body. You can hardly move. You don't know what to do. But then you get some hope. The person goes to the doctor, they get some medicine; you think it's going to be okay. But then things get worse, and you need people to help you, and someone to talk to, and other kids to talk to, and that's the next step. And then you find a net of support, and you're in the net, and it holds you. And the support people will talk to you about that you're scared, and you're sad, and that you don't know if everything is going to be okay.

"And then, if it's not okay, you have to cry a lot, and that's what the tears are."

8.

Chronic Illness: When It Won't Get Better

Children and "Always"

Up until now, we've been thinking mostly about medical situations where something will *happen*. Within a time frame of weeks or months, Dad's illness will get better, or it will get worse. The chemotherapy will succeed or will fail. The body will accept the transplant or reject it.

But this chapter is about a situation that is, in many ways, more difficult for everyone—for the patient, for the partner, for the children. In this chapter, the science of medicine has come to its limit, has helped as much as it will help. Now the wheelchair, the darkness, the body's betrayal of itself have become permanent. Change, if it happens, will probably not be for the better, and it will come imperceptibly—not over days and weeks, but over years.

Now we are dealing with always.

Difficult as "always" and "forever" are for adults to accept, they are far more difficult for children. A child's world is one of new ideas, new skills, new developments almost every day. The only "forevers" in your child's world are the things he's always taken for granted, never even thought about—home, family, two healthy parents. Those are the "forevers" that are changing now.

Before we can even start to consider bringing children safely through this new reality, we need a way of thinking about chronic illness and how it affects family life. There is one image that I came across years ago, and that has stayed with me as I've worked with families struggling to adapt to an illness that won't get better.

Greenland

Imagine that you and your family have planned for years for a wonderful trip to France. You've studied the maps and the brochures; you've even learned a little of the language. You know all about driving through Normandy and you've packed your swimsuits for the Riviera; you're ready for Paris and the Seine and hot croissants at sidewalk cafes.

At last you and your family board the airplane and wing out across the Atlantic. The plane touches down. The attendant opens the cabin door . . .

. . . And you're in Greenland.

> *Oh, Greenland is a dreadful place,*
> *A land that's never green,*
> *Where there's ice and snow, and the whale-fishes blow,*
> *And daylight's seldom seen,*
> *Brave boys!*
> *Daylight's seldom seen*

What might you feel, looking out that door across an icy, alien tundra? There would be, first, a feeling of total disorientation, then, perhaps, a crushing sense of loss.

This is exactly what many families feel as they face the prospect of a parent's lifelong illness.

Yet a moment's thought will probably suggest one additional idea to you:

Even Greenland has possibilities.

Coming to Terms with Your Own Altered Future

I can promise you now, as I have in every previous situation: Your children can handle this new reality, can live and grow and *thrive* despite—and even because of—the travail of a parent's lifelong illness. In my experience, *the children usually emerge whole and sound.*

But the parents who face a chronic illness must help themselves before they can possibly help their children.

No child can adapt to your new condition if you are angry all the time, or constantly depressed, or more dependent than your medical situation compels you to be. As long as the parent is struggling against this new reality, the children will struggle and fail to adapt.

So before you can begin to help your children, you must first look at yourself.

- Do you understand this new future?
- Can you accept it, or at least get past the injustice of it?
- Can you reach this understanding: "My life has changed, but it's going to go on"?

There is the tendency now to echo John F. Kennedy's homily: "Life is unfair." I think that puts life in terms that are far too narrow, too centered on ourselves. Life is neither fair nor unfair. Life is life. And if life takes us unexpectedly to Greenland, perhaps we can learn to ski.

Helping Your Child Come to Terms with a Different Future

What you are struggling with, your children are struggling with. Usually it's on an unconscious level; rarely will they be able to talk about it. The unexpressed feeling is: "I'm *never* going to have a dad like Dad was." Inevitably, there is a huge sense of mourning, of loss. Most of this chapter will be about getting *beyond* the mourning, accepting the loss, and living and coping with this new reality—this new emotional Greenland.

Preparing Your Children

You should proceed now in very much the same way that you did when your illness was first diagnosed, as we discussed in chapter 1. As you face a future of living with permanent illness or disability, you must take your children into the process. Some parents are hesitant about this; they fear they might be *leaning* on their children for emotional support. A common reaction is, "I don't want to make our child think he has to solve our problems."

Quite the opposite: You are opening yourselves up so your children can *lean on you*.

You must tell them, with complete honesty, your understanding of what is coming:

- How the illness will proceed, and on what timetable.
- The plans you've made and are making for how the family will readjust and cope—who will do "the Mommy things" or "the Daddy things."
- Once again, as in chapter 2, you and your children should plan the help you will need and expect of them.
- Very important here, your own feelings and reactions—in sharing your own uncertainties and sense of injustice, you give them permission for their own emotional responses, their grief, their rage, their sense of loss. Again, your purpose in opening yourselves in this way is *not* to gain emotional support from your children. Instead, you are offering them a *model*, an understanding that what they feel is acceptable, *because Mom and Dad feel that way too.*

The Continuing Dialog

What your children will need in this new reality is the same kind of absolute honesty and openness we've been talking about since page 1. But now they need one thing more: The dialog must continue over time.

Remember, the situation will never be static. Even if the parent's condition remains unchanged for months or years, *the child is changing every day.*

Right at the beginning, you and your children will need to talk out what has happened to Mom or Dad, the emotional impact, and how ordinary, everyday life is now going to change. But that *is* only the beginning; parents can never enjoy the feeling, "Okay, we've talked it out; I've explained to them what MS or progressive blindness or Huntington's or spinal cord damage is, and what's going to happen, so *that's over.*"

Continuing the dialog is one of the most important things you can do for your growing children. As they grow, their understanding and their physical and emotional abilities grow with them. Inevitably their development will be affected by the abilities and condition of the sick parent.

Choose some regular intervals to talk, and be governed by how much the children seem to need. The parent's visits to the doctor or hospital are a good time to bring the family up to date. And watch how your children react; if you get, "That's great, Mom; gimme the details later, 'cause I'm late for band rehearsal," that's fine. Your child has put his dad's illness into the background music of his normal life.

Remember: Just because a parent has a chronic illness, that *doesn't* mean the children have a problem with it. And if you *expect* a problem, if you keep pushing information at a child who isn't particularly worried, you may create a self-fulfilling prophecy. You may get the child to *start* worrying.

Fear of the Parent

Sometimes it will happen: This new, somehow "different" parent returns from the hospital, and the children back away, physically or emotionally. They may not know how to handle the situation, or they may actually fear the parent.

It's important to get past that, and it's important for the child to get comfortable again with whatever level of interaction the parent can now handle.

In general, infants and toddlers adapt best to the situation; it may take a three- or four-year-old a little while to adapt to the parent's limitations, but pretty soon, if Mom can't pick Jimmy up for a cuddle, Jimmy learns to climb into Mom's lap.

The older the child, the more difficult the adaptation—the more the child fears for his own well-being, the more bad things he can imagine.

If the child is simply afraid, that's pretty easily overcome with just a moderate amount of education and instruction. Before the parent comes home, tell your children exactly what to expect: how things will look, feel, smell; what special equipment may be coming home, and what it's for and how it works; what helpers may be coming to the house. Explain the parent's condition in detail: the physical limitations, lack of stamina, emotional struggle.

Let the children approach the situation slowly, at their own pace. You can offer suggestions (which they may accept or reject):

"How about just going over and giving Mommy's hand a squeeze? I bet she'd like that."

It's important not to be shocked at a child's initial fear or reluctance, and *not to make too much of it.* I've seen situations where a child gained a lot of positive reinforcement by persisting in the attitude, "Don't wanna be next to Daddy." Concerned grandparents, aunts, uncles, friends would rally around, coaxing the child to go see Daddy, talk to him, hug him. The child quickly learned that simply by *not* going to Daddy, she became the family's center of attention—and kids *love* to be the center of attention.

If you encourage the child to experiment, and don't overreact, pretty soon she'll probably overcome her fears and reestablish a normal relation with the parent. If that *doesn't* happen, if the fear and revulsion *don't* diminish over time, then something else is probably going on. You may need professional help to find out what's wrong and how to deal with it.

Hope, Limited

As the child looks at the parent's new limitations, and begins to face up to "always," it's important to keep hope going, to find good things in the future. Your ten-year-old may have always wanted Dad to take her to Disneyland, to walk around the Magic Kingdom with her. Now Dad will never walk around Disneyland. Still, even in a wheelchair, perhaps he can take the whole family to McDonald's on Saturday. And that's a start. If he can do that, then one day, perhaps, he can *roll* around the Magic Kingdom with her.

When your child digs in, seems absolutely determined to be miserable because of what Mom or Dad *can't* do, the child is still in the stage of rejecting the new reality. So it's important to take these baby steps, find the little things the parent *can* do, to keep the family working as a family. Dad can't coach Little League anymore, but he can sit in the stands and holler.

It's a matter of adjusting expectations, of finding the good in the smallest things, *and it's hard*—for you and for your children. Perhaps Mom has had a stroke, gone through rehabilitation. She can walk, a little. Her thoughts may be clouded. Her speech is slurred. Now she's home, with her new limitations.

You've had time; you've prepared the children. They know Mom will need home nursing, with health aides coming and going. Perhaps Grandma is moving in for a while to help. The children know that Mom's brain has been damaged, that the most you can look for is tiny improvements. If Mom could count to three when she came home, and today she can count to six, that's a great improvement, and the family should try to be excited by it.

Dealing with this kind of loss is terribly difficult for children, but it's part of a process. And for the process to work, the children have to *grieve* for what they've lost.

How Children Grieve

Children's grief is different from adults', and the younger the child, the more different the grieving. Young children usually don't maintain a continuing level of sadness. Instead, what you see is happyhappy-happy*DEVASTATED!* The same child may be shrieking with laughter at a party, then go up to his room and sob heartbrokenly.

As children grow older, their grief becomes more like our own; you'll see a more mature, more level sadness as they learn to go on with their own lives despite the loss of parenting. There will be "down" moments, but not those enormous peaks and valleys of a younger child's grief.

Enabling Grief

When your child sinks into those valleys of despair, you should *give her permission to grieve,* not try to stifle the sorrow or cut it off. At those moments when you sense that your child is teetering on the edge of grief, there are ways you can *invite* the child to tears. There are so many things you can say to trigger the emotion and bring it out:

"It really hurts, doesn't it, to think of Mom like this?"

"It's just so sad, isn't it, about Daddy?"

When the tears do come, the best thing for your child is simple, physical comfort. Your instinct will be to cuddle, to soothe, and that's the right instinct—*as long as you don't try to cut off the grief.*

When a child *really* cries, when he abandons himself in misery, most parents' natural inclination is to think, "I want you to stop crying; I don't want you to hurt so much." But your child *does* hurt that much; you can't change that. It's simply counterproductive to say, "Stop crying now. Mommy wouldn't want you to cry."

What you can do is let the hurt come out. You don't have to say a thing; just by being there and holding your child through the pain *you're doing the best job you can possibly do.*

It may go against your instincts, but it's important to help your child work through that misery, before he can come out the other side and adjust to the new reality.

Avoidance and Denial

As we discussed in chapter 3, sometimes children simply refuse to face the fact of a parent's illness and an altered future: "Nothing's sad, everything's just like it was; it's gonna be fine." And for a while, that may be okay; you can respect a child's desire to proceed at his own pace. If your child really needs *not* to think about the new reality, you might offer a nonthreatening, "We're going to have to talk about the changes in our lives pretty soon," just planting a seed.

Since we're talking about a chronic situation that isn't going to change very much very soon, I'd rather go a little too slowly than too quickly in working toward children's acceptance. Open the doors for them, respect their defenses, and they will probably adapt in their own time.

But if you as a parent can't get through to your child, don't beat yourself up about it; start to think who else might be able to. You and your child might be *too* close at this point; perhaps he'd open up to an uncle, a cousin, the mother of a pal. Teenagers often tell me they can talk only to their friends, because only other teens understand what they're going through. That's perfectly normal, healthy teen behavior.

The Boy Who Got Stuck

I met with a fourteen-year-old boy whose father has a connective tissue disorder. The disease first struck when the boy was six or seven; the father's condition stayed about the same over the years. There was some loss of function, but he retained a great deal. He could go to work and play with his son.

Suddenly, several years ago, there was a new attack; the father underwent a series of operations. He emerged stable once more, but much weaker and more limited, far less able to engage in activities with his son.

The family tried to adjust, to take the most optimistic view: It could have been worse, Dad could have lost so much more; the doctors caught it in time; now we can look forward to Dad being no worse than he is now—et cetera.

Yet the boy seemed to "get stuck"; he couldn't get past the new changes in his father. His behavior and his schoolwork both began to deteriorate.

When I began working with the young man, he wouldn't talk about his dad, or almost anything else. But I knew he had one passion: a really distinguished collection of baseball cards. As soon as I began asking about baseball cards, he became animated, talking first about the cards, then about other, more active things he really liked to do, and finally about how much he wished his dad could still do those things with him. He began getting his frustrations out in the open, to recognize his own rage at what was happening.

In their need to remain strong, to put the most positive face on the new crisis, his mother and father had never given their son the chance to say, "This is bull! You *weren't* this sick before. Just when I really need to have you around as my dad, doing stuff with me, it all fell apart!"

So I asked, "Do you think you can tell your dad how you feel?"

The boy shook his head. "I could never do that," he said. *"It would hurt him too much."*

I think he was absolutely right. It was a remarkably mature and compassionate understanding. But *by talking his frustrations out with me*, he seemed to come "unstuck." He could unbottle his feelings, look at his anger, and recognize that it was both justified and acceptable.

Weeks later I ran into the boy and his mother in a drugstore. He seemed a bit shocked to see me—child life specialists don't buy hair spray!—and hung back out of earshot. His mother told me that both the behavior and the schoolwork had improved since our talk. A little later he sort of wandered up the aisle past me and murmured, "Well, thanks for everything."

In this case I was the one who "allowed" the conversation he could never have with his father. But I think that any warm, sympathetic confidant—anyone he trusted—could have gotten the same results, just by offering an attentive ear, and permission to *hate* what had happened to his dad.

Affirming Their Emotions

Children do best when their parents can confirm the emotions that go along with chronic illness. The child should feel that Mom and Dad understand, that it's *okay* to resent having to stay home with Mom while the other guys are playing ball. It's okay to be mad about things like that, to think it's not fair: The other guys don't have to do things like that, *but I do.*

The child really needs that permission from you: It's okay to absolutely *hate* the fact that you have to take care of your mom. *You have to do it, but you don't have to like it.*

No matter how well your family adapts, each of you from time to time is going to have these furious, frustrated flashes: "This isn't right. This really makes me mad. This shouldn't have happened to me. *Why is it happening to me?*"

Those feelings will never completely disappear, for you or for your children. As long as you give yourselves permission to have those anguished moments, as long as you can make the struggle to get back on track and accept the reality, as long as you allow yourselves and your children those moments of despair, your family can remain whole and flourish.

Two Particularly Bad Times for Children

Most of the time, children can "float." If there is no dramatic change in a parent's illness, children adjust, adapt, and "float"—living their lives from day to day, as normally as possible under the circumstances. But there are two periods—one during latency, or school age, and one in the early teens—when your children may seem to be newly stressed by the parent's illness, *even though nothing much has changed.*

Trouble in Mid-School Age

School years are usually a pretty mellow time for kids; in this latency age they're not quite as vulnerable as they were as toddlers or will be again as teens.

But somewhere around the middle of school age—roughly between age eight and ten—something changes. At this point, children are still extremely focused on themselves, but now their peers are beginning to become important too. Your children start thinking about what their pals might be thinking.

Somewhere in here you may see your child begin to struggle with having a sick or handicapped parent. She'll become much more aware of the parent's condition, hesitant to bring friends home anymore. She'll worry about what the other kids will see in her home, how they'll react to a parent who talks, acts, or looks "different."

If the child begins to fear the loss of those developing friendships, a parent's illness can now become a real, major conflict for her.

But then, after that tough year or two, things return to normal for a while. The child matures and comes to learn that her friends really aren't going to reject her because her mom or dad is "different." For several years, your child can "float" again. And then comes the second, even more touchy period of difficulty:

Trouble in Early Teens

Thirteen to fifteen is never a day at the beach, for the child or the parents. It's a time of life when your child wants to be just like all her peers, look like all her peers. She doesn't want anybody to rock her boat, and at that age it's already a pretty wobbly boat. The extra needs, the very fact of a parent's handicap can be very destabilizing for the young teenager.

(Of the two "times of trouble," the early teen period may be less severe, especially if the parent's condition has existed for quite some time and the child has adjusted to it.)

Other Causes of Trouble

Beyond running into these developmental "times of trouble," a parent's continuing illness may cause problems for children when:

- There is a change in the parent's actual condition
- There is a change in the family environment—a new job, a new town, a new home.

The Signs of Trouble

How do you know when your child is feeling these stresses, is losing the fight to "float"?

Many of the warning signs are the ones we discussed in chapter 3, *but now they will be more subtle.* Because the parent's condition has become part of the family "background sound," children's stress reactions will show themselves more slowly, more insidiously. The child won't suddenly go from A's and B's to D's, F's, and Incompletes. There will be a gradual decline, perhaps over several semesters, in school achievement. A well-behaved child gradually becomes less well behaved; an average-behaved kid starts developing into a problem. It is important to bear something in mind:

> ***The child's problems may have nothing
> to do with the parent's illness.***

Checklist of Warning Signs

It's a mistake to think that just because a parent is ill, that's automatically the central fact of a child's life. With one child maybe it is; with another, it isn't. Even with the same child, *sometimes* it is, and *sometimes* it isn't.

When a child starts developing problems, or getting into trouble, you as a parent probably have a mental checklist you run through:

- Having problems with friends?
- Bad company?
- Drugs?
- First love?
- Hormonal change?
- One of those days (weeks)?
- Hard year in school?
- A rough time developmentally?
- Physical problems?

There are a lot of other possible causes. The checklist is still valid but, with one parent chronically ill, you must add one more *possibility*:

- Something about my illness?

Work it out, as you do all the other possible causes of trouble. Is the child suddenly embarrassed by the parent's condition, even though she hasn't seemed to be in the past? Is the child burdened by responsibility? Could I be asking too much, going beyond what she's ready to handle?

Don't give the illness too much weight, or too little. But don't make the very common mistake of thinking that "Something about my illness" is the only or even the most important behavioral factor in your children's lives.

What Can You Do?

If you determine that your son or daughter is showing warning signs of stress, and that the parent's illness is an important factor, there are several things you can do. One is very specific:

If you suspect that your child is becoming afraid of how her friends might react to her "different" parent, it's a good idea to confront the problem head-on: Encourage her to invite a pal over to the house. And if you think that some of her circle of friends might indeed handle the situation badly, then you'll want to hand-pick the pal.

Once the two of you have decided who should come over, spend a little time with the friend; explain the other parent's medical condition, and what she's going to find in your house. Just as when you took your own children to the hospital a few chapters ago, preparation is everything.

Great Expectations

Most parents fly by the seat of their pants, and usually that's fine. But a parent's chronic illness forces you think.

- What is it I want for my family?
- What is a good family life?
- What do I want for my children?
- What do I believe about raising children?

Being forced to confront these questions directly is one of the good things that happen now. Because chronic illness or no: *You should still want the same things, still have the same expectations of your children.*

You should maintain the same approaches to parenting, enforce the same discipline, distribute the same chores, require the same curfews. Your children need stability, need to know the boundaries. *So all these things need to remain in place.*

That's why, when parents ask me, "How should I behave now?" I simply ask them, "How would you have behaved if this *hadn't* happened?" Just because one of you is sick, that's no reason to change your children's world.

Gains Amid the Losses

Any chronic illness, with its permanent loss of some part of the body's skills, is a tragedy. I would never dream of minimizing it; there is no place for Pollyanna, the Glad Girl, in our approach. And yet . . .

Seldom is a disaster as disastrous as it first appears. Greenland isn't *worse* than France; it's *different*. If we can adapt to the differences, we can make this new reality valuable, even positive—particularly for our children. Sometimes we can still give them more than we think we can . . . it just takes some ingenuity.

I'm thinking of Roy Campanella. Arguably the greatest catcher in baseball when he played for the old Brooklyn Dodgers, Campanella smashed up his car one icy night in 1958 and emerged a quadriplegic. Yet every spring until he died, Roy Campanella parked his wheelchair beside the batting cage at the Los Angeles Dodgers training camp in Vero Beach and taught the young rookies how to hit. For the last thirty-five years of his life Roy Campanella couldn't even pick up a bat, but the baseball that was in his head remained a priceless asset.

A father who has lost his eyesight will never teach his daughter to drive. Yet sitting in the backseat of the car, he can tell her things she needs to know—to apply the brakes *before* she turns, or that, as soon as she can see the front of the truck she's passing in her rearview mirror, it's safe to pull back into the right lane.

A parent forced into medical retirement may well be devastated, his sense of his own worth terribly diminished. And yet, over time, I've seen such parents come to another realization: "I'm here with my kids. I'm going to spend time with them during certain marvelous periods of their lives that I'd never have known without this illness."

This is not the mindless optimism of Pollyanna. It is the unsentimental, correct analysis that good things frequently do arise from the ashes of the bad.

The Computer People

I know a father, a professional man, whose son and daughter were ten and fourteen years old when he was diagnosed with multiple sclerosis.

The disease took a rapid form; just a year after the onset, he was forced to take a medical retirement, and soon he began to lose the ability to speak. Luckily, we now live in an age where there are alternative ways to communicate.

The father began using a computer, both to speak and to write. Simply to keep up with him, the rest of the family—his wife and children—had to sharpen their own computer skills, far beyond anything you or I might be able to do. They learned all kinds of databases, spreadsheets, computer languages—just because that's what his disease was forcing *him* to learn.

The girl and boy now have tremendous computer skills at a remarkably young age—and the whole family is inordinately proud of those skills. *Of course* the disease continues its inevitable progress; *of course* the family wishes the past were still the present—yet in the midst of its struggle, the family has this really positive new thing, a direct result of the father's illness.

"A Mile in My Moccasins"

Part of being a child is the focus on self—most normal children see the world as revolving around their own needs. Only gradually, as they grow, do they learn to be more other-directed, to identify with people other than themselves. We say they learn *empathy*.

Most children are allowed to remain self-centered and self-absorbed all through those early years. They are never pushed to really feel what it would be like to be someone else, and struggling. There's no reason they should be.

But with a parent who will never get better, and may gradually get worse, children's ability to empathize becomes crucial to their own well-being and the health of the family.

At the Cleveland Clinic, and now at The Gathering Place, we've developed techniques that allow children, particularly school-age children, to understand—to *feel*—what life has become like for the handicapped parent. With minor adaptations, you can use the same ideas with your children and achieve the same results.

What we try to do in these group sessions is mimic the symptoms of the parent's illness in the child's body. Of course the children must *want* to play the game, and usually they do. It's interesting, it's fun, it's even funny—and it ends.

If a mother has a degenerative muscular disease like MS, we'll tape a couple of ten-pound weights to the arms and legs of her twelve-year-old, then have him try to run around the room or build a Lego fort. He feels what it's like to live inside a body that's tired and uncoordinated.

If Mom or Dad is a paraplegic, we give the child a wheelchair to roll around in—and then tell her to go into the kitchen and scramble a couple of eggs without leaving the chair, or take herself to the bathroom.

If the parent has a visual impairment, we'll give the child a pair of glasses with distorting prisms over the lenses—or we'll just smear Vaseline thickly across the child's own specs—then ask her to find her way to the door or read some Harry Potter aloud.

Where a parent's problem is neuromuscular, we may have the child reverse handedness—then ask him to button his shirt from the wrong side or write a letter with the wrong hand.

Where disease will impair a parent's speech function, we let the child load up his mouth with marshmallows, then ask him for directions to the cafeteria, or shout a sudden, startling question at him.

You see the idea: We try to let the child *experience* what the parent is experiencing—for just a little while. With a bit of ingenuity, you can do the same thing for your children—and share a lot of laughter in the process.

The Not-So-Great Race

On days when we have families in to The Gathering Place for group sessions, we've started something new: the surprise obstacle race. First we give the kids a bunch of blank wooden blocks and ask them to write their "burdens" on them—minding little brother; the house is like Grand Central Station; no trips to the mall; I have to do *laundry!* The more burdens, the better. We're very sympathetic.

What the kids don't know is that they are going to have a race. They're going to have to hand-carry all those burdens around a pretty serious obstacle course. Naturally, their first idea is to stuff the burdens in their pockets, but that's a no-no—they must *carry* their burdens, just as their afflicted parents must carry theirs.

So off the kids go, balancing on beams, climbing over something and under something else, always holding their burdens (and frequently dropping them, amid laughter), until they reach our human obstacle: a volunteer, sitting in a chair, square in their path, who tells them, "No, you can't go past me. You haven't done your homework, you haven't helped Dad enough today, you didn't watch your little sister." That's when the negotiation starts: "I promise, I'll do the homework right after I watch *Gossip Girl*." Silence. "*Before* I watch *Gossip Girl!*"

Well, maybe yes, maybe no, depending on the volunteer's mood.

And the children don't compete only with each other. A lot of the afflicted parents try the obstacle course too; kids and parents judge each other's performance amid lots of laughter and "Nyaa, nyaa"s. The children are always so pleased because, burdens and all, they can still run the course better than their handicapped parents can. That's when we say, think about how hard it is for your parent to handle all that stuff in his life right now. He's the one struggling, and he'll keep struggling.

We describe our obstacle course as the course of life: This is your life, going through it day by day, walking the path you have to walk.

Does it work?

At the end of these workshops, we ask the children what they've learned. One session at the Cleveland Clinic included a quiet eleven-year-old whose father has the degenerative disease multiple sclerosis.

After most of the other children had given their impressions, and the room had become pretty quiet, the boy suddenly spoke up. He said something like this:

"You know, if you were always able to do something, like play ball, and then all of a sudden you couldn't do it anymore, and if it was something you *really* liked to do, and you knew you'd *never* be able to do it anymore . . .

"Wow!

"It would be so frustrating. You'd just get so mad, and you'd take the mad out on everybody around you . . .

"Now I know why my dad is so mean and angry sometimes. It's because he's so frustrated. He used to be able to do all this stuff. I can get out of the wheelchair. *He can't ever get out!*"

It was remarkable to listen to the boy talk his way to an understanding of what his father was going through. It was as if he had taken himself out of himself and into the heart and mind of another human being, much earlier than he ever would have otherwise.

And this, I think, may be the most positive thing that can come out of a parent's chronic illness. The children can learn empathy at a much earlier age, and that ability to empathize, to feel another's pain, to "walk a mile in his moccasins," will stay with them throughout their lives.

The Fort

Let me tell you one more game we've started to play at The Gathering Place. It began once again at a Saturday group session; we had ten or eleven families with us. We also had a whole lot of bedsheets that our volunteers had brought in. We set up some tables and gave the families three or four bedsheets apiece. And I said, "I want you to make forts with the sheets around the tables.

"On the outside of the forts, put all the pressures on your lives—

you can write notes, draw pictures, make clay models. All the bad pressures go on the outside. On the inside of the walls, put all the things that are helping your family get through this—communication with each other, friends, doctors, feelings—whatever."

Well, it took about forty minutes. Everybody scrambled to get *tchotchkes*—toys and dolls from our playroom, syringes (minus the needles) from our medical table, books from our library—some really imaginative ways to represent the bad stuff (outside) and the good stuff (inside). They wrote on the bedsheets, drew on them; some of these forts became really elaborate. And when they were finished, I said, "Now go inside your fort, close the sheet, just be your family inside the fort. And no talking; I just want you to be together as a family. Look around you at the things that help you, and think about what helps your family cope. When I hit the gong, you can come out."

So everybody, large and small, crept inside their forts and found ways to get comfortable, huddled under the tables. The silence was deafening.

And after a few minutes, when I hit the gong, everybody came crawling back out. But now they were crying, touching, holding on to each other. It was so incredibly moving; I was in tears too. And finally one mom spoke:

"We forgot hugs! When we got inside we remembered: It's hugs that help us. We just sat there and held each other the whole time we were in there!"

We humans do have things to help us get through the bad that happens to us. We have all kinds of good things inside our family forts. And the junk outside our forts is just that—junk.

One mother put it in more colorful terms, after she came out of her fort:

"Everything else is crap; we have our family."

Our family is our fort.

Losing Some Childhood

There is a price to be paid for this increase in empathy, and it is an important one: the loss of some childhood.

So often a parent diagnosed with a chronic illness will say to me, "I just want my child to be a child. I don't want *my* disease to affect *her*." My answer is always the same: *"That's not possible."*

There is no way your child can have the childhood he or she would have had if you had not become ill.

For one thing (and it is not a bad thing), your child will have to learn to become more independent. If your ten-year-old daughter really *must* have clean jeans morning, noon, and night, she'll have to learn to run the washing machine, and that's perfectly okay. It's also okay— and probably inevitable—for her to resent having to do it; all her pals' mothers do the washing for them!

The loss of childhood involves learning an equation: "If this is what you want, this is what *you* have to do." It is the price they pay for the skills they learn.

Helping Kids Help Themselves

It's always a mistake to think of children as helpless *objects*, acted upon and shaped by outside forces beyond their control. Children are bright, resilient beings capable, with only a little help from their friends, of finding their own answers, their own coping skills.

When Daddy Couldn't Help

I met a little girl named Maryanne. When she was just two and a half years old, her father was shot in the neck, severing his spinal column. He became a quadriplegic. How this tiny girl adjusted to her new reality is one of the most remarkable processes I have ever witnessed.

At first, Maryanne seemed utterly terrified of this strange new father. In the hospital, she didn't want to see him. When they went to visit, she'd hide behind her mom.

During those visits, we began getting together in the playroom. Maryanne didn't have a lot of verbal skills yet, but almost all her play focused on "Daddy." She'd identify a doll or toy as Daddy, then play Daddy-this, Daddy-that. She'd put the Daddy-toys in different hiding places around the playroom, bury them in our rice table, then carefully retrieve them. She seemed to need the reassurance that wherever she left her toy "Daddy," that's where she would find him.

At the end of the sessions, she'd always want to take all her "Daddies" home: I'd tell her she had to pick just one and bring it back next time.

At home, her mother told me, that "Daddy" toy would be very important to Maryanne. She always knew exactly where the toy was. She would carry it around, then put it somewhere, then go back to check on it.

When her dad was sent on to a rehabilitation hospital, Maryanne continued to come by our playroom, play with all her toy "Daddies," take one home each time. And by the time her father came home for good, she had made the connection between the old daddy and the new one. She lost her fear. Because Daddy couldn't pick her up anymore, Maryanne would climb into his lap and give him a hug big enough for both of them. It worked for her, and it worked for him.

I'd never presume to know what goes on in the minds of very young children. But as Maryanne worked with these daddy-symbols in the playroom, she found a way to get through her fear of this different, damaged daddy, to accept his limitations, and to re-establish her loving relationship with him. This was the magical thing she decided to do for herself, and it worked. All she needed us to give her were the tools, and the time.

On Their Own

In earlier chapters we were dealing with acute illness—a crisis that would resolve itself, for better or for worse, within a foreseeable time frame. When your children became angry or upset, I could suggest interventions, ways you and your children could handle the crisis together.

Facing up to a parent's chronic illness—to "always"—is a little different. Yes, you can offer the support, the model, the permission to grieve, and to be furious at the situation. You can guide the process and be there for them, but your children now must find the resources *within themselves* to cope with a parent's chronic illness all through the months and years of growing up.

The only strength we can rely on, to be there whenever we need it, all down the years, is the strength that comes from within. With your support, your children can and will build that internal strength of their own. And at the end of the process, you'll be proud of your rugged young Greenlanders.

". . . so many emotions and issues." Sarah Hanna Marinski put together this angry collage—a knife transfixing an orange, a dead pet—to illustrate some of her feelings throughout her dad's illness and their whole difficult life together.

9.

Dealing with a Parent's Mental Illness

"I'd give anything to have cancer instead," she said.

Working as I now do primarily with cancer patients, I was shaken. What could be worse than having cancer?

"If I had cancer, if I had a heart attack, at least it would show," the young mother went on. "People would rally round me, want to help me. Right now I can barely get out of bed in the morning. I burst into tears at the drop of a hat. I'm going to lose my job, and *nobody cares!*" And she did indeed burst into tears . . .

Since that young woman, in the grip of a crushing postpartum depression, I have, over the years, heard something similar from dozens of parents with mental illness—everything from bipolar disease to clinical depression to schizophrenia to a whole array of addictions. It still shakes me, but it no longer shocks me.

We call them, correctly, mental *illnesses* or mental *diseases,* but as a society we don't quite seem to believe it—believe it the way we believe that that totally bald woman has a disease called cancer.

And our culture's ambivalence toward mental illness, coupled with the frustrating difficulties of treating it, has terrible consequences for the children of mentally ill parents. Recent studies show that when a parent has a mental illness, the risk of damage to the children is *50 percent higher* than with even the most severe purely physical illness. That damage can show itself in children's

- Relationships with other children and adults
- Educational performance
- Behavior
- Developmental skills

Our object, then, in trying to help children through a parent's *mental* illness should be to enhance the children's own *resilience*, their inborn ability to manage difficulties (in this case very great difficulties) and not let the difficulties overwhelm their normal life, now and in the future. And that is the subject of this chapter.

(These ideas also apply where a *physical* condition or injury—anything from Alzheimer's to brain trauma—results in a parent's mental impairment.)

Wanted: One Grown-Up

One of the most important elements for the child of a mentally ill parent will be continuing help and attention from one key adult. Ideally, that will be the well parent, the person most attuned to the child, most concerned with the child's welfare. But the well parent may simply not be able to handle the job: coping with a mentally ill spouse is exhausting, frustrating, and time-consuming; there's not a lot of energy left over for worrying about the children. So the most important single element for children of a mentally ill parent is the continuing presence of *some* caring adult—frequently an aunt, a grandparent, the mother of a school friend, a coach or counselor—who will make sure the child gets what she needs to make it through these coming difficult years. And that adult should read and work with the information in this chapter.

Another change from our earlier ideas: Remember those "ripples" of help in chapter 4? They began with the well parent and touched professional help—therapy—only after several other alternatives had failed. But when dealing with a mentally ill parent, that professional help must begin at the beginning—the therapists working with the mentally ill parent must also help you deal with your children. One of the most important things the well parent must now do is make sure all the mental health professionals on the case know that there are children involved.

David's Way

My friend David Deckert is a psychiatrist, and his routines reflect how this idea can work—and how it can help both the mentally ill parent and his or her children.

David told me something remarkable:

"The children are the most powerful potential healing factor in helping the adult come to grips with his diagnosis and his treatment. And we're not exploiting the children, because I think their involvement is good for them as well."

The Mandatory Meeting

Before discharging a mentally ill patient to home care, David insists on one or more sessions at the hospital, under his guidance, with both the parents and all their children.

Frequently the mentally ill patient is in a state of despair—facing years of disruption with no guarantee of ever coming out the other side.

"Mental illness is as hard to deal with as any other illness," David says. "It's just as hard if not harder to work through and deal with on a long-term basis as cancer, heart disease, diabetes, or any physical illness.

"Having the children kind of step up to the plate and be on the side of that patient while that person is deciding whether it's even worth it to try means everything to the prognosis: Will he or won't he be willing to go on with life?" For the fact is that in almost every case, even the very worst parents *want* to be good parents to their children; it's an impulse deep in the primal brain, and it's what David works with.

In his practice, David is the one who prepares the patient and the children for the children's visit—which never takes place unless he or a clinical nurse is there to manage the meeting.

Using the Tension

"I don't mind if the tension between the parent and child becomes very significant," he says, "as long as I moderate it and use it therapeutically. What I don't want is for the parents and the kids to have a big fight and stalk out, with no therapeutic benefit. For me this is part of therapy."

What David tries to impress on the despairing, mentally ill parent is this:

"Your children will never be better off without you. They will never be better off thinking you abandoned them than they will be coping with your illness." David says this is his most powerful single argument, and works most of the time, whether the parent is contemplating self-destruction, or a hopeless retreat into his mental illness.

"I've seen time after time where a child's visit has turned the patient around," he says.

Getting the Patient to Commit

We do have better and better treatments for mental illness, but they all demand discipline, sacrifice, and frequently discomfort, over a long, painful period of time. Despair comes easily. So David's job, at these predischarge meetings, is to get the sick parent to commit to trying to get well—taking those meds despite their miserable side effects, going to therapy, sticking with a twelve-step program. And the children's presence helps the parent to commit, which is what the children want too; they want the possibility of getting their parent back.

David finds the situation is easier with very young children, who don't have a history of problems with the parent and will just give a hug or crawl up into Mom's lap and say, "I miss you." Older children may have to work through emotional baggage from the parent's previous conduct toward them. They'll start off angry, but that's when the mental-health professional can help the child work through the anger toward what she really wants—an attentive, responsible parent who can be in her life again. Usually that's a possibility, at least with acute ailments—anxiety, depression, psychosis.

Never the Same Parent

With chronic mental conditions, severe personality illnesses like borderline personality disorder, obsessive-compulsive disorder, and others, the sick parent may never again be the parent the child remembers and wants. In those cases, David meets with the children, and tries to help them understand why the parent is and always will be "different." His first job is to prevent the child from feeling responsible for the parent's illness. And so, in front of the adults, and especially the well parent, he gives the children one thing:

The Message

This is not your fault. It will never be your fault, and nothing that happens in the future with your parent will be your fault. This has nothing to do with you. There is something broken inside your dad; there is a disease inside your dad. We can help make it better, but dad is never going to be done with it.

And he goes on to give the children this reassurance: "You *can* go on and live a healthy, happy life."

To make sure the children understand that Dad or Mom is coping with a real disease, he compares it to pain: "You know how, when something is really hurting you, and you *want* to focus on your schoolwork, you *want* to score a goal, but your ankle hurts so much, or your headache is so bad that you just can't do it? Well, deep down, your mom really *wants* to be a good mom, but this disease is hurting her so much, and it's getting in the way."

Grieving for the Loss

David also helps children with their very real sense of loss. The child of a hemophiliac, a paraplegic, *knows* he'll never be able to rough-house with Dad. But the child of a mentally ill parent feels the loss of normal parenting constantly. So what David tries to do is help them grieve for that loss, to accept it, and get past it.

The guidance David or his staff provide at these meetings demonstrates why it is so important to involve a professional right from the beginning—no layperson is equipped to get these messages right for the children.

Protecting the Children

Nevertheless, the children must be protected during the coming years of contact with a chronically mentally ill parent . . . protected not so much from physical danger (a parent who poses a physical threat probably will not be allowed to live at home), but from long-term emotional harm. What they must understand is that the sick parent CANNOT be the parent they want, perhaps the parent they once had.

Normally, as we mature into adulthood, we go from a focus on self to empathy—a focus on a caring for others. But mental illness short-circuits that process; in a way, the sick parent becomes a mental toddler, with toddler rules: I am the center of all things.

Over and Over Again

The child must also understand—must be reminded over and over through her growing years—*she is not to blame* for her parent's illness. That becomes especially difficult when the parent accuses the child, as many mentally ill parents do: "You're driving me crazy! You're such a bad kid; you're the reason I drink—smoke—take drugs! You're why I'm always depressed—angry—messed up! It's *your* fault I'm the way I am." Nothing is more important here than that the healthy, caring adult in the child's life repeat and repeat and repeat, all through these terribly difficult years, David's mantra:

It's not your fault!

We're talking here primarily about chronic mental illness, where a child is exposed for years to a parent's disturbing presence in the home, and that parent's unpredictable mood swings. It is certainly easier for children to adapt to a parent's chronic physical illness—the demands of kidney disease or cancer, the predictable rhythms of dialysis or chemotherapy, even a parent permanently confined to a wheelchair. Those children, with adult support, appear able to cope and plunge ahead with their own lives.

Cocoon

That doesn't seem to be the case when the parent is mentally ill. Uncertain what will happen next with this unpredictable father or mother, children put up emotional defenses; they retreat into a kind of self-protective shell or cocoon. They are waiting for the next big crash—for the parent to act out wildly, or disappear into the bedroom for days at a time—to get another job, or lose it again—to climb on the wagon, or fall off—to pick up a weapon, or put it down. These children live on the edge of a trauma response—freeze/flight/fight—all the time. They are waiting, waiting, waiting.

Opening the Cocoon
This is where that caring adult, from outside the immediate household, becomes crucial to the child's life: Someone who can expose the child to a more "normal" home, can demonstrate that there is a

life beyond a parent's mental illness. Someone to be a sounding board, with whom a child can let down the defenses, open her cocoon, and relax—not, at least for the moment, awaiting the next disaster.

This is not easy for the mentoring adult. There is still a stigma to mental illness which is no longer present for physical diseases like cancer, or even HIV/AIDS. Some potential mentors—the aunt or next-door neighbor with two kids of her own to worry about—will just want to steer away from the situation. But for the children of the mentally ill, nothing is more important than exposure to a "normal" life outside the orbit of the parent's disease—and to the release of just being able to talk about it.

A playdate with best friends. A date for a burger and shake every Saturday at Mickey D's. A bike ride through the park. Basically, a taste of normal life and proof that it really exists. This is what an adult who cares about the child can provide—to prevent the damage we spoke about at the beginning of this chapter. And yes, it may take some courage.

Caring

The child needs to see that someone cares: Did you get into the school choir? How did you do with that history paper you were struggling with? All the things that most kids get from both parents, but that her own parents may no longer be able to give her.

This caring adult must do, continually, the things we saw David, the psychiatrist, doing. Keep reassuring the child:

> "Mom is sick, she has a mental illness. Down deep, she'd like to be a real mom again, but the sickness won't let her."
> "None of this is your fault. *Nothing* you did made her this way."
> "You CAN get through this and I'm here to help."

That adult mentor should be constantly nudging the child toward a regular life. Encourage new friendships outside the circle of family problems and secrets. Push her to join school clubs, choirs, teams, bands, wherever her interests lie. Do everything possible to expose the child to a "real" world beyond the family's continuing crisis. Sports are an especially good outlet; there's nothing like being physically exhausted to make you forget your other troubles for a while.

Never Leave the Child in Charge

Now, this is difficult, but it's important for the well parent to understand: *You must never make your child responsible for the well-being of a mentally ill parent.* You can't leave the child in charge while you're at work; you can't assume the child will notice if the parent brings something—alcohol, a gun—into the house. This must never be the child's role for one very straightforward reason: If the child fails as the guardian, and something bad happens, you're setting her up for a level of guilt from which she may never recover.

Addictions

An addicted parent—whether to alcohol, drugs, gambling, or something else—poses special problems. I've seldom known an addict who wasn't absolutely sure he could stop any time he wanted to—no need for twelve-step programs or therapy or some in-patient clinic. Denial comes with the addiction. And because the addict is convinced, people—especially the family—tend to take him at his word. His children's unspoken question then becomes:

"If you can quit anytime you want to, *why don't you?*" Believing dad *can* quit but doesn't means *he doesn't want to*, and that really poisons the relationship.

Nowadays there are reliable support groups, not only for the addicts themselves, but also for their families—Alanon is one example. And one thing an adult mentor can do for children in this situation is direct them to the support groups, so they can meet other children in the same situation, and can begin to understand the realities, rather than the fantasies, of the parent's addiction.

When the Child Doesn't Live with
the Mentally Ill Parent

When a parent has a severe mental illness, her children probably won't be living with her, and that poses a whole new set of challenges. For mentally ill parents, loss of child custody runs as high as 70 or 80 percent— far higher than in the case of physical illness. In America, only about a third of children with a severely mentally ill parent are living with that parent. Whether you're the well parent still raising your child, or a grandparent or aunt who's taken over the parental role, remember: The child who, because of a parent's mental illness, can no longer live with her, needs a special approach from the adults she is now living with. First she needs to know WHY she can't live with Mom or Dad anymore.

"Why Don't They Love Me?"

Invariably, every child living separated from one or both of her natural parents wonders: Why doesn't my mom, my dad raise me, like my friends' parents do? Why don't they love me? Why aren't they in my life?

So she must know the truth: Mom is sick, she is sick in her mind, and she can't take care of you anymore. It's NOT that she doesn't love you, but the sickness won't let her be herself. What's happening in her mind is a real disease.

To be avoided, at all costs, those little fictions a family makes up to conceal mental illness: "Your mom's on a long vacation." "Dad's on a secret mission for the government." Even the ultimate lie: "Your mom is dead."

The Heredity Factor

There is one more reason children must understand the nature of a parent's condition. Mental illness may involve a genetic component—it can be hereditary. So the child must, at some point, be briefed on the nature and timing of the risks; both the child and the adult guardians must understand the early warnings of the disease onset, must know how to interpret initial signs of an emerging addictive personality, bipolar disorder, or any other gene-linked mental problem. Self-awareness is crucial, and the child, when she strikes out on her own, must always tell her doctors of what may run in her bloodline.

For detailed guidance on how, what, and (sometimes most important) *when* to discuss hereditary illnesses with children, see chapter 13, "Genetic Diseases."

Checklist: Helping Children of Mentally Ill Parents

At the beginning of this chapter, we learned that a child with a mentally ill parent is at far greater risk for emotional damage than a child with a physically ill parent—no matter how grave the physical illness.

The American Academy of Child and Adolescent Psychiatry has developed recommendations for helping the children of mentally ill parents avert that damage, based on research and clinical practice.

The most important single factor in *decreasing* risk for these children, the academy found, is making sure they understand clearly these two crucial points:

- The parent is *sick*.
- *It's not the child's fault.*

Some other factors that can *lessen* the risk of damage to the child:

- Help and support from family members
- A stable environment, living in one place, not moving from home to home
- Therapy for the child
- Positive self-esteem

- Good relationships with peers; help building friendships
- Healthy interests outside the home
- A strong relationship with a healthy adult

Websites

Compiled by Michele D. Sherman, Ph.D.

Parenting Well Project: parentingwell.org

Helping Children Understand Mental Illness: A Resource for Parents and Guardians: mhasp.org

Invisible Children's Project: mentalhealthamerica.net/invisible-childrens-project

COMIC: Children of Mentally Ill Consumers: howstat.com/comic

Children of Parents with a Mental Illness: copmi.net.au

National Network of Adult and Adolescent Children Who Have a Mentally Ill Parent (Australia): nnaami.org

Because her father was in a hospice, Kaitlyn Butcher's family held her tenth birthday party at his bedside. Kaitlyn's father gave her a stuffed bunny—his last present to her. Kaitlyn still carries it with her everywhere she goes. When I asked her to draw a picture about remembering her father, Kaitlyn drew the bunny.

10.

When Things Get Very Bad

Two Fathers

Two young fathers, in adjoining beds.

I had come to see the one in the nearer bed.

He had been in his own home one morning, playing with his two children ages five and three, when suddenly he collapsed. The children had watched as the rescue squad arrived and rushed him away to this hospital. Now he was awaiting very risky surgery for an aneurysm—a weakened blood vessel that was leaking into his brain, threatening to burst.

He might die.

His wife and I took the children to visit. He was weak and not fully conscious. He couldn't talk to them, but he could open his eyes at the sound of their voices, could see them, could smile because he loved them and because they had come. Such moments are incredibly valuable, not only for the children but also for motivating the patient to *try*. I have seen parents on the edge of death make an effort to come back, to respond at the sound of their children's voices.

I took a picture of them together; the children kept it.

In the next bed lay a man with a brain tumor, dying. His wife was visiting him. The man's nurse took me aside and suggested I talk with this second young mother.

The nurse had overheard the first family—she had heard the children talking to their father, heard their questions, heard their mother and me explaining that, yes, this is very serious. We just don't know how Dad will be. Yes, he could die.

What bothered the nurse was that the second young woman refused absolutely to tell her children *anything* about their father's illness and impending death.

Well, sometimes I get paid to be pushy. So when the woman had finished her visit, I took her aside and suggested some of the ideas I've been sharing with you—the children have a right to know, have the need to know, and their future may depend on your courage and honesty right now.

She was courteous, listened to all I had to say, thanked me for my concern, and told me, "The children are fine." They did not need to know their father was dying; she saw no reason to upset them. And good-bye.

We try; sometimes we fail. I've gotten philosophical about that. But the nurse was anything but philosophical; she was furious. As the mother left, the nurse told me in an angry whisper: "Do you know how hard this is for us? That man's brain stem could explode at any time. He and his children had a chance for something important—their last time with him—and their mother says, 'They are fine'!"

Last Things and First Things

If you have turned to this chapter, it means we will have to talk of last things and first things. There is no easy way to write it; there is no easy way to read it. So I will try to do for you what I told you, all those pages ago, you must do for your children: Be absolutely honest.

My qualification to speak to you now is this: I have held the hands of many dying friends, and I know of their going, and of the children they left behind. The purpose of this chapter is still the purpose of the book: to help your children emerge from crisis mentally, emotionally, and spiritually whole. But I know, beyond any doubt, that in helping your children into the future, you will help yourself into that future as well.

Is It Ever Too Late?

Whatever has happened with your children up to this point, I come back to one very central point: It is *almost* never too late to start doing things the right way.

Here is when it was too late:

The nurse called from intensive care: A young mother was there, in the last stages of pancreatic cancer. She had hours, perhaps less, to live. Her children, a teenage girl and boy, were coming in from out of town. But what the nurse told me next, I could hardly believe:

They didn't even know their mother had cancer.

I went to the unit and met with the father. He was devastated. Obviously, he loved his wife deeply, was agonized at the thought of losing her. Yet in the six months of her disease, he had told the children as little as possible, had never *used* the word "cancer." He said they'd never asked him any questions; their lives seemed fine, and he didn't really think they needed to know anything. He himself had obviously spent the past six months in pretty serious denial, refusing to accept even the possibility that his wife might die.

By this time my heart was aching: for him, of course, but especially for the children. *Six months* knowing their mother was ill, guessing frantically, with no freedom to talk to anyone. And now—now it *was* too late. *There was so little we could do.*

What the father wanted us to do was very simple: He wanted somebody else to tell his children their mother was dying.

The children came in. I sat with them in our conference room; their dad came in too. He was willing to be there, but he just couldn't say the words.

I remember the two teenagers were almost silent, their heads bent; no eye contact anywhere.

I said, "You must be wondering why we had you come here." They nodded their heads, without raising them.

"You know your mom is sick. Do you know what she has?" They shrugged. It was just so hard.

Finally I had to tell them: Their mom was right on the verge of death. They could see her, but it would have to be now—she would probably die within the hour.

They fell apart. They cried, they sobbed, doubled over in anguish, doing in that moment all the grieving they'd been denied for half a year.

They chose not to see their mother before she died.

And afterward, I remember the father saying:

"I don't think I did this right."

I don't know what "this" was, in his mind. But I believe it was a very generic statement about the entire six months: He was saying, for his whole family, *"We didn't make the time valuable."*

So: However much time there is now, *there is time*. Let's see how we can make it valuable.

Helping Yourselves, Helping Your Children

First, let's talk for a moment about you: you the sick parent and you the well parent. You're going through the very worst of times now, and it would be just plain silly to talk about helping your children without suggesting that *first* you must help yourselves. Because you are over-whelmed with the demands on both of you. Because you are dealing with rising tides of anger and confusion, of hope and no-hope. So some-times the needs of your children must take a backseat to those intense feelings, those pressures, *and that's okay*, that's *normal*.

That is why so often, when I'm asked to help a family's children, I work first with the parents. They are so distraught, they *can't* think about their children until they settle their own emotions. So I give them all the time they need to talk about how tired they are (and they are), how unfair all of this is (and it is):

"We just got our life started . . ."
"We waited so long . . ."
"We bought a new house . . ."
"We moved to a new community for its marvelous schools . . ."
"This just isn't right!"

The parents must get all of this out, look at it and learn to get past it, or at least live with it, before they can really help their children.

How Children Come to Terms

Normally, in children—and in adults, too—the possibility of a loved one's death arises gradually, almost silently. The long medical process of treatment, of hope, of fear; of upturn, then downturn gradually leads to the loss of hope that the parent can recover.

It's a terribly difficult time for the children, because both parents become more and more ambivalent about talking to them, about keep-ing them informed. The parents, of course, don't want to admit the pos-sibility of death *even to themselves*; how can they possibly admit it to their children?

Remember: *Your children* always *know when something is happening*. They won't know in detail; they may not realize that what has happened is that death has become possible. But your children have very delicate antennae for picking up mood. When optimism becomes pessimism, *they will know*. When you begin to exclude them from unhappy truths, *they will know*. They will have an increasing sense that something is *not* being said. And it is always better for them to know the facts than to sink deeper and deeper into uncertainty and fear of the unknown.

As the prospects grow darker, your children may be uncomfortable asking questions; now you must take the initiative. With older children, when the parent's medical situation grows worse, I routinely ask, *"How much do you want to know?"*

It's a question that's perfectly safe for you, or a counselor, or a friend to ask. Some children answer, "Don't talk to me about bad things," but they're the minority. In my experience, *most children want to know what's going on.*

I remember how one little boy answered my question. He never talked much, yet he'd shown me right along that he understood: His mother was really sick. He had told me she could die. I told him the people at the hospital were going to try a lot of ways to keep that from happening. But, I asked, if things get very bad, do you want us to tell you? How much information do you like to have? Do you like to hear everything, or just a little bit?

He thought about that, then he said, "I think I want you to tell me everything—*but sometimes I don't want to talk about it."*

It was such a perfect answer—such a good description of what so many children feel.

You may be comfortable deciding for yourself exactly what and how to tell your children about a deteriorating medical situation. But if you feel uncertain, it helps to run your ideas by a professional you trust—a hospital psychologist or social worker: "Should I tell him this? Can she handle that?"

Regular family meetings are really useful now. Your children know that on Thursday night, they can sit down with you and ask for the latest information from the hospital.

When to Push It

Keep in mind: a child's *failure* to ask questions *doesn't* necessarily mean there's something wrong. Looking away may be this child's style of dealing with stress: "Be happy, mon." The well parent's job is to keep the door open for conversation when the child is ready: "Anything you want to ask about Mom? Well, whenever you're ready, we'll talk."

But when something dramatic is about to happen—when a serious illness becomes grave or terminal—then you should begin to push past the child's defenses. The child *must* have advance warning that things are about to become very bad. It will go against your protective instincts as a parent; the information may be terribly upsetting for your child. Nevertheless, he'll be better able to cope at the end if he's had time to anticipate, and to work through the pain of what's coming.

Painful as it is, the information should be clear and straightforward:

"Honey, Mom isn't coming home from the hospital this time. We think Mom is going to die."

There may be no immediate response. Children throw up protective shields against such devastating news. Acceptance is a *process*.

If possible—if death is not a matter of moments—try to respect that protective mechanism; give the child time to accept.

I've seen children who hear words like, "We think Dad will probably die; the doctors say there's nothing more they can do," who've responded, "Oh. Okay." And go on as if they hadn't heard. And hours later—that night—the next day—they burst into tears, acknowledging that they *did* hear, all those hours ago, but weren't ready to handle it. Perhaps the hospital environment wasn't safe for them, perhaps they needed privacy, or the presence of a certain person to comfort them.

It's okay to repeat the message, to try to get through again.

But if your child completely blocks the information, refuses over time to react or even acknowledge that he understands what's happening, then you should seek the help of a counselor or psychologist. A trained professional can help you get through the child's defenses—and can also determine when the stress is becoming too much for the child, and you must back off.

This Time You May NOT Be the Best Judge

Until now, we've assumed that parents are the best judges of their own children's state of mind. When you think something's wrong, *something is wrong.*

But when we're dealing with extreme stress in children—the stress of a parent's serious, or grave, or fatal illness—a couple of important recent studies suggest parents may *not* be the best judges. The researchers had parents fill out questionnaires on exactly how worried or stressed they thought their children were about their illness—in this case, cancer. Then the researchers interviewed the children to establish their actual level of worry or stress.

In almost every case, the parents UNDERestimated the stress their children were experiencing because of a parent's illness.

Sometimes the children were deliberately hiding their worries from their parents, so as not to put even more pressure on them. And sometimes the parents were simply seeing what they wanted to see— viewing their children through rose-colored glasses: "My, aren't they handling this well!"

We saw the perfect example at the beginning of chapter 3, the father who felt sure that "Moira is fine." Moira, of course, was anything *but* fine; her father was just too close, or perhaps too distracted, to realize it.

That's why, when trying to bring children safely through one of these very bad times, it's wise to bring in someone who's a little more objective, a little more detached from the crisis. Don't depend exclusively on your own evaluation; ask a trusted relative, friend, counselor, social worker to talk with your children, to find out whether they are indeed harboring dangerous stresses, deep anxieties that you yourself haven't caught. You may think the kids are handling the situation, you may even be right, but have someone else check your conclusions.

Helping Children to Feel

At this point, nothing is more important than letting your children know how *you* feel. You must have the courage to drop your own defenses.

The Little Boy Who Wouldn't Listen

The grandparents brought the grandchildren to the hospital. Their daughter, the children's mother, had had a brain aneurysm—a burst blood vessel. Surgery had failed. She was on a ventilator, and now it was going to be turned off.

She was a single parent; no husband in the picture. The grandparents, Midwestern farm stock, loved their only daughter deeply—but they were determined to be strong.

We started talking about turning off the ventilator and what that would mean. The older child listened intently, but the five-year-old boy kept trying to change the subject, trying to distract us, running across the room. Finally, he simply covered his ears.

I took the grandfather aside. I told him I was sure the little boy understood what was happening but was pretending with all his might that he didn't. And I said, "*It has to be okay with you if he cries.* You have to show him how *you* feel; he needs this permission from a man, someone he respects."

We went back into the room; I asked the grandfather to take the little boy on his lap —I wasn't going to continue until somebody was holding that child.

Then I started, once again, to talk about the mother's condition. I explained what had happened to his mom: Her brain had died, and the rest of her was about to die too. I try to explain clearly and in great detail, so the family can use the explanation when the children ask questions in the future—as they will.

I thought the boy was going to cover his ears again, but this time he listened.

Finally, he looked up and met my eyes. I still didn't know whether I was getting through. I said, "You know, everyone around here is really, really sad, even your grandpa. Grandpa doesn't show his sadness very much."

At that moment, his grandfather began to cry. The little boy looked at him, saw his tears, and said, "No, no, not my mom!" And then his own tears came.

They cried and cried; we all did. But this child just needed that permission; he needed to see that it really was okay to start feeling this, and that there would be someone there to hold him when he did start feeling it.

That little boy did not need stoicism and strength. He needed to see vulnerability and grief, so that he too could be vulnerable and grieve.

To know you have reached your children, to be sure they understand, you must get an emotional response—and *your* emotional response will be their guide.

Some children can grieve without crying, but not many. And there is no "right amount" of grief. *The cause of the pain comes out in the tears.* When they are ready to stop, they will stop. Probably they will sleep.

Final Communications

As I look back, so much of this book has been about communication— the flow of information within the circle of well parent, ill parent, and children. Now we'll begin to think about final communications within the family—the ones that must last your children a lifetime.

"Are You Going to Heaven?"

I'd like to tell you the story behind the picture on the next page.

I was working with a mother in the hospital who knew she was terminally ill. She had one child, a daughter of about fourteen. She wanted to prepare her daughter for her own death, and yet she couldn't

talk about it. She was afraid, I think, both for her child and for herself.

They both liked pictures, loved colors.

One day I suggested they do a picture together. The daughter didn't think much of the idea:

"Mo-om, I'm really too old for this kind of thing."

But I gave the mother a handful of brightly tinted Magic Markers, and she began idly to sketch some colored lines. It wasn't a picture, really, just noodling around.

After a while, the teenager said, "That's kind of pretty, it looks like a rainbow," and picked up a couple of markers to make more lines. In a few more moments, Mom said, "Now what does it make you think of?"

Her daughter said, "It looks like heaven." And then she said, "Mom? Are you going to heaven?"

And then they began to talk about death: Mom's death. And they agreed they were both pretty scared. They decided that what their painting needed was a little boat, to carry Mom to heaven.

As communication, it was almost accidental. And it was perfect. There was no longer any shadow of fear or misunderstanding: Mother and daughter were together, looking at the future, which was a wash of beautiful colors and a little black boat.

"I'm Not Sure Dad Can Handle That"

Many families, I find, raise barriers of miscommunication in these days of crisis, in a mistaken effort to "protect" a child or a parent.

I remember a young mother whose uterine cancer had recurred. Treatment had failed; medically, there was nothing more to be done. She looked extremely sick, and no one knew exactly how much time remained. Her husband and three children were devastated, the way people are devastated when hopes are raised, then dashed. The husband told me he didn't think his wife understood that she was dying: "She can't handle this, I don't think."

So he felt he couldn't tell their children. It would be disloyal while his wife still kept hoping. He thought it important now that the family do fun things together, but that the children mustn't talk about death. And I told him children can do that.

He and his mother had brought the three children to the hospital, and I said I'd be glad to meet with them sometime. At this point, the grandmother suddenly said, "I think Suzanne needs to see you *today.*" And Suzanne, the fourteen-year-old, nodded.

We walked down the long corridor to a private room. Suzanne needed to talk. And one of the first things that came out was, "Mom's going to die, isn't she?"

She said, "I keep thinking about all the things I'm not going to have now, all the times that Mom's not going to be there anymore. My school trips. Graduation. When I get married." I realized, Suzanne was *practic-*

ing, was getting herself ready for a future without her mother, and was doing it alone, and courageously.

So I told her, "Your dad doesn't think Mom knows she's dying." And Suzanne said indignantly, "But she *does*. She *told* me she was dying!"

It seems that one day, after the cancer recurred, Suzanne was helping her mother into the tub, and her mother said, "Know what? I don't think I'm going to make it this time, baby. I think I'm dying."

I asked Suzanne, "Do you think we can tell your dad that?" She was uncertain. She said, "I'm not sure Dad can handle that."

The mother is home now, and we've all been working to bridge the gap. She and her husband seem to be talking more, making plans, but the d-word still hasn't passed between them. They're getting to it. Gradually, I think, they will all arrive at the truth together.

Messages to the Future

A few chapters ago, we talked about messages—little surprise notes and presents while Mom or Dad is in the hospital, to let the children know that, even though you're sick, you love them and think about them. That kind of message can continue into your children's future. It is at once the most difficult and the most rewarding effort in a parent's final time.

Some parents write notes; some make audiotapes, some—if they still look well—videos. With the ability now to burn CDs and DVDs at home, the possibilities are really limitless.

And it doesn't require a whole lot: You know what the landmarks will be in your children's lives, the important moments when you might not be there. Pick just one or a few:

- The first day of junior high or high school
- High school or college graduation
- Bar mitzvah
- Confirmation
- Engagement

- Marriage
- Birth of a child

You can leave messages of love and encouragement for anyone, or all.

One mother, a physician herself, facing terminal breast cancer, left this kind of series for her then two-year-old daughter. And she added one more message, for when her little girl will first be thinking of having sex. She spoke of the wonderful new feelings, of the cautions, of the importance of love and the right young man. She told me, "I want her to hear this from me. I know my husband can't do it; guys just can't talk to girls about these things."

Hesitations

Some parents hesitate, wondering whether such messages from the past won't simply reopen old wounds, recall a sorrow left behind many years ago. The pain of, "Yes, Mom was thinking of me—*but I'll never see her again.*"

My answer to them is this: The important part of the message is *Mom was thinking of me.*

It does cause pain, but it does *not* rip open old wounds. Almost invariably, I have found, the message is positive. When a growing child, or young adult, learns that Mom or Dad left them a special message, they do feel the loss again, at a reduced level, *but they also feel the love again.* It strengthens the ego: Mom or Dad really loved me, *and I am a lovable person.* He or she cared so much, in those last days so many years ago, to think of me right at the very end!

In later years, these children tell me, "It was so hard to read, so sad, but he loved me enough to do it, and I was so glad. *I could almost hear his voice.*"

So write or speak the message. Think about your two-year-old son, and what you'll want to tell him when, at thirteen, he becomes a man in the Temple. Hold your six-year-old daughter in your mind and tell her what you'd like her to know on the day your first grandchild is born.

Making the Effort

This is something the well parent can and should help with. Because it takes an effort; it's hard, *hard*, to look beyond your own personal tragedy into your children's future without you. A grave illness must turn our thoughts inward, to this ultimate personal catastrophe, yet messages to the future require that we turn our thoughts to others—to our children—in the midst of our own anguish. And the well parent is the best one to say, "I know it's hard to think about. But important things are going to happen in Julie's life, in Danny's, and *they're going to need your help and guidance.* Can we talk about some of those things?"

Frequently someone other than the spouse can help the parent leave messages. It may be a professional like me; it may be an adult sibling. Clients tell me, "My sister Ella came to town; we started talking and she suggested leaving a video behind for my daughter. I didn't know if I could do it, but Ella got out the camera and started asking me some questions—that's all it took."

Some parents simply cannot do it. And if they can't, they can't. I find the situation, for some reason, is a great deal more difficult for men. Fathers leave messages far less often than mothers do, and that's a tragedy. So many women have told me, despairingly, "I tried and tried to get him to write, or talk into a tape recorder; he just couldn't do it."

I find it's also harder for a well husband to suggest such legacies to a gravely ill wife.

Of course, there are exceptions; some fathers leave wonderful spoken legacies for their children; some mothers simply can't. In the end, it is an extremely personal decision; all I can do is tell you what I am certain of: Such messages to the future will be good for your children, and good for you.

Completion

When mothers or fathers do leave these messages, they almost always experience an enormous sense of release, of *completion.* There is a glow about them, the kind of glow you see at births and at weddings. And the sense of completeness comes to the well spouse too. One father told me, after listening to his wife's taped message, *"I don't know if this is more important for the children or for me."*

A Message

I remember a young mother who wanted to leave a message for her six-year-old daughter, but she said, "I just can't write." Then she began telling me about the day her daughter was born, and all it meant to her.

I produced a little tape recorder and said, "Maybe you could just talk." Well, she tried; nothing would come. I said, "Would it help if I ask questions?"

So I started the tape, explaining to the little girl that Mom is thinking about her and wants her to hear her thoughts sometime in the future. Then I asked one or two questions, and the mother's thoughts began to flow, and I didn't have to speak again.

She was a little teary at first, but then, as she spoke on, her voice grew very calm and spiritual. She said:

> *I wish I could be with you on your wedding day. But I guess nobody ever knows when they can be with their children. I was thinking of how you'll look the day you get married. Did you ever see the picture of me in my wedding dress that Dad has? If you haven't seen it, you should ask him to show it to you.*
>
> *I hope the man you're marrying is someone you really love . . .*

It was just very sweet. She talked about the good times and the bad times. She said:

> *You know, Dad and I used to have some fights; we'd get so mad at each other, we'd wonder why we got married. But we always patched them up. And then when you came along, it was so special: It made us a whole family.*

By this time I was teary, but she was very calm. Once she got going, she spoke to the tape for ten or fifteen minutes, and then stopped and said, "I don't know what else to say."

I said, "I don't think there's anything else you need to say."

She never recorded another message. She died three years ago, but her daughter has a wonderful legacy in her future.

What to Say

Here are some other things I've heard parents leave behind:

Almost always, there's an expression of love. Some parents try to leave a spiritual explanation, or interpretation, of their death. Some can talk about the imminence of death; some cannot.

Many will share religious beliefs: "I believe I have been a good person; I believe good people go to heaven. We learned that in church together. And that's where I think I'm going to be." And some will go on and tell their children what they think heaven, or the life beyond death, will be like.

What Not to Say

But be a little careful. Some of this can be scary.

I wince when a parent tells her children something like, "I'll be watching over you. And if you do something bad. *I'm going to know it.* So don't disappoint me."

That kind of concrete warning can make children feel constantly guilty, can cast its shadow on their lives far into the future, can cloud their judgment and undermine their egos. And if there is time left, I try to help the parent see the risk of that kind of message.

If the parent is close to the end, and this may be the very last message, then I don't interfere—but I try to work with the child afterward, to make that message a little less concrete, a little less fearsome.

Messages: One More Thought

In a way, our children are our own messages to the future; they are our immortality. So the greatest tragedy is not to die before our children; it is to outlive them. And this tragedy, now, is avoided.

We pass that message in two forms. Heredity—the qualities about us that won us the love of our mates, our children: The twist of a smile, or the way our eyes can laugh, or a squinchy new way of seeing things, or the love in our own hearts—they go on in our children, taking wonderful new forms in each new twist of the genetic spiral. And so those legacies of ourselves will spiral down, through the years and the generations. It's totally out of our control; that's *why* it's wonderful.

The second form of the message is what we say and do, what our children learn, both from what we try to teach them and from the way they see us conduct our lives. This is the message over which we *do* have control, right to the end and, if we wish to make the effort now, beyond the end.

So however great the effort of sending these final messages, and the effort *is great*, the result, I believe, is worth it.

Last Days

We're going to look at two different situations: where a parent is able to spend the last days at home with the family, and where those days are spent in a hospital.

The Hospital: Final Visits

As we discussed in chapter 6, the most important part of a visit to a very sick parent is *preparation*. Particularly if the child hasn't seen Mom or Dad for a while, she's got to be put on notice *in advance* as to what she's going to see. The key object is the same: If the child is going to have a strong emotional reaction, have that reaction in a safe place, *not in the hospital room*.

Again I'd suggest the use of digital pictures to show the child what Mom looks like now, and to explain all that sometimes-frightening medical equipment surrounding her. The older the child, the more careful the preparation must be; somehow younger children seem to *accept* these situations more readily than their older siblings.

After the preparation, the decision must be the child's own. Most younger children, I find, want to make these final visits; older children are more ambivalent. The important thing to remember is this:

Whatever decision the *child* makes is right for that child, *providing that the child makes it.*

With late-stage hospital visits, as with funerals, I find that the well parent frequently puts pressure on the children on the basis of his own earlier experiences. If, as a child, he was denied a final visit to his own dying parent, or if he was compelled, unwillingly, to peer at a dead parent in a casket, he may very well try to press his own child to the other extreme.

Remember: If the child wants to visit a parent at the end, that's all right. If not, *that's all right too.* And if you don't like the child's decision, don't press: He may very well change his mind, or vacillate back and forth, and you can work with that. But:

If the child wants to visit and isn't allowed to, or if the child *doesn't* want to visit and is compelled to, that can cause lasting trauma and real anger in the child. Now is the time to let the grieving happen, not to block it with anger and hostility.

"I Never Had a Chance to Say Good-bye"

One source of anger that I encounter repeatedly in children long after a parent's death, and even in adults many years later, is this single despairing sentence:

"I never had a chance to say good-bye."

So without exerting excessive pressure, it is probably wise to freely offer a final visit to a dying parent. And if the child does want to visit, it's probably *not* wise to discourage it. Because the anger of that moment, of "I never had a chance to say good-bye," can leave a lasting emotional scar. The emotion of anger blocks the emotion of grief, prevents grief from happening. And what is vital when a child loses a beloved parent is to allow the child to grieve, and so get beyond the loss.

But what of the child who really *doesn't* want to make that last visit?

"Something to Remember Me By"

It's important to offer alternatives. Any but the youngest child is going to feel some guilt, deciding not to visit an extremely ill father or mother. So let's find surrogates for the visit, little things the child can send in place of himself.

Sometimes we pick flowers; I promise the child I'll put them in a vase, right where Mom can see them. Or I ask the child whether he'd like to draw a picture, or write a poem, as a message to Mom; I promise I'll show it to her, read it to her, tape it to the wall where she can see it.

Whether or not children visit the parent, *they need a response.* And that's the job of the well parent, because the sick one probably can't do it:

"Daddy's pretty tired now, but he thinks you drew a *beautiful* picture of all of us; he's got it right there on his wall."

If the parent can still respond, then that's going to be a very valuable interaction, an important memory for the child in the future, and usually the child will want it.

What If the Parent Says No?

Sometimes it happens that the children want to make these final visits, and one parent or the other rejects the idea. Usually it's the well parent; sometimes the sick one. In either case, the rationale is something like:

"I don't want them to see me [or see Mom] like this."
"I don't want them to remember me [or her] this way."
"I don't want them to be frightened."

It's not often in this book that I've *urged* you to do something, but now I urge you: *Put this attitude aside.* What your children will gain from these last visits (if *they* want to make them) will far outweigh any hypothetical harm to them.

The children need the closure of these last times together. The physical situation may be daunting, may be frightening, but your children *can* get past it. They're trying to reach the real parent whom they love, within that depleted physical shell. And simply by making the decision to go visit, they are already setting themselves up for the experience, saying "Yes, we can handle it."

Preparation

After that, once again, it's simply a matter of preparation. Look back at chapter 6 and how we prepared children for a visit to a critical-care unit. Tell them exactly what they're going to see; if there's going to be an emotional reaction, let it happen at home where it's safe, *not* in the critical-care unit.

Digital photos can now help everybody. If the sick parent is hesitant, if she doesn't "want them to see me this way," then suggest the photo as a halfway step: "How about this: I'll show both kids the picture and ask if they still want to come visit. If they say yes, you'll know they're ready to handle it."

These last visits are worth the effort they involve.

(I've been asked what to do when a dying parent wishes to see his or her children, and the children don't want to go. In my experience, *that has never happened.* Whenever the parent has been conscious, capable of communicating, the children have wanted to visit and say good-bye.)

If the parent can no longer communicate, the children have to be prepared for that lack of response. Often I tell them, "Even if Mom can't talk to you, or say thank you, somewhere inside her heart, the place where she keeps her feelings, she knows that you're here, that you're trying to help, and she appreciates it."

I say this because I believe it. I believe it is true even when a parent is unconscious, or on a ventilator, or deeply sedated, or comatose. Somewhere inside she knows her children have come, and is grateful.

The Very Last Visit

Even after death, there may be the question of a final visit to the bedside. About half the children, in my experience, want to go in. With younger children, toddlers under three or four, I don't encourage a visit to a parent who has died. Their concept of death simply isn't clear enough for such a visit to have meaning. *They don't understand that the body isn't alive anymore.*

But it's still important to offer the other options—to ask whether they'd like you to leave a picture, a poem, a flower, or some special token beside Mom.

I know a family where the father's work involves a great deal of travel. He never leaves home without a little box containing one token—a toy, a barrette, a little charm—from each child and one from his wife. It's magical thinking, and it works for this family; the children have no doubt they're keeping Dad safe while he's away, and I suspect Dad thinks so too. Something like that may help your family now.

It's very normal for children to vacillate at this point: They are confronting life's final mystery. They want to see Mom, they don't want to see Mom. So at some point that seems right to you, you must be strong enough to say: "It's time for us to go home now and make some plans. So this is your last chance to see Mom while she's here in the hospital. If you'd like to do that, it's still okay; but if not, it's time for us to go home."

Last Days at Home

Given our choice, most of us would prefer to spend our final time at home and, more and more often, that is what is happening. It's a good and humane development.

The Hospice

Another good and humane development of our times can be your family's best friend now: the hospice. Once the possibility of medical treatment is at an end, *no one* should leave a hospital without hospice referrals.

Many hospitals are now affiliated with hospices, and your hospital social worker can put you in touch with one. In an outpatient situation, your physician, nurse, or social worker can refer you. In a pinch, you can find hospices listed in the yellow pages or online.

The basic guidelines for hospice care usually are that the patient has less than six months to live, and that she has discontinued active medical treatment. (Two exceptions: Some hospices will accept clients who are enrolled in clinical research projects involving new, unproven treatments. And some will accept clients whose medical treatment is entirely palliative—aimed at comfort rather than a cure or remission.)

Even if the patient is still in active medical treatment, however, and therefore not eligible for hospice care, certain hospices will stay in contact, against the time when no further treatment may be possible, or the client decides to discontinue treatment and spend her last days as comfortably and peacefully as possible.

Some hospices extend their services to the children of their clients, but others do not. So as you consider hospice care, and various hospices, that should be one of your first questions: Will you counsel my kids?

As I write, there is new research suggesting that some terminally ill patients who abandon active medical intervention to go into hospice care may actually live slightly longer than those who stay with aggressive medical treatment—though the difference in survival is measured only in weeks or months.

There are also indications that people often don't seek hospice care soon enough and later express regret that they waited so long to accept these end-of-time comfort services.

A personal note: In my lifetime of work, I have seen many, many friends decide on hospice care at the end. I have not heard any of them express regret for the decision. To me, accepting hospice does *not* mean giving up hope. It means exchanging hope—from hope of a cure to hope of peace, comfort, and the management of pain for as long as possible.

Children Aren't as Afraid . . .

You'll find your children are probably more receptive to descriptions of the processes of dying than adults are; generally, *children aren't as afraid to think about it.*

If possible, try to avoid the situation where your child is alone for any extended periods with a dying parent; try to have someone else in the house. But if that's impossible, your child *must* understand the process of dying; that's where the hospice teaching comes in.

(Usually, when a parent dies at home, her body will be treated with great care and respect by the mortuary people who remove it. Whether the children actually witness the removal is, once again, a matter of judgment, and of negotiation with the children. What is their age, their level of maturity? If you think they are up to it, ask them: Do you want to be here when Mommy leaves? Either answer is fine, so long as it is the children's answer.)

The Good Days

I will tell you that these final days can be very good days indeed.

I'm thinking of a man, in the terminal phase of cancer. He was divorced, but his ex-wife suggested that he now move back in with her and their fifteen-year-old daughter. It was a warm and generous thing for her to do. At the time all this happened, he was growing weaker, but could still get out occasionally. Whenever he did that, he wore a hat; the chemotherapy had left him entirely bald.

A hospice was involved, helping the family to deal with the prospect of death, explaining just how things would happen. One day when I was meeting with the father and daughter, she said, "What I'm really scared of is that I'll be here alone with you when it comes, *and I won't know what to do.*"

This is what her father told her: "If that happens, *I want you to do nothing heroic.* I just want you to stay with me, and talk to me, and tell me that you love me. I don't want you to call 911. I just want you to stay with me."

And they agreed on that. Then the father said, "But I'm not dead yet. What we have to do is plan our time together."

The girl thought for a little while. She said, "The most important thing in my life now is getting my driver's license."

We nodded.

She said, "You're a better driver than Mom."

Dad nodded.

She said, "So that's what we could do together. You could give me a driving lesson!"

The father wasn't at all sure that was such a good idea in his debilitated condition. But the girl had it all figured out. "Come on! If a cop stops us, you just tell him you're dying of cancer! He'll never give you a ticket! And if he doesn't believe you—well, just take off your hat!"

And the following Saturday, that's what they did. I'm not sure it's the strangest parting gift I've ever heard of, but it was surely one of the neatest.

As to the kind of help your children can provide for a parent who does come home, I'd suggest referring back now to the list we worked out in chapter 2, with special attention to how your own family style affects what should and shouldn't be asked of them.

One Family's Way

I want to offer one further example of how a remarkable family coped with a father's impending death. Their plan is certainly not right for every family, but it was dramatically right for them, and I think you might like to know about it now, in making your own decisions:

Brian, the father, had leukemia, and he had relapsed—his doctors told him his condition was now terminal. In that situation, we usually suggest that parents delay telling their children until closer to the end, so the children aren't living with the worry and the fear over a long period. And for many, perhaps most, families, that may be the right way to go.

But Brian and Leanne didn't do that. They had three gorgeous little girls, ages four to ten. And they decided, when we met at The Gathering Place, that they would tell the girls exactly what was happening. They went home and explained to their daughters, one by one: Daddy is going to die. We don't know when; it might be months from now, but treatment is over and, yes, Daddy is going to die. And they were going to do everything they could to make every remaining moment with Daddy as wonderful and valuable as possible.

Emily, the eldest daughter, reacted with a lot of fear and misery as her parents said it. But then, when Daddy *didn't* die the next day, or the day after that, or the day after that, even Emily, and certainly her younger sisters, Annie and Molly, slipped into this comfortable place of making every minute count.

They traveled; they did the Disney World thing. Brian went to every athletic event, every school activity the girls were involved in, for as long as he could; he made a point of being everywhere his kids were. Then, as he grew sicker and weaker, they stayed home together, reading books, watching movies. They were consciously making the most of every moment, with the clear understanding that these moments together would be their last.

Brian lived for six more months. Today his three daughters are lively, emotionally healthy young ladies who talk freely about their father's life and about his death. And what they remember is all the time they had with their dad—knowing he was going to die, and making the most of the rest of his life. Essentially what Brian and Leanne did with their girls was make memories—and they did it powerfully and well.

I do think this response may be the right one for certain families, where the parents have been continually open and honest about the illness, and the children are resilient. You might want to consider it.

"Don't Hug Me!"

There's one more thing to be learned from this family's experience, as we think about how to help and console children after a parent's death. And that is to let the children guide what we do for them. There is no single right way; there is a right way for each child.

When Brian's two older girls talk to our school conferences, the contrast couldn't be more stark. Emily is adamant: Do *not* treat her any differently. She doesn't want well-meaning teachers to ask how she's doing. Above all, do *not* hug. "It's *my* body; don't hug me!"

Annie, three years younger, is just the opposite; she *loves* to be singled out, loves to be hugged, by anybody, anytime: Hug me, it's great, I love it! Annie is the willing star of her own reality TV show.

So when teachers ask us what they can do to help a child after a family tragedy, we tell them: You have to ask the child. No one magic formula will help all kids.

"Don't hug me!"

"Hug me!"

Facing Death: How Children React

The way your children react to the prospect of a parent's death is going to surprise you, the well parent. And not all the surprises are going to be pleasant.

Remember that a child's world is absolutely centered on himself. Only as we grow toward adulthood do we gain the ability to see through others' eyes, walk the mile in someone else's moccasins.

Cathy's Plan

I remember Cathy, five years old, who started telling me, with great composure, exactly what was going to happen after Mommy died. She announced very firmly, "I want Daddy to find me a new mommy and get married again. And I want to have a baby sister; I want to be a big sister. So I want my new mommy to have a baby."

I told all that to Cathy's father (who laughed and shook his head), and explained that this is very normal for a child her age. Actually, I said, what it showed me was the security you and your wife have provided for her. It's not that she doesn't love her mom, and it's not that she thinks you could transfer your affections that easily; that's not what this is all about. *She's five*, and she's very clear about what she needs in life, and *what she sees herself as needing is a mommy and a daddy and a baby.* And so she's just going to arrange the world to get those things, which is what five-year-olds do.

He laughed again, so I told him, if Cathy brings it up, you can just tell her that you're not ready yet to get her a new mommy. But don't be surprised or hurt if she says it. *It's not an indication of a problem.* It's good stuff, not bad stuff.

Many children tell me they've thought, well before a parent dies, about having a step-parent. Usually the idea surfaces about the time they first realize the parent is seriously ill. And school-age youngsters tend to have reactions that are the polar opposite of preschoolers. These older children tend to become really angry when they think about a step-parent. One nine-year-old told me, "The one thing I'd be so mad about, after my dad dies, is for my mom to get married again. *She's never going to get married again.*"

The important thing to remember, as your children begin to look toward the future, is that every family is unique, and every child will respond in his own way. There are no hard-and-fast rules as to what is the proper response and what isn't; there are only guidelines. And the first guideline is that the child works outward from his own needs.

The Question

At some point, your children will ask it: *Why?*

I won't pretend to help with an answer; we each must find our own. All I can do is warn you: It is coming, and you must be ready for it.

Some families, in my experience, understand their own beliefs in great detail. Most do not. Now it will become important for you to know, coherently, what your own faith believes about death and what follows. Here is where your clergy can be of enormous help, not only in providing the comfort of faith but also detailed instruction from that faith, which you can give to your children.

I've dealt with families of every denomination: Families that believe in a joyous afterlife and families that believe in none; Jewish families who tell me a loved one lives on in the people who loved her, and Buddhists who explain reincarnation to me and their children. Sometimes, if a child asks me, "Why?" I will turn the question around and ask, "What do *you* think? Why does God do the things He or She does?"

Usually, I find that children have some beginnings of an explanation, based on what they've learned at home, and at church, and in life.

You must be prepared to deal with fury and despair. Children have told me, "I think God is terrible, and I don't want to believe in God anymore." I acknowledge that, tell them, "It sounds like you're really angry at God, like you really blame God for all this." And I suggest that, after a while, the child talk it out with the family priest, minister, rabbi, or counselor.

Sometimes children just want to lash out, and I tell them, "I understand how mad you must be, not only at God, but everybody you think had anything to do with why your mom is dying—the doctors, the nurses, the other driver, the carmaker, the cigarette company . . ."

Usually I find that children will give in to their feelings and then leave the need for explanation behind them. "Life is unfair." And that's fine; it's useful for them. And there really is no final explanation for why we ebb and flow as we do.

How Children Grieve

If you were to come to my office at this point, I would give you a little essay called "The Grief of Children." It was written by Susan Woolsey, of the Maryland SIDS Information and Counseling Project, and it's the best short summary I've found about how children process the terrible tragedy of a parent's death and how the surviving parent can help them through. So let me give it to you now:

The Grief of Children

One of the most difficult tasks following the death of a loved one is discussing and explaining the death with children in the family. This task is even more distressing when the parents are in the midst of their own grief.

Because many adults have problems dealing with death they assume that children cannot cope with it. They may try to protect children by leaving them out of the discussions and rituals associated with the death. Thus, children may feel anxious, bewildered, and alone. They may be left on their own to seek answers to their questions at a time when they most need the help and reassurance of those around them.

All children will be affected in some way by a death in the family. Above all, children who are too young for explanations need love from the significant people in their lives to maintain their own security. Young children may not verbalize their feelings about a death in the family. Holding back their feelings because they are so overwhelming, the children may appear to be unaffected. It is more common for them to express their feelings through behavior and play. Regardless of this ability or inability to express themselves, children do grieve, often very deeply.

SOME COMMON EXPRESSIONS OF CHILDREN'S GRIEF

Experts have determined that those in grief pass through four major emotions: fear, anger, guilt, and sadness. It should be remembered that everyone who is touched by a death experiences these emotions to some degree—grandparents, friends, physicians, nurses, and children. Each adult's and child's reactions to death are individual in nature. Some common reactions are:

Shock: The child may not believe the death really happened and will act as though it did not. This is usually because the thought of death is too overwhelming.

Physical Symptoms: The child may have various complaints such as headache or stomach ache and fear that he too will die.

Anger: Being mostly concerned with his own needs, the child may be angry at the person who died because he feels he has been left "all alone" or that God didn't "make the person well." .

Guilt: The child may think that he caused the death by having been angry with the person who died, or he may feel responsible for not having been "better" in some way.

Anxiety and Fear: The child may wonder who will take care of him now or fear that some other person he loves will die. He may cling to his parents or ask other people who play an important role in his life if they love him.

Regression: The child may revert to behaviors he had previously outgrown, such as bed-wetting or thumb-sucking.

Sadness: The child may show a decrease in activity—being "too quiet."

It is important to remember that all of the reactions outlined above are normal expressions of grief in children. In the grief process, time is an important factor. Experts have said that six months after a significant death in a child's life, normal routine should be resuming. If the child's reaction seems to be prolonged, seeking professional advice of those who are familiar with the child (e.g., teachers, pediatricians, clergy) may be helpful.

EXPLANATIONS THAT MAY NOT HELP

Outlined below are explanations that adults may give a child hoping to explain why a person she loved has died. Unfortunately, simple but dishonest answers can only serve to increase the fear and uncertainty that the child is feeling. Children tend to be very literal—if an adult says that "Grandpa died because he was old and tired" the child may wonder when he too will be too old; he certainly gets tired—what is tired enough to die?

- *"Grandma will sleep in peace forever."* This explanation may result in the child's fear of going to bed or to sleep.
- *"It is God's will."* The child will not understand a God who takes a loved one because He needs that person Himself. Or *"God took him because he was so good."* The child may decide to be bad so God won't take him too.
- *"Daddy went on a long trip and won't be back for a long time."* The child may wonder why the person left without saying good-bye. Eventually he will realize Daddy isn't coming back and feel that something he did caused Daddy to leave.
- *"John was sick and went to the hospital where he died."* The child will need an explanation about "little" and "big" sicknesses. Otherwise, he may be extremely fearful if he or someone he loves has to go to the hospital in the future.

WAYS TO HELP CHILDREN

As in all situations, the best way to deal with children is honestly. Talk to the child in a language that he can understand. Remember to listen to the child and try to understand what the child is saying and, just as important, what he's not saying. Children need to feel that the death is an open subject and that they can express their thoughts or questions as they arise. Below are just a few ways adults can help children face the death of someone close to them.

The child's first concern may be "who will take care of me now?"
- Maintain usual routines as much as possible.
- Show affection, and assure the child that those who love him still do and that they *will* take care of him.

The child will probably have many questions and may need to ask them again and again.
- Encourage the child to ask questions and give honest, simple answers that can be understood. Repeated questions require patience and continued expression of caring.
- Answers should be based on the needs the child seems to be expressing, not necessarily on the exact words used.

The child will not know appropriate behavior for the situation.
- Encourage the child to talk about his feelings and share with him how you feel. You are a model for how one expresses feelings. It is helpful to cry. It is not helpful to be told how one should or should not feel.
- Allow the child to express his caring for you. Loving is giving *and* taking.

The child may fear that he also may die or that he somehow caused the death.
- Reassure the child about the cause of the death and explain that any thoughts he may have had about the person who died did *not* cause the death.
- Reassure him that this does *not* mean someone else he loves is likely to die soon.

The child may wish to be a part of the family rituals.
- Explain these to him and include him in deciding how he will participate. Remember that he should be prepared beforehand, told what to expect, and have a supporting adult with him. Do not force him to do anything he doesn't feel comfortable doing.

The child may show regressive behavior.
- A common reaction to stress is to revert to an earlier stage of development. (For example, a child may begin thumb-sucking, or bed-wetting; or may need to go back into diapers or have a bottle for a time.) Support the child in this and keep in mind that these regressions are temporary.

Adults can help prepare a child to deal with future losses of those who are significant by helping the child handle smaller losses through sharing their feelings when a pet dies or when death is discussed in a story or on television.

In helping children understand and cope with death, remember four key concepts: be loving, be accepting, be truthful, and be consistent.

Restarting Life

The days immediately following a loved one's death are a period of shock for the entire family. There is the funeral to be taken care of, paperwork, the routine of loss. The family goes through this period on autopilot.

Then it is time to go back to life: to work, to school.

That transition, children tell me, is really hard. It's just easier not to face the routines of life again.

Returning to School

Most children say that when they go back to school, they feel *singled out*. There's a sign dangling somewhere: HIS MOM DIED. They feel the other kids are all talking about them, and they're going to be treated differently. And there's some truth to it: *Everybody knows, and nobody knows what to say.*

Earlier in this book we met Annie Marks, whose mom died of cancer when Annie was nine. Annie found it helped to write about her mother's death, and this is what she wrote about returning to school two weeks later:

"It was really hard to go back . . . *I felt like the only girl whose mother ever died.*"

So now we need help from the school, and we need to help the school as well.

Someone from the family should go to the school in advance, before the child returns, to talk with all the teachers involved as well as the guidance counselor and the nurse. They will need to know just what has happened and how to help the child back into normal school life.

It's good for a teacher to say, "I'm sorry about your mom. And if you ever want to talk about it, we can." It's particularly valuable for another child, who's suffered a similar loss, to offer to share: "My dad died too, if you ever want to hear what it was like for me when it happened."

But what is vitally important, and what the teachers must be told to encourage, is that the other children *start treating this child as normally as possible.*

They should call him by his old nicknames, draw him back into sports, band, clubs, silly jokes, and just hanging out.

Sometimes the child is going to "lose it," suddenly burst into tears. The teacher should not ignore that, but also should not make the child the center of attention. When it happens, ask the teacher to excuse the child with a quiet, "Would you like to go down to the office? To the nurse?" Most children would rather be out of the class-room, out of the eyes of their peers, while they pull themselves to-gether. The teacher will help the child most by acknowledging what's happening, handling it, *not* making a big deal.

Above all, there must be *no permission to fail*. Impress on the teach-ers: you expect them to demand that your child perform to his full capacity. There must be no misplaced compassion, no, "Well, no won-der she's flunking exams, poor thing."

If the child has been out for a significant period of time, she will have difficulty coming back up to speed; even a good student will re-quire special attention and coaching. Marginal students need a *lot* of help to get back on the track; school is not the release and pleasure for them that it is for the good student. Nevertheless, expectations of full performance must continue, both from the teachers and from the family. *Permission to fail now can mean the start of a lifetime pattern of failure.*

As long as the teachers and staff are notified in advance, I've found most schools to be very helpful, very concerned with helping the child past the tragedy. Some schools even have trained crisis teams; counsel-ors meet and talk with the child on the very first day back. The school can be your best ally now; lean on it.

Keep Looking for Trouble

As you and your children begin adjusting to this life after death, you will probably find they return to normal faster than you do. It's the nature of youth to put the past away and grow quickly toward the fu-ture.

Nevertheless, keep watching for those signs of trouble we looked at in chapter 3:

- Sleep disturbance
- Eating disturbance
- Fear and anxiety

- Aggressive play
- Patterns of failure
- The quiet child
- Risky behavior

As always, you are the expert; you simply have to pay attention. When you think something is wrong, *something is wrong*. And by now you know what you can deal with yourself, and when you need a little help from your friends.

A Personal Note: To the Parent Who Is Still Here

Now is the hardest time. Probably the worst thing that will ever happen to you has just happened. The dear partner of your life is gone. And now, here comes a stranger, a child life specialist sitting in a distant city, to tell you that you must begin to look outward—to share this terrible grief—for the good of your children.

And yes, that is what I am telling you. And I do it with a clear conscience, for two reasons:

As you know better than anyone in the world, the central concern now of the wife or husband whom you loved so much would be for the health—physical, mental, emotional—of your children. Children who emerge from this tragedy whole and sound will be your last, best memorial to your absent friend.

And the help you can give your children in *their* grieving will help you in turn. Certainly the wrenching sadness will not go away, yet sharing it with your children will make good things happen *within* the sadness. You will support each other, become closer, and emerge stronger—a family still. And that too is what your absent friend would wish.

SPECIAL
SITUATIONS

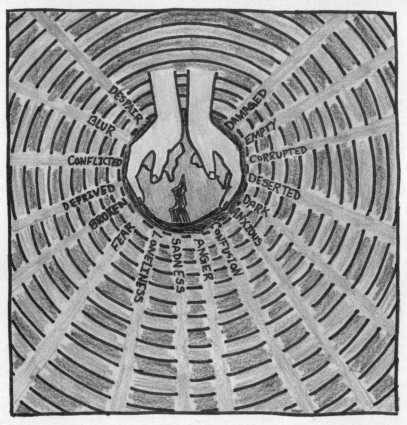

When Marissa Barrett was just four, her dad was the victim of a savage carjacking, emerging alive but nonresponsive—a condition that has continued for the past seventeen years. His head injury has left him totally dependent; he cannot walk or talk.

Now twenty-one, Marissa drew this picture about how her father's trauma impacted her life. "Basically, my whole world fell apart when this happened," Marissa remembers. "My mom is a great mom; she was trying so hard to help us all keep it together. She never realized we all needed to fall apart, and maybe she did too. Everyone wanted to be so positive: 'We can handle this, this will be our new normal, **Daddy's still in there somewhere.**'" Nobody, she says, ever let her address her confusion, her anger, her four-year-old's rage at the unfairness—that the world wasn't the way it had been, and never would be again.

With those feelings unaddressed, Marissa had a rough time growing up; she got into trouble with drugs and alcohol. At sixteen she entered rehab, where, for the first time, she was encouraged to talk about her pain, her fury, over what had happened to the father she loved. "It was so hard and painful, but it was exactly what I needed to do," she says.

Marissa is now in college; since that catharsis at sixteen—that permission to express the fury she felt when she was four—she has pulled her life back together.

II.

Children and Trauma

Let's start with definitions. There are two. Trauma is:

- An injury to a living body, caused by the application of external force or violence
- A disordered state resulting from mental or emotional stress, or physical injury.

What's immediately clear: The first definition, physical injury, can *cause* the second definition, mental or emotional stress. And in this chapter we'll be dealing with trauma as both cause and effect.

The word itself comes from the German for "dream," and that link is our clue to how very deep in the brain an emotional trauma lies—it is far, far beneath our conscious control, in that primitive, million-year-old reptilian brain—it's called the limbic brain—that does not, cannot, respond to logic. It knows only three responses:

- Freeze
- Fight
- Flee

The traumatized child—or adult, for that matter—simply cannot "think her way through it." We can no more reason our way through a trauma than we can reason our way through a dream.

The memory of trauma will never go away. But what we can do, gradually and with help, is pull it out of that primitive brain into our thinking brain—our human brain—where we can examine it, understand it, and, after a while, deal with it. And this is what we must do if we are to help ourselves, or our children, through trauma.

I'm going to bring some first-hand knowledge, painfully acquired, of both kinds of trauma, because when you've seen it from the inside out, there's no mistaking what trauma is, or how it can damage the self. And I hope you will come to understand the heart of the problem when we try to help children through their own, and their parent's, trauma:

The central loss in trauma is the loss of a sense of safety.

My Trauma

Some years ago, I was a volunteer firefighter. On one call-out, in the depth of winter, I was hauling a hose up an icy ladder. Two stories up the side of a burning building, I missed a step and fell.

Oh, what a long fall!

I remember thinking very clearly as I fell: This is taking a long time. This is taking too long.

I'm going to die . . .

Well, I hit the ground, and I was still alive. Paramedics braced me, rushed me by ambulance to a local hospital, but the damage was beyond its capabilities. The doctors wanted to helicopter me to a major trauma center, but this was Ohio in midwinter—ice, snow; no choppers could fly. So over the road we went, lights and siren, in a second ambulance. It was at the trauma center that doctors confirmed: I had broken my back.

I was very lucky. With casting and care I regained my ability to walk, and even to indulge my greatest passion: scuba diving. Physically, I would be myself again. But as to the mental trauma . . .

It struck first the first time I drove myself back to the trauma center, to see the specialist who had repaired my back. I still don't remember driving up to the center, pulling into the parking garage. My heart was beating so fast I could hardly stand the hammering. My hands were shaking, and I broke out in a cold sweat—all this just from *seeing* the trauma center. All those feelings from the night of the accident—the endless fall, the two screaming ambulance rides, the not knowing whether I'd ever walk again, or even live—they all washed back out of my limbic brain and over the grown-up, highly educated, very professional person called Kathleen McCue.

At this time I was actually working professionally with trauma; intellectually I knew all about it—still, it took me over. So I did what I'd been trained to do: I sat there, in the car, in the hospital parking garage. I took deep breaths. I forced myself to think: The worst part of this is over. You are healing, you are getting well. You have got to wrap your head around those facts; you have got to slow your body's panic response down. Your heart doesn't *need* to race, your hands don't *need* to shake, your skin doesn't *need* to sweat . . .

And after some minutes, it began to work. I began to recover intellectual control from that terrified, primitive part of my brain—because I'd been trained. I don't know whether most people, lacking the training, could have recovered control.

But the trauma wasn't finished with me.

Several months passed. One afternoon I found myself walking along a sidewalk, quite close to the roadway. Beside me was the curb, three or four inches high. And suddenly I felt myself falling—falling over that curb, falling not three or four inches, but down, down, down forever, to the frozen sidewalk that broke my back months earlier.

No, I didn't fall, not even over that low curb. It was a flashback from the limbic brain, shrieking, "Danger! Danger if you fall! It will happen again!" It's not the thinking part of the brain; it can't say, logically, you won't hurt yourself if you fall off a four-inch curb.

So I got professional help. I actually learned procedures to switch off the limbic brain and switch on the reasoning brain. And it hasn't happened again.

Traumatized Children

We're going to look at two different ways children may experience trauma:

- First-hand. The child is actually involved in the traumatic incident that hurts her parent or parents. She's riding in the family car when it rolls over. The family is together inside the home when the tornado strikes. She sees the mugger shoot her father.
- Second-hand. She wasn't there when it happened, but now she must see a badly burned parent in the hospital, cope with the empty place in the hospital bed where her father's leg should be, visit the flattened wreckage of her home after the windstorm.

What the well parent, or the helping adult, must understand is that in the first situation—the child actually involved in the traumatic experience—you will be dealing with TWO traumas: the child's own trauma and then the trauma of having a seriously injured, possibly disfigured or mutilated parent. AND THESE ARE TWO SEPARATE TRAUMAS. You will have to help the child work through her own experience and then help her cope with her new and perhaps frightening parent.

Unless she works through her own trauma first, she will remain "frozen," unable to handle the emotions caused by the damage to her parent.

She'll have to do the toy car play, the crashing play, the immobilization play, the play about police and firefighters helping rescue her, before she can begin to handle the second trauma—a new and perhaps frighteningly altered parent.

(The death of a parent is an enormous trauma for the child—so much so that we've given it its own separate chapter. See chapter 10, "When Things Get Very Bad.")

First, Help Yourself

In chapter 8 we learned that, before you can help your children cope with a massive change in your own life story—a chronic illness that will alter your lives forever—you must first help yourself. You must come to terms with those permanent changes, must overcome your own natural anger, depression, dependence.

That's even more true—far more true—when you and your children have shared a trauma.

If, after your auto accident, you can't sit in a car without shaking uncontrollably—if, after the fire, you can't enter a room with a fireplace—if, in short, your own trauma is still controlling you, then you cannot possibly help your son or daughter sit in that car, enter that room, face whatever trauma you've shared. And severe trauma, as we've seen, lies far beyond our conscious grasp. You may very well need professional help to get beyond your own deep trauma—and recognizing that need is your first step toward coping with your trauma, and your child's.

The Child Who Was There

What the child who shared the traumatic moment needs most from you, the injured parent, and you, the well parent, is completely counterintuitive. The most natural thing in the world is to tell your child, "Don't think about that. Just put it out of your mind." It feels like the humane, kind thing to do—and it is exactly what the child does NOT need.

Children who have been through a shocking experience *need* to talk it out, play it out, do it with dolls, rehearse it over and over again until they begin to gain some mastery over it. And children do this naturally. After the monstrous attack of 9/11/01, teachers all over America were horrified as their pupils began *en masse* to draw planes crashing into skyscrapers, write essays about people jumping out of burning towers. But these children were actually beginning to heal themselves of the terrible, unimaginable horrors they'd been seeing all day and all night on television.

And the job of the well parent now is to encourage that natural tendency, to say, "Can you draw what happened? Would you like to write a poem or story about what you saw, how you felt?" If the answer is no, that's all right. But usually the answer will be yes.

Your child will tend to go over and over the traumatic experience, day in, week out, until you really don't want to hear it again—but that's what you must do, until your child has brought the trauma out of the lizard brain and into the reasoning, thinking prefrontal human cortex.

A Surrogate "Well Parent"

The best person to help a child through trauma is the well parent. You are the person your child trusts above all others. You, more than anyone, have the power to make her feel safe again. But it's *hard*, perhaps too hard: You are traveling back and forth to the hospital, doing the work of two people, handling unfamiliar finances. You may not even want to hear the horrors of the accident over and over . . . especially if you, too, were involved in it.

This is another situation where someone who cares about the child, but is a little farther from the center of things, can perform an invaluable service. An aunt, a grandma, an old friend, Dad's pal who coaches youth hockey, some special person who can listen to your child, guide his play, drawing, writing—this person can help you bring the child safely through the trauma. Suggest: "Just play with him, just let him get his cars and trucks and people out and play: Ask him to tell you about what happened."

Whoever that helper is should read this chapter with you now.

Guilt

Remember those three, and only three, possible reactions when the lizard brain encounters trauma:

Freeze. Fight. Flee.

The immediate response is usually to freeze, followed by one or both of the others: the fight response: screaming, struggling; the flight response: running away.

Encountering trauma, we will do one of those three things, or all in some sequence—and we probably won't be proud, as thinking human beings, of what we did. The tornado struck the house, and eight-year-old Jill froze—she made no effort to save her little brother. The elevator lurched, stopped suddenly, the lights went out, pitch blackness, and Sammy began to flail his arms and scream—a classic "fight" reaction. The car ran Joey down on his bike, and Tommy, his very best friend, ran away—he didn't help Joey; he *ran away.*

What you must do, first for yourself and then for your children, is understand and accept: At the moment of trauma, you are in the grip of a part of your brain that has been trying to save our lives since we were small reptiles crawling through a Jurassic swamp. In an emergency that requires instant response to keep the organism alive, your ancient brain takes over, and it knows only three things to do. We don't do what, morally, we feel we *should* do, what, as rational human beings, we'd *want* to do—what we *hope*, sitting here at ease, we *would* do.

We freeze. We fight. We run. And there's no guilt because, in the purest sense of the phrase, *we couldn't help it.* This is the message that must be conveyed, again and again and again, until the child understands and accepts:

You couldn't help it.

Being Safe

One thing parents can count on (we've been counting on it since page 1): Children are *resilient*. The life force burns brightly in them; with our help, they can bounce back even from shocks that might devastate an adult. Drawing the pictures, writing the stories, doing the puppet play are how children assert that resilience, and put themselves on the road to recovery. But the first thing that has to happen is that the child *must feel safe again*. Nothing good will happen, no resilience will occur, while the child is sitting in the ruins of her smashed or burned house, or on the edge of the road where the wrecker is rolling the family car over.

Helping Time Heal

The good news is: Most of us—children and adults—will recover from trauma on our own. For a reasonably well-adjusted individual, the trauma will gradually recede; the forebrain will take over. The key factor is time.

Without some intervention on your part, it may take your child weeks or even months (depending on her own resilience and the severity of the trauma) to get back to something like normal. And a lot can go wrong in those weeks or months: An A student can become a C student; normal development can suffer; so can friendships.

So the second bit of good news: We can help; we can materially shorten that bounce-back time. Let's think about how we can support and speed up recovery, make it a little bit easier for your child to get back on track.

(At the end of this chapter, you'll find a detailed checklist, broken down by age groups, of how children manifest trauma. I'd suggest you go over it to see whether your own children are indicating a need for help.)

Coping Skills

As you play through, or talk through, or listen through the trauma with your child, try to inject coping skills. Let him crash those toy cars together, again and again if he wants to, but then, perhaps, have one of the cars say, "I'm so tired of being afraid. What can I do to not be afraid, to feel better? I know, I can drive out into the country and listen to the birds sing. That would make me feel better." And drive the little car away, and let it park under a tree and listen to the birds sing.

When I visit a group of children who've seen something traumatic— a horrendous auto accident, a schoolyard shooting—I may ask them to talk about it, write about it, draw pictures of it. And then I try to help them find ways past the trauma.

I visited one group who had seen a schoolmate struck by lightning, and asked them all to draw the picture. But when I came back a week later, I said, "What have you done this past week that's made you feel better, less scared, less worried about your friend? Pick one thing that made you feel better, and draw a picture of that." I wouldn't say, "Don't draw the lightning bolt anymore"; they may still *need* to draw the lightning bolt. But together we found ways to make the lightning bolt less overwhelming—less traumatic.

There are, in general, four areas where parents can help speed children's recovery from trauma:

1. **Ventilate the stress response.** Perhaps the child is furious with the drunk driver who ran into your car; she can't move beyond the trauma because she's just too angry. I'll offer that child a punching bag—we have a heavy bag hanging in our playroom, but you can just fill a soft, sturdy bag with packing peanuts. Ask your child to write on the outside of the bag everything she's mad at, then let her whale away on the bag until she gets out the anger.

Then talk to her: Okay, now we know what makes you angry; what are some things that make you happy? In The Gathering Place playroom we have pillows with big smiley faces—for younger kids. I'll have them hug a "happy pillow" and talk about everything that makes them feel good, makes them feel safe and secure. Let the child guide you, and herself, through the anger to her safe place.

2. ***Avoid additional stress.*** If whatever caused the trauma can show up on TV, keep the TV off. Stay away from family and outside situations that may be stressful, *even if they're not actually related to the trauma.* If Saturday normally means a visit to an unpleasant relative, postpone it. If your child is one of those alphas who have a different after-school activity every single afternoon, try to get her to cut back on a couple of them and consciously relax.

3. ***Find positive ways to give comfort.*** A warm bubble bath. Relaxing on the couch, reading together or just cuddling. Taking a leisurely, comfortable walk to nowhere in particular. Petting the dog or the cat. Above all, warm human contact, and plenty of it. A lot of traumatized adults have told me they benefit by going home, picking up their children, and just hugging them. After a while, of course, a child will start to wiggle, and say, "Okay, Mom, you can put me down now," but these traumatized parents don't want to let go; they want to hug and be hugged back.

   And this one works in reverse; hugs can be huge stress-relievers for a traumatized child. Tell her, "I had a really bad day. You know what would make me feel good? If you could give me a really big hug." The child will think she's helping you with the hug, but hugs are bi-directional. You can't get one without giving one.

4. ***Reinterpret the stress.*** Find ways to make it less threatening. Talk about the good that came out of the bad. The 9/11 attacks

were a national trauma, but within a couple of weeks you began to hear, "I didn't realize neighbors cared so much for each other." "Weren't those Canadians wonderful to our stranded passengers?" "My son was hiking in Kenya, and everybody looked out for him, helped him get home."

And there were real advances for our society: Perhaps your children's school put an automatic cell-phone notification system in place. Next time something happens, we'll be ready.

Any positive outcome of the traumatic event will put the trauma itself into a healthier perspective.

Trauma First

Before the child can begin to cope with all the stresses of a changed life, she must first overcome the trauma. Until she does, she will not be able to handle the new stresses: having to live with a relative while her dad is in the burn unit, having to take over chores that Mom always did, having to supervise younger kids. She'll be "frozen," and her natural resilience won't be able to assert itself. Nancy's story will give you an idea of the process.

Nancy's Story

It was the first day of our regular horseback camp for clients of The Gathering Place, and eleven-year-old Nancy had been looking forward to it. But when the bus was about to leave, Nancy hadn't shown up. I called her house, and she answered, but she didn't sound like the Nancy I knew. She sounded blocked, dazed.

Nancy said, "My mom's really sick. I'm waiting for someone to come home, and then I'll get them to bring me right to the stables; is that okay?"

I said sure, that would be fine, and asked whether she needed any help. She said no, she was all right; a neighbor was coming over to help.

I was uneasy, but Nancy kept saying no, her mom was sick, someone was coming, it was okay.

That afternoon Nancy finally arrived at camp, in a neighbor's car, looking and acting shell-shocked. After a little while I took her aside and said, "Can you tell me what happened this morning?" Nancy just stared at me for a long minute, and then she exploded in tears.

I held her, and she cried and cried. And then I began to learn what had happened.

Nancy's mother, a cancer patient, had a central line, called a broviac catheter, implanted in her chest wall so chemotherapy could be delivered without a new IV each time. The catheter tapped directly into a major blood vessel. That morning, suddenly, while they were having breakfast, the catheter pulled partway out, spraying blood all over the kitchen. It must have been a scene out of *CSI*, blood gushing in all directions.

"Mom was just bleeding and bleeding, buckets of blood, blood everywhere," Nancy told me. I cannot imagine a more shocking, a more traumatic moment, for an eleven-year-old or, for that matter, for you or me.

Nancy's mother stayed calm; she knew exactly what to do. First, she clamped her hands over the catheter, stanching the flow of blood to a trickle. Then she told Nancy to call their next-door neighbor and have the neighbor call 911. Meantime, Nancy's mom was still holding pressure over the site; by this time she'd lost a good deal of blood and was growing weaker, but she never lost consciousness. All the time, she kept telling Nancy, "It's okay, I'm going to be okay." And this was when my phone call reached Nancy.

I don't know how much blood there actually was, but in Nancy's narrative there was blood everywhere, a huge pool of blood.

The neighbor came, the ambulance came; neighbor and paramedics assured Nancy that her mom would be all right. But sitting there, in that blood-spattered kitchen, Nancy could not possibly begin to recover from the trauma of what had just happened. She was shell-shocked.

Only when she arrived at camp, when she told me the story—when she cried, and *began to feel safe*—could Nancy start to emerge from the trauma.

Things became a little better when I got her calmed down a bit and asked her, "Would you like to call the hospital to make sure Mom is okay?" Yes, she wanted to do that. So we called Mom's room; Nancy's dad was there, and he let her talk to her mom. Her mother, sounding like herself, reassured Nancy: everything was fine; the doctors were re-inserting the catheter, making sure it still worked.

After the call Nancy, too, was more like herself. Then she asked me, "Can I tell people about what happened this morning?" I said, "You bet you can."

At camp each afternoon, we do a closing circle, where the campers talk about their day's adventures, their families' medical situations. When Nancy's turn came, she described what happened in the kitchen. "It was kind of scary," she admitted, "blood all over the floor." There was a murmur from the other kids: "Oh, gross!" But then they imme-diately began to ask, "Is your mom okay?" And Nancy said, "Yes, she's going to be okay"—and you could see her start to believe it.

Then a couple of the other kids chipped in with traumatic stories about their own parents—projectile vomiting, gunshots. And those stories, too, helped normalize the horrible thing Nancy had seen.

Nancy told us she felt *safer* at camp—people hugged her; people helped her. She knew nobody would get hurt. Above all, there would be no blood.

There, in a nutshell, is trauma—from that freezing moment in the kitchen, through stunned hours in the grip of the limbic brain, to the enormous catharsis of tears, and the process of talking about it, reliv-ing it, and so bringing the horror out into the forebrain, where Nancy could begin to cope with it rationally:

"Yes, she's going to be okay."

Trauma in Children: A Checklist
of Signs and Symptoms

Megan Bronson, APRN, BC, a trauma nurse, compiled this list of how trauma manifests itself in children within our three age groups:

Young children, about two to six years old

- Hyperactivity
- Fear, anxiety, nightmares, fear of going to sleep or sleeping alone
- Regressive behaviors: bed-wetting, talking baby talk, thumb-sucking, whining
- Repetitive trauma play, possible difficulty verbalizing about the trauma
- Confusion, difficulty understanding that the trauma is over
- Attachment anxiety: clinging, excessive concern about parent leaving
- Physical symptoms: stomach aches, headaches, etc.
- Personality changes: may be withdrawn and passive, or reckless and aggressive
- School difficulties: difficulty concentrating, may not want to go to school or preschool
- Arguing, fighting, agitation, restlessness, quick to anger

Latency-age children, about six to twelve years old:

- Fears more specific, related to the trauma
- Sleep disturbances: nightmares, fear of sleeping alone
- Obsessing about the trauma, talking about it repeatedly, compulsive behaviors
- Guilt related to not being able to control the traumatic event
- Impaired ability to concentrate, focus, problem-solve, learn

- Changes in behavior: withdrawn and isolated, aggressive and reckless
- Feeling overwhelmed, afraid of losing control of feelings, moody
- Fear of death, sometimes a fear of spirits or ghosts

Adolescents, about twelve to eighteen years old:

- May include symptoms of latency-age children
- May be self-conscious about feelings, fears, being different
- Aggressive, destructive, self-destructive, risk-taking, acting-out behaviors: substance abuse, sexual acting out, delinquent behavior, truancy
- Avoidance of relationships, withdrawal, social isolation
- Personality changes; depression, apathy, moodiness
- Leaving school or home, or fear of separation from family/parents
- Pessimism, cynicism, plans for revenge
- Failing grades, lack of interest in school, friends, and previously enjoyed activities.

When illness strikes a single parent, storm clouds gather for both the parent and the child. Nine-year-old Madeline Boka used that powerful image to show the impact of her mom's breast cancer on both of them.

12.

Single Parenting, Multiple Households

It's our new reality. As I write, two of every five babies in America are born to single mothers, and that number is increasing every year. The traditional family, a mother and a father who stay together while raising their 2.7 adorable children—to the extent it ever really existed, that family is going away. With more than half of the nation's families now headed by one adult, the single-parent family has become our new norm. And when that single parent falls seriously, or gravely, or fatally ill, that is the toughest situation of all. Tough, and yet it *can* be handled.

If Yours Is a Single-Parent Family

Many of the stories in this book involve single-parent families. Working with so many single parents who've faced serious illness, I've learned two things:

- Everything in this book that applies to children in two-parent families applies equally, or even more strongly, to children being raised by a single parent.

• There are special conditions that apply uniquely to a single parent who faces a medical crisis. Those are what we'll look at now.

Remember that for children growing up with only one parent in their lives, things become very murky and worrisome when that parent becomes ill. One of childhood's most basic concerns is security: "Who'll take care of me? Who'll do the Mom things? The Dad things?"

Find Someone to Be the "Well Parent"

For the two-parent family, there's a sort of automatic backup system in place—the "well parent" who can take over some, or most, or all the roles of the sick parent. The first thing for you, the sick parent, to do now as you face a major illness is to try to find someone, or a group of someones, who can fill that role of "well parent." It may be your own mother, a brother, sister, or cousin, your closest friend, the mother of your child's playmate, a coach—one or more folks you can count on to stick with you and your kids and pick up part of the load through whatever is coming.

Nobody in this group of potential helpers has to be, necessarily, the person you'd want to raise your children if you were no longer with them. Perhaps you'd plan for them to go to your own parents, who live in another city. But *right now* you want some people close and *close by*, available to you and your children on a continuous basis. Make it clear that you're asking them for their help *only* through the course of the illness; they're taking no responsibility beyond that, no matter what the outcome.

It's important for these helpers to know as much as you now know about helping your children through your crisis. So I would urge you to share this book with the helping relatives or friends, and ask that they read at least those parts that directly bear on your own situation. The less you feel up to reading, the more your helpers should read.

These helping folks should be alert for the early warning signs of a troubled child (chapter 3), aware of the kind of help that can be provided within the family's own circle, and the levels of help available on the outside (chapter 4).

Make Long-Term Arrangements for the Care of the Children

You've probably already done some thinking about it, even made some preliminary arrangements. Every single parent has in the back of her mind the auto accident, the sudden illness that could leave her children in a world without her.

But now, with a medical crisis, the situation is imminent. Hard as it is to do—and it's far harder in the face of your own illness—you must think the situation through, and get the machinery started. Even if your condition is very treatable, and you have every expectation of coming through with colors flying, now you *must* make the unsentimental analysis: "If something happens to me, what do I want for my children?"

Remember: By *not* deciding, you are making a decision—and it's probably not going to be a good one. Without an advance plan, your children may wind up at the mercy of *whoever decides to fight over them*—the courts, the welfare system, a former spouse. Later in this chapter, we'll look at the very worst that can happen when a parent refuses to plan—and that worst is very bad indeed.

Even though legal considerations are beyond the scope of this book, I would urge you to consult a lawyer, to make sure that your wishes for your children's future will be carried out. Custody issues, the rights of a divorced parent, child welfare laws all are far beyond the competence of even the most caring hospital social worker. Every state has its own rules, and you need professional guidance through the minefield. This kind of planning, with legal assistance, will ensure your children's security—and your own.

And now you are ready to reassure your children, to answer the questions that your illness has raised about their future:

Tell Your Kids About the Plans You're Making

"If Something Happens to Me . . ."

First, be assured: *Long before you speak these words, your child is thinking about them.* Your son, your daughter, will get there long before you do. And while your speaking the actual words aloud may upset your kids initially, by addressing this central issue clearly and openly you will help them in the long run.

Our children are exposed to ideas of violence, change, and death from the time they start watching cartoons on television. You aren't giving your child any new idea when you say, "If something happens to me . . ." All children in all lands and times have worried about the illness or death of a parent, and America's children today probably know more—and worry more—than any previous generation.

So when you, as a single parent, tell your children, "If something happens to me . . ." and then go on to explain the arrangements you've made for them, *you're reassuring them.*

Choose the time and place carefully; this is deep and emotive stuff for your children. At some point when you discuss the illness with them, and you begin to probe for their fears, the subject will probably come up on its own: "Who'll take care of us?"

Here's the kind of thing you might say then:

"If something does happen to me, you guys are all set. You'll be living with Aunt Ellen. She loves you very much, and she's promised she'll take care of you just the same as her own kids. We've talked it over, and she knows just what I want for you."

Then you can reassure them, by explaining what you truly believe. If you feel you will beat this thing, survive, prevail, then tell them so: "I expect to be with you a long time. I plan to be here until you grow up, until you have grandchildren for me. These plans are just in case."

But even if the prognosis is bad, even if you think perhaps you won't make it through, you can be honest and still be positive and reassuring: "I intend to be with you guys just as long as I can. One of my biggest goals in fighting this disease is to have as much time with my family as I possibly can. You're the reason I'm fighting so hard."

Remember, even if they don't bring it out in the open, the question of the future is surely there inside their heads. So it's up to you to go fishing, gently:

"Do you worry sometimes about who'll take care of you?"
"Want to know some plans I've set up, just in case?"

The timing is up to you. You don't want to use this book like a cookbook: "Well, Kathleen says I've got to talk to them about it, so here we go, right in the middle of dinner." You'll feel when the time is right—when your children ask, or too obviously *don't* ask, "Who'll take care of us?"

I can't tell you *when* to share these plans; I can only explain how important it is that you *do* share them with your children. Let me say it once more: By raising the issue, "If something happens to me . . . ," by allowing their deepest fears to surface, you will *not* be scaring your kids, not more than they already are. In a sense you'll be *unscaring* them.

Reassuring Younger Children

Probably, for the younger kids, that will be enough. From toddlers up through early school age—seven, eight, or so—children simply want to be reassured and then go on about their business. If you tell them confidently that Auntie Ellen, who loves them a lot, has promised to take care of them, that's probably all they'll need. Young children usually don't want to have a lot of input about planning the future; they're content as long as *you've* done the planning.

If you do encounter a strong negative reaction, if your young child announces, "Don't *want* to be with Auntie Ellen" or "I *hate* Uncle Phil," pay attention to that; something real is probably going on. This is different from, "Don't want to go; want to stay with *you*," which is a perfectly normal reaction. But if the child understands that you're talking only about a time when you might not be here, and still objects strongly to the guardian you've chosen, better do some more thinking. It doesn't *necessarily* mean anything inappropriate is going on with Auntie Ellen or Uncle Phil; perhaps Uncle Phil inadvertently frightened the child somehow, years ago.

But whether or not anything is really "wrong," how much chance is there that a child with such negative feelings can ever develop a good relationship with his new guardians?

Reassuring Older Children

Beginning with the later school years—around age nine, ten, or eleven—children *do* want to have an input into your plans for them, and they're entitled to it. That doesn't necessarily mean you'll accept their wishes, but you owe them a hearing.

You'll probably find they have very strong feelings about where they'll go and who'll take care of them if you're not here. And (surprise!) the people they'd pick for their primary caretakers may not be the people you'd pick at all.

Think through, carefully, your children's wishes. Their ideas may be quite good, or pretty bad. Your fifteen-year-old daughter may want to go live with the most permissive of your sisters—the one who, in your view, lets her own girls get away with murder. In that sort of situation, address the problem directly:

"I know you'd like to live with Aunt Sylvia. I know you like the rules she has for her kids. But you know those aren't my rules. And what I need is to make sure that you guys continue to grow up with the rules *I* believe in. That's my job as a good parent. You may not like it, but that's what I need to do."

Doing What's Best for the Child

There will probably be a lot of family pressures—some overt, some in your own mind—colliding around your decisions now. Many parents, in my experience, feel obligated to name a certain individual, or at least a blood relative, as their children's guardian *even though there's somebody else who they think would do a better job.*

The decision, of course, is yours, as the pressures are yours. My own view, however, is that the children are primary here, and all the other considerations are secondary. When parents talk to me about these family obligations, I tell them they should do *whatever they think is best for the child.*

Your mother may think she *should* take the children, but a grandparent in her seventies may simply not be up to coping with a houseful of toddlers or teens. And, in fact, the grandparent may not be thrilled with the idea. So those dear friends who are doing such a super job with their own children, and who'd love to have your kids if something should happen to you, may be the best answer for everybody. The real question should be: Is it the best answer for my children?

When Parents Are Divorced

If you are divorced, your illness may now bring your former spouse back into the family picture, at least temporarily. Be aware: The change can be both confusing and difficult for your children.

You both must be careful how the estranged parent re-enters the scene, so your children don't begin to erect a dangerous structure of false hopes. Perhaps that parent may envision some permanent role, may plan (with your approval) to care for the children if you become too ill. If so, fine.

But if the return is temporary—Dad coming to help out for a week or two, with no intention of a longer-term commitment—*it's crucial that the children understand.* Both parents must give a very clear message from the start: Daddy's only going to be here for this week, while Mommy has her operation. After that, he's going back to his new family. Daddy still loves you, but *Daddy and Mommy don't love each other again.*

If the children *don't* understand this, then *Dad's second departure will be as traumatic as his first.* Your children will go through two divorces, not just one.

And, assuming the children would want the other parent back in their lives, you must both be careful that your illness doesn't begin to take on positive aspects for them.

Younger children in particular may connect Mommy-being-sick with Daddy-coming-back. Then your illness *may seem an acceptable price to pay.* The child may think along the lines, "It's worth Mommy being sick to have Daddy back." Again, you must both make clear from the start: The situation is temporary. Daddy is *not* back to stay.

Two Embarrassing Ideas

The thesis of this book—and of my life, really—is that no matter how grim the reality, it is possible to bring children through it whole, healthy, and ready to lead full, rewarding, emotionally rich lives. My experience shows that this is possible, even in that worst-case scenario, the afflicted single parent. But:

To bring children safely through the illness, and even death, of a single custodial parent requires, I think, two qualities that we're embarrassed to talk about: *courage* and *self-sacrifice*. I became involved in three life stories that helped form my own thinking and may guide yours. In each case, a single parent was trying to do his or her very best for a child or children. Yet the outcomes were shockingly different. They involve:

- A single father who made compromises he both hated and feared to make.
- A single mother who, as she died, made very careful plans for a child born of a tragic experience.

- A single mother who denied, denied, denied until the moment of her death.

Not all of these stories have resolved themselves. But to the extent they have, two of them seem to be turning out well *for the children*, which is, after all, the object of this book, and surely your object as well.

The third ended in utter disaster for a little girl. It left me with a mental image I wish I could escape.

"Single Parent"? There's No Such Thing

The heart of the problem is that there is, of course, no such thing as a single parent. Each child is the product of two human beings, with all the emotion, the storms, the chaos that implies. In some cases, where one parent is raising the children, the other parent remains in the picture, may even be a source of help, a welcome backup when things go very badly. But many single-parent situations carry enormous emotional baggage— a whole trainload of guilt, of hurt, of betrayal, fury, even hatred and fear.

Whether you who are reading this are the sick parent, the well parent, a concerned relative, a colleague, a neighbor, a coach, or a family friend hoping to help, our orientation will be this: to keep that crushing load of emotional baggage *off* the children, so it cannot ruin their adulthood.

And we must always remember: A child's relationship to a mother or father is *primal*. It resides deep in our lizard brain, and we must respect it. No matter what we think, no matter what society thinks of the parent, it is usually NOT in the child's interest to "protect" her from knowing that parent—especially when that parent is going to die.

Allan, Deirdre, and Kristie

Allan and Deirdre certainly loved each other once. They shared everything—food, money, liquor, drugs, and finally a baby girl, Kristie.

When Kristie was just two, her mother's lifestyle finally caught up with her—she went to prison for several serious, though nonviolent, offenses. Meanwhile, Allan, now a single father, cleaned up his life to an astonishing extent—got off drugs, became a lay minister, a youth counselor invited by churches all over his neighborhood to help troubled kids. And he had full custody of Kristie.

Now, with memories of her mother fading into the background, Kristie was getting ready to start kindergarten. And now Deirdre, diagnosed with terminal pancreatic cancer, was released from prison on compassionate grounds—and now she wanted, before she died, to re-enter her little girl's life. She wanted a relationship—visitation rights, Kristie to stay with her every other weekend.

Deirdre was living with her own mother and sisters, and between that family and Allan was nothing but bad blood—each side hated, despised, loathed, and feared the other. Both parents, in particular, now really hated each other, talked terribly about each other, blamed each other for everything that had gone wrong in their lives.

We Get Involved

Deirdre went to court to sue for visitation, and that's when Allan came to us at The Gathering Place for help and advice. Should he battle to keep this almost forgotten mother out of his daughter's life? The father said, reasonably, Why on earth would I want my daughter, who doesn't talk about her mother anymore, doesn't even think about her mother, hasn't lived with her mother in almost three years—why in the world would I want her to reunite with *someone she's going to lose again?* Why would I let her reattach to a mother who's going to die?

This to me is the toughest, most complex kind of issue. Whose needs are to be met? The child's? The dying mother's? The father's? I did a lot of thinking about Kristie, and my role, which was as advocate for the child. Certainly, this did not seem to be the situation we spoke of earlier, where the parents can put aside their differences for the good of the child. And what *was* the good of this child?

But in the end I realized: This little girl knows she has a mother. No child growing up, no matter which parent she's living with, doesn't want to know about the other parent. And starting school would only exacerbate things; inevitably her kindergarten classmates would want to know, "Who's your mommy?"

Kristie already knew her maternal aunts and grandparents. So: A time will come, inevitably, when Kristie knows that her mother lived, and died. And for the rest of her life, she will resent her father for not giving her the chance to know her mother in the time remaining. Once she makes that leap, it will, I thought, be disastrous for Kristie's relationship with her father.

The Decision

On balance, I felt we could honor the mother's desire for a relationship with her child, could give the child a chance to know her mom with the full understanding that Mom is very sick, and we all want Kristie to have time with her, even though Mom may not get better.

There's another consideration. If Kristie now shares her mother's last days, she will get to know her *real* mother, warts and all. She will not develop some idealized vision of a super-mom, from whom a cruel, uncaring father kept her separated.

These are the arguments that persuaded me, and these are the arguments we used to persuade Allan. Because he always put his daughter's welfare first, he agreed to do something that went against all his instincts. He allowed us to set up a meeting for Kristie and her mom at The Gathering Place.

Kristie Meets Deirdre

Before that meeting, we worked to prepare everybody—Dad, Mom, Mom's sisters, and above all Kristie. In these situations, the actual meeting is the easy part. Everything depends on the preparation.

First, I talked to everyone by phone about what was going to happen, and the safest way to approach it. On the morning of that first meeting, Deirdre and her sisters arrived early. I explained again what

Kristie would require—the need, above all, to take everything slowly and gently. Deirdre got it. Her sisters, not so much.

Allan arrived with Kristie and said a stiff hello to the other women. But, at my suggestion, he didn't stay. This would be Kristie-Deirdre time, and Allan trusted me to look out for his daughter's welfare. I promised him.

First Meeting

The meeting started out cautiously. Deirdre was appropriately gentle, not too pushy, allowing Kristie to set the pace. But the aunts were overbearing and overwhelming; they didn't give the little girl a chance. And they began offering all kinds of incentives for further visits—toys, parties, fun. They were pushing the child to continue a relationship that didn't yet exist.

So after a few minutes I pulled the aunts out of the room, leaving Kristie and her mom to work things out on their own.

We watched from another room. Mom had obviously taken my advice to heart; she was gentle, restrained, waiting for Kristie to make a move toward her. Deirdre had, again as we had discussed, come prepared with some things they could do together. But I had also set up activities I knew would appeal to Kristie. She loved to paint; we set up side-by-side easels, so they could paint together. She also really enjoyed making bead bracelets; I had suggested to Kristie that maybe she and her mom could make bracelets for each other, and that turned out to be a big hit. We set up opportunities for what, in children, would have been called parallel play—Deirdre and Kristie could do things together, but still separately.

Kristie, at five, was an easy, outgoing child who liked people, liked people to play with her, talk to her. And that's what her mom began, very gently, to do. You could see Kristie begin to remember her mom, from toddlerhood. And as Deirdre began to play with her more directly, they talked. I heard parts of that conversation:

They didn't talk at all about where mom had been the past three years. As far as I know, Allan had never talked about that to Kristie either; it was a family secret. But for a five-year-old, that secret is okay.

They talked about mom's illness. Kristie asked whether Deirdre's hair would fall out; Deirdre told her, It already did; this is a wig. Kristie didn't ask to see, and Deirdre never took off the wig. Kristie and I had already talked about the fact that you can't "catch" cancer, so she didn't ask. I sensed some reluctance to hug her mother, but that seemed to be more about re-establishing a relationship than any fear in Kristie

And by the end of the meeting, an hour and a half later, Kristie flung herself into her mother's arms, and they held each other for quite a while.

When Allan returned to pick up Kristie, she told him all about what had happened, in very concrete terms: I saw my mommy, we made bracelets, we played. It was like any other five-year-old recounting an adventure: They had fun, they had snacks, she had a good time with her mom.

Kristie also told him what the aunts had said about coming to visit. And she asked me, "Can I do that?" Already she was wanting more contact with her mom.

But all those incentives the aunts had loaded her down with were also playing a part in her question, and not in a good way. A child *must not* become a pawn in a power game between two sides.

So I told Kristie, we'd really have to wait and see what Daddy wants. And Daddy and Mommy will have to talk to the judge and see what *she* wants.

(After this meeting, Kristie did something very predictable: She tried to use Deirdre's cancer to bring her parents back together—a total impossibility. Over the course of the year, she would try things like, "Mommy doesn't feel good; can you come? So you and me and Mommy can be together?"

(That's why it's so important to make it absolutely clear to the child: Mom and Dad are *not* getting back together; any help Dad may be offering now is because of Mom's illness. They both love you but they don't love each other and they will *not* get back together.

(Failure to pound home that hard truth, allowing the child any false hope, means she will lose her family twice.)

Allan Decides: It Can Go On

Allan was now willing to let the budding relationship proceed, and the family court judge agreed. But it quickly became evident that Deirdre, who lived two hours away, simply could not handle that car trip. So Allan began driving Kristie to the town where her mother lived. The two parents did not meet; one of the aunts or the grandmother would pick Kristie up at a gas station or a McDonald's and bring her back eight hours later. Occasionally Kristie would stay overnight—the father didn't like Deirdre's family, but he knew they were drug-free and would take care of his little girl.

Think about this man's sacrifice for his child. He has his own business, he does endless hours of volunteer work. Yet not only is he going against all his instincts, he is now spending hours and hours driving to a distant town and killing time in that town, all so Kristie can spend time with a dying woman he doesn't trust.

Deirdre and her family knocked themselves out to make the arrangement work. Sometimes Deirdre could sit in a chair; more often she was bedridden, but Kristie would play in the bedroom and Mom would participate to whatever extent she could. They played games and they chatted—mom to five-year-old. As long as Kristie had the freedom to choose whether she wanted to be with the mom or not, she did really well. I have the feeling that Deirdre was totally wiped out after those visits, but she got herself up when Kristie was there. And the mother's family planned; they bought toys for Kristie, gave princess tea parties. Early on, they'd all even go to McDonald's for lunch. As the mother got sicker, her sisters and mother did all they could to keep Kristie's visits upbeat.

That went on for almost a year, until Deirdre died.

And during that year, a sort of relationship even sprang up between the parents. From time to time, without her own family's knowledge,

Deirdre would phone Allan, tell him what was happening, tell him, too, about her pain and her fears. And this gives us something to remember:

Dying Is Different

Dying changes things. The person who knows to a certainty she is dying is no longer the person she was. And especially in these terrible situations, where there is nothing left of a once-loving relationship but mistrust and fear, it's worth remembering:

The person who is dying is no longer the person who was living.

So we took the chance of exposing this child to a loss, because it *was* going to be a real loss: This was a real mom, her mom, whom she would be allowed to know and so could grieve normally. Otherwise, there's just a blank place in the heart and soul where a mom belongs. So even though we all knew, almost for sure, that this would end in a loss for this child—and probably pretty quickly—it was worth her knowing, loving, connecting with, and then losing her mom—far better than never knowing her at all.

A Year After

It's a year later now, and I still see Allan and Kristie. There's a really strong, very loving relationship there. Kristie is maturing; she talks openly about her mom, alive and dead. She's working on her grief. And her grief, I think, isn't terribly deep, because there wasn't a deep attachment. I think Kristie grieves mostly for not having had a mom, not for this particular mom. But at least now she attaches that loss to a real person. It isn't, "I never had a mom." It's, "My mom died, and I got to know her before she died."

And I truly believe that because both parents yielded on this, because they let go of some of their deepest, most bitter passions, *their child is better for it.* Both parents, at the start, would much rather not have interacted with each other, each would have preferred that Kristie not know the other. But because both could give a little, relax a little, try to work through these huge differences, *their child today is far happier than she would have been otherwise.*

Allan thinks so too. He tells me that, if we hadn't pushed him, he never would have permitted the relationship; everything in him was saying, "Protect Kristie, protect her, protect her." But, he says, if he hadn't gone against his instincts, given them that year together, his daughter never would have been whole.

Myra, Alexa, and the Law

That family, shattered as it was, *worked* on the future. There's one thing about the future: It will arrive, right on schedule. And in these life-and-death situations, if the parent fails to plan for it—worse, if he or she refuses to recognize its inevitability—that's a formula for disaster. This is what I mean:

Myra was a brilliant woman. She taught mathematics at a major university. She had a daughter, about seven at the time this story begins. Alexa was the only positive thing to come out of what was apparently a really ghastly marriage. The situation was as bad as it gets: Myra had divorced the father, fought any ongoing contact. He had no visitation rights, and she would never allow him to have anything to do with the child—his child as well as hers.

I never met the father. Myra told me he had been abusive both emotionally and physically; she took out a restraining order but, crucially, she never filed a formal complaint. Consequently, as far as the legal record was concerned, there was nothing against him when Myra was diagnosed with uterine cancer.

Despite the best efforts of her friends, and counselors at The Gathering Place, Myra entered a state of denial in which she remained until the day she died. First, she absolutely refused to accept the fact that she *might* die. Her particular type of cancer, discovered late, is usually fatal. Yet the sicker she got, the more she isolated herself and Alexa from the world, from reality. Myra did not want to plan for Alexa's life without her—she could not, would not, admit that possibility.

I reached out to Myra, went to her home several times, which is not my usual routine, to try to help her make a plan. Because there was another shadow looming over this tiny family's future:

Another faculty member, who knew both parents, was growing increasingly concerned. At last she called us at The Gathering Place with a warning: Alexa's father knew of Myra's illness, knew of the grim prognosis, and *was waiting for her to die so he could claim his daughter.*

Denial

In the face of that, the plans Myra actually was making for Alexa were utterly unrealistic. She refused to admit even the *possibility* that this man, whom she hated with all her heart, could possibly get custody of the child she adored. She talked of Alexa going to live with friends whom she knew and trusted. *That could not possibly happen:* When one parent dies, then unless there is something really horrible in the surviving parent's record, virtually every family court in America will award custody to the living parent. He or she may be a bad parent, a drug abuser, prone to unpredictable rages, and yet he or she probably will get custody.

As she grew sicker, Myra made a bad situation much worse:

She promised Alexa that the child would *never* have to live with her father; she would just go live with a friend they both liked.

Even worse: She kept filling Alexa's head with horrible stories of how evil her father was; she painted a monster.

The End of the Story

The friend, whom Myra wanted to take Alexa, was at their home the day the mother died. This is her account of what happened next:

A police car arrived at Myra's residence, with two officers and Alexa's father. They entered the house.

A few minutes later, they emerged. One of the officers was carrying seven-year-old Alexa. She was kicking, screaming, thrashing, biting, crying. All four entered the police car, and it drove away.

No one from the mother's side of this story has ever seen or heard of Alexa again . . .

. . .

Could the story have gone differently? Of course, no one can know, but a worse outcome is impossible to imagine. So what if:

What if Myra had faced the possibility—the near certainty, in fact—that she would die? And what if she had opened negotiations with her ex-husband concerning Alexa's future, the way Allan negotiated with Deirdre's family?

Two possibilities: They might have come to some kind of understanding satisfactory to both, perhaps even keeping some of Myra's friends in touch with Alexa. Or if he did indeed prove to be an unyielding monster, Myra could have begun legal proceedings so a court would have *some* reason to question the father's claim to custody.

And if it turned out mother and father could reach some broad agreement, what if Myra had told Alexa she *might* be going to live with her father, that even though Mommy and Daddy didn't love each other anymore, he loved Alexa and would take care of her?

As I said, there is no certainty that any of this could have happened, could have headed off those horrible final moments in the driveway. But because this mother, until the day she died, refused to face the future in any realistic way, she in effect guaranteed that terrible finale for her child.

Anna: The Planner

Contrast that with this story of a dying mother who planned the future very, very carefully:

We were counseling Anna, who was being treated for ovarian cancer, and her daughter, Lily, who was then about eleven. The mother-daughter relationship was warm and loving, the daughter bright, outgoing, well-adjusted. But we never heard about a father. When other kids in the group asked Lily, she'd just say, "I don't have a father"—the message she'd always heard from Anna. Anna never said anything negative about the father, she simply didn't say anything at all.

Finally, one of the other girls pressed Lily: "Everyone has a father. You have to have a father." And we could see that idea start to dawn on Lily: She had to have a father.

Anna's Story

And that's when Anna told us the story. Lily's conception was the product of force (much later, Lily's adoptive mother would use the term "forced love" in telling Lily about her birth). Although there had never been any further contact, Anna had to assume the father knew his child existed.

Despite the girl's tragic origins, Anna and Lily loved each other as much as any mother and daughter I have known. But now Anna began to worry:

$$$$$

When a parent dies, and a child moves into someone else's care and custody, a whole lot of public and private money can move with her. First there's Social Security and state funds, which can easily exceed several thousand dollars a month. But beyond that, there's the dead parent's estate, savings, possibly a pension plan—all of which the child inherits. Some very serious money may go along with the child.

Usually the money is secondary, but I have seen far too many cases where the only reason people fought for custody of children was the money that came with them. And this man, this accidental father with no other connection to his child, could nevertheless have had a claim to custody of Lily.

Planning Lily's Future

Anna had two friends, a married couple with no children of their own. She wanted them to raise Lily, and they passionately wanted to have the little girl. Anna's first move was to consult an attorney specializing in family law.

Most jurisdictions require public notice of an intent to adopt. Without going into details, I can say that Anna and her lawyer managed to set up the adoption and fulfill all the legal requirements, without catching the attention of the father or his family.

On the day Anna died, the lawyer and her friends initiated the formal adoption process. The couple became Lily's interim guardians while the adoption proceeded.

That was about eight years ago; I'm still in touch with Lily's new family. They've set up a small scholarship in Anna's name, with an annual fund-raiser. The money helps children of parents who've died of cancer to study to become teachers—the career Anna always wanted.

Lily's new mom calls me from time to time, to talk about her daughter's perfectly ordinary teenage problems This year Lily will enter college—to study to become a teacher. Overall, a very good result from Anna's meticulous planning. But one issue remains open: What, if anything, to tell Lily about her father.

Her new mom decided to tell her most of the story when Lily turned fifteen. That's when she told Lily of her conception by "forced love." I asked how Lily handled it. Here is what Lily told her:

"Look, I just don't want my mom's death to be my whole life. I want to have a life that's separate from my mom's death. And I don't want to talk about it anymore."

And they haven't.

Lily's new mom left open the possibility of trying to put the girl in touch with her father; Lily is nineteen now, and has never asked.

But her new mom, Anna's old, dear friend, told their daughter one thing more:

Here is what your mom told me:

When you were conceived inside her, she knew there was the beginning of the baby you. It didn't really matter to her that the man who started your life was aggressive, did something wrong and terrible. He was out of control, but none of that mattered to your mom, because from the very

*beginning she saw you as a whole, separate, lovable, potential person. And
she wanted to have you and raise you.*

Anna's story still gives me chills. Good chills.

The First "Do": See a Lawyer

These three stories form, I think, an entire architecture for the single
parent, or his or her surrogates, of what to do and what to avoid when
grave illness strikes. One thing I would urge: Wherever there is a potential question of custody, or any kind of disagreement over the children's future, **the single parent should consult a family practice
lawyer at the very beginning.** With the best will in the world, no social worker, no child life specialist, no spiritual adviser, no lay friend is
equipped to handle the legalities of custody. **Bring in a pro.**

And as those cops on TV keep saying: If you can't afford a lawyer,
one can be provided for you. Our organization, and others like it,
have a number of attorneys who work pro bono on these cases. State
and local agencies can also provide free legal help. **But you must
ask.**

What I have seen in the worst situations, where a single parent is
gravely ill, and may die, is a really dangerous pattern of denial. The parent is scared, doesn't *want* to die, doesn't *want* to leave her child. And so
she pulls away from everything in her life that would remind her of that
reality, which means pulling away from all her support systems, which
means increasingly isolating herself *and her child* from any potential support. Yet this is the time when it is so important to keep all lines open,
to seek and accept help from whoever is in her life—parents, siblings,
friends, counselors, coaches.

And if the mother simply cannot cope with the situation on her
own, then it may be up to you, the supportive person in her life, to volunteer help. If Mom just cannot talk to the children about her illness,
maybe Grandma or Grandpa or Aunt Ruth can. Perhaps they can open

negotiations with the other parent, even explain to the children that they may go to live with their father for a while, *and that's okay.*

Probably nothing is more important than to prepare the children for that, and to put the possibility of living with the other parent in the most positive light. Because no matter how much one dying parent may detest the other, unless that other parent has some very specific mental diagnosis or criminal record, *the courts **will** give custody to the biological parent if he or she wants it.*

When the Law Steps In

You've probably noticed: This chapter on single parenting refers far more often than other chapters to the courts, the law, and governmental bureaucracies set up by our society to protect children. All these can be a source of difficulty, an additional burden for a single parent who's stricken with a serious illness, *but they can also be a major positive resource.*

Here is one final story of a single parent at the breaking point and beyond:

Callie's situation was about as bad as it could be. She had three children. The oldest daughter, seventeen, had developmental problems and was in a special school. The second child, a son, fourteen, was a pretty normal teenager. But the younger son, age ten, was a handful—a big kid, wild, quick with his fists, usually in trouble at school, though he caught a lot of blame for other kids' wrongdoing. He'd been diagnosed with several behavioral disorders, yet with it all, Brandon was basically a good kid. I liked him a lot.

The father had vanished. Courts had ordered him to pay child support, but he never did. Times were always hard for this family, and into this picture came the mother's advanced lymphoma.

Now the financial crisis really hit: They lost their car, were behind in the rent. Callie, depleted of energy and in constant pain from her spreading cancer, had to cope with all this while at the same time seeking out the various social services required just to keep her family going. If you remember the client who told me she was about to go "*BOINGGG!*," that was Callie—times two.

"I'm Gonna Hurt Him"

One evening around 5:30, just as I was leaving, Callie showed up at The Gathering Place and announced that she had to speak to me, right that minute. And what she told me was, "I'm gonna hurt him. You have to help me."

That afternoon, Brandon had been doing what rambunctious ten-year-olds do, testing the limits, seeing how far he could push his mom. But this time he pushed too far. This time Callie, at her physical and emotional limit, grabbed Brandon by the shoulders, began to shake him, and slapped his face, hard.

Brandon, as astonished as Callie, broke away with a yell and ran out of the house. A few minutes later, Callie learned, he turned up at her mother's home a couple of blocks away.

Callie told me that if Brandon had not run out, she really feared that she would not have stopped hitting him: "I'm gonna hurt him." Callie knew she was losing it, knew she needed help.

But that slap changed everything. Because the moment Callie actually struck her son, it brought into the picture the laws of the state of Ohio. I was now *legally obliged* to report that blow to a government agency.

I explained that to Callie. And I told her, "Look, we need to get you help. I know that when people call child protective services, it's pretty scary. You think they're going to come, say you're a bad parent, an abusive parent, maybe try to take your kids. But the reality is, they're here to help families under the kind of pressure you're under. I have to call them; I want to call them with you here, listening to what I tell them."

First I called Callie's mother, made sure Brandon was still with her, and could stay there for a day or two. She said yes.

The County Steps In

Next, I called County Protective Services. When I reached a social worker I reported, as required by the law, an incident of child abuse: Callie's slap. Then I explained that this child is at risk. The mom barely got herself to stop at one slap; if the boy hadn't run out, she doesn't know what might have happened. The boy is now safe with his grandmother, but the mother doesn't know what she might do when he comes back.

The county worker was wonderful. She said yes, absolutely, we need to help. We'll send someone out to talk to the mother, and someone to see the grandmother and the boy. We'll make sure he's safe and he's okay to stay there. And we'll get Callie and Brandon back together as soon as we think it's safe.

Within a couple of days, that social worker had a whole set of programs in place to help. Brandon was transferred into a program for troubled youngsters, Callie got parenting guidance, and someone from the agency who'd come in from time to time, handle the kids, and give her a break.

The Lesson

There's a serious lesson here for overstressed single parents who fear the consequences of reaching out to the authorities for help. The most important point: The very last thing these agencies want to do is take the children away, to take on that responsibility. They don't want to deal with problems of foster care, protective custody. And if the kids do need to be moved temporarily, the first choice will be a close relative who's willing to take them for as long as necessary.

Yes, if you're dealing with any professional, such as myself, and you report an actual, physical blow to your child, that person MUST report it. But this story (and, in my experience, most such stories) had a great outcome. Callie and her family got the outside help they needed. Callie was the perfect example of how the sick single parent can be pushed beyond her own limits—and how our organized society can help, if the parent, or someone in her support system, will let it.

Two Households: A Rock and a Hard Place

One consequence of our national trend toward broken and reconstituted families is more and more children dividing their time—their lives, really—between two households. They find themselves with not two, but three or even four "parents." Shared custody is enormously stressful for children in the best of times. But when one of those parents becomes seriously or terminally ill, the stresses on the children multiply—and so do the demands for all those parent figures to put aside their own (often very real) grievances and think of their children's welfare.

I frequently find myself involved in court proceedings around custody issues. My role as an expert witness is the same as it is in this book: *to be, unambiguously, an advocate for the children.* And that is my role now, as I urge you to set aside the grievances, the ugliness, the trauma that have brought you to this moment, and *selflessly, courageously do what is best for your children.*

Here is one case I became involved in some time ago:

Two Boys in the Middle

Two sons, ages thirteen and twelve. The natural parents divorced, and the divorce was as bad as they get—hateful, spiteful, simply awful.

Under the custody terms, the boys lived with their mother; their dad had them every other weekend.

The father remarried . . .

. . . and was diagnosed with terminal cancer.

The boys were as different as brothers can be: Hank, outgoing, mature for his age, and (like his dad) a jock; Mal, more introverted, a whiz at computers, but socially shy.

Both knew their dad was dying.

Hank now wanted to spend every possible minute with Dad, so he began lobbying his mother—"Can I go every weekend?" Reluctantly, Mom agreed. But Mal didn't want to go every weekend.

The two families limped through the summer that way, but fall brought football. Hank loved it; Mom didn't approve of it; she found all kinds of reasons not to take him to practice. That was when Hank appealed to me: "Can you get Mom to let me spend weekdays with my dad? My stepmom will take me to practice, and I can be with Mom on weekends!"

What Hank was asking, though he didn't realize it, was a complete reversal of the court's custody decision. And of course he never thought of the impact on his mother, who had been hurt beyond words by his father—and who still nurtured those feelings.

Well, I took Hank's idea to the mother, and she put her foot down. Not only wouldn't she agree; she stopped bringing either boy to see her ex-husband at all, and canceled all her future appointments with me. The boys got no more time with their second family, no chance to say goodbye.

A month later I learned the father had died. I called the mother to see how the boys were doing, left a message on her machine. She never called back.

The Stepmom Sues

A year passed, and one day I got a call from the stepmom: The mother had never again allowed her to see the boys, so now the stepmother, who had become genuinely attached to her husband's sons, was suing for visitation rights. Ohio law allows grandparents and stepparents to demand visits with children who have lived with them.

The birth mother found out that her boys had been calling, texting, and e-mailing their stepmother, whom both liked, and she issued an ultimatum: Unless they ceased all contact, she would cancel their admission to a prestigious magnet high school—which both had their hearts set on; it boasted a state-ranked football team for Hank and a nationally recognized computer curriculum for Mal—and send them to the local high school instead. She made the mistake of putting that in writing; the stepmother got hold of it and took it to the judge, triggering yet another round of court proceedings.

The Money

And there was a trust fund. Money invariably complicates these situations, and the complications are frequently bad for the children. Before he died, the father set up a trust fund for both boys and made his new wife the trustee. The birth mother filed a countersuit; *she* wanted to be the trustee of her sons' inheritances.

The point of all this ugliness, the reason I tell the story, has nothing to do with the money, and very little to do with the angry adults. Just imagine the impact of all this on two vulnerable youngsters, now thirteen and fourteen years old, who have lost a father they both loved. How can they possibly enter these terribly complicated years of adolescence with anything like an emotionally healthy outlook?

Pawns

It is just so easy for parents in these situations—human beings who may have been wronged, perhaps even harmed by the mates they once loved—it is so easy to use the children as proxies, as weapons to repay those hurts. But *nothing* can damage children more than finding themselves used as emotional pawns—as foot soldiers in a war they don't understand between two people they love.

Let me recall here a paragraph from our opening chapter:

Counselors, psychologists, and psychiatrists see them in their thirties and forties. And they say, "Doctor, I can't love anyone." And so often, when you look back, there was a real break in that love during that person's childhood. Very often the break can be traced to the illness or death of a parent—a break never brought out and handled by the child.

I said early in this chapter that helping children through a parent's grave illness in these single parent, multiple household situations might require (perhaps unfairly) both courage and self-sacrifice. In thinking about whether and how to summon that courage, that sacrifice now, you might ask yourself this:

Do you want the lives of your children to perpetuate the sorrows of your own?

SOME ONLINE RESOURCES FOR THE SINGLE-PARENT FAMILY

---

singledadstown.com: *Guidance for single parents of both genders.*

childsgrief.org: *Helping children anticipate grief, informing them of a death, going to a funeral.*

childrensgrief.net

Artist: Alina Raulinaitis, age twelve. Alina's story of the Phoenix:

"The Phoenix is a mythological bird that was greatly honored. When the bird is about to die, it bursts into flame and crumbles into a pile of ashes. Then from the ashes comes another baby Phoenix that will repeat the cycle.

"The first picture of the old sad Phoenix represents my father when he had cancer. He looks old and gray and looks like its glory is gone and withered.

"The second picture of the burning Phoenix is of my father's death, because everything at that time was terrible and seemed to go up in smoke.

"The third picture of the ashes represents my mother's cancer, because we were already suffering from one blow and it seemed as if it could not get worse.

"The fourth and final picture is of the baby Phoenix rising from the ashes. It represents my family surviving. Though we are small and frail and broken, we will survive, completing the cycle of the Phoenix."

13.

Genetic Diseases: "No, but . . ."

Helping children deal with a parent's genetic or genetic-involved disease is similar to coping with other illnesses—but with several crucial differences.

I've placed this new chapter near the end of the second edition, because almost everything we've talked about so far will still apply, as far as helping children cope with the *parent's* condition, BUT:

The answer to the child's inevitable question, "Can I get it from you?" has now changed from "No" to "No, but . . ." And the "but" is this:

No, your child can't catch it like a cold. But she may have inherited it.

That new "but" presents parents with a whole new set of challenges. How to deal with those challenges will be the subject of this chapter.

Susan's Gene

My friend Susan's life, over the past few months, is almost a microcosm of the genetic problem—and suggests some solutions.

Susan is an oncology social worker; she *knows* cancer. Her mother and grandmother both died of breast cancer, suggesting that Susan might have inherited a change, or mutation, in a gene, thus increasing her own risk for developing the disease. Yet she delayed for years getting the very reliable genetic test that would tell her, one way or the other. She wanted children, wanted to raise her family. And the certain knowledge—yes she did, no she didn't carry the gene mutation for breast cancer—would not have affected how Susan intended to live her life.

Earlier this year, with her son, Spencer, now nine, and her daughter, Emily, twelve, Susan finally underwent the genetic test and, sure enough, she learned she was positive for a mutation in the BRCA2 (for BReast-CAncer) gene. That meant there was up to an 85 percent chance she would develop breast cancer (there was also an increased risk of ovarian cancer).

The best, perhaps the only way for Susan to avoid this aggressive, sometimes fatal cancer was a prophylactic bilateral mastectomy—having both breasts surgically removed *before* the cancer could manifest itself. And that's when she and I began to talk about her daughter, Emily.

The Worrier: I

Certainly Susan would have to explain the surgery to her children, *before* it happened. But should she tell Emily of the genetic ramifications—the one chance in two that Emily, too, carried the BRCA2 mutation?

"Emily's a worrier," Susan said. "I don't want her to spend her teen years worrying about breast cancer or a future mastectomy."

Susan's dilemma brings us squarely to the core issue of how to help children in an era when more and more diseases are found to have genetic roots:

- What do you tell the children?
- How do you tell the children?
- And perhaps most important of all, *when* do you tell the children?

Jill: A New Profession

Jill Polk is a certified genetic counselor—a profession that scarcely existed two decades ago. Her job is to explain the intricacies of genetic diseases to families, and to help them understand their options—including the information their children will need. She's a busy woman, because we're living in an ongoing explosion of knowledge about how single genes, combinations of genes and the environment, even the way genes fold together on our chromosomes, can shape our lives and our deaths. But Jill's interest in genetics is more than professional. She has a two-year-old son and, as I write, a new baby daughter. And there may be a genetic-linked disease in her husband's family.

There's one curious, crucial anomaly about genetic or gene-related diseases: Very few of them manifest themselves during the school years. Most childhood diseases, such as sickle-cell anemia, Tay-Sachs, hemophilia, show up early, long before the child can, or needs to, understand the genetics involved. Adult-onset disease, such as hereditary breast cancer or Huntington's disease, are just that—they show up in early or mid-adulthood. And that gap in onset can guide our answers to those three questions.

Jill's Rule of Thumb

"I have a rule of thumb," Jill says. "If nothing can be done medically *right now* to help the child or reduce the risk, I urge parents to tell the children as little as possible until they need to know. And that may be years from now."

No, Jill is not violating the central theme of this book: Never lie to a child about a parent's illness.

The Press Agent

My coauthor once spent a brief, unhappy period working in public relations. Out of that generally negative experience, he took away one useful principle from his boss, a man named Mike, who was an acknowledged master of p.r.:

"You never lie to the press. But that doesn't mean you always tell them the truth."

Not telling the whole truth—not telling the whole truth right now—these are what make up Jill's rule of thumb.

Avoidance, Again

A few chapters ago, we talked about children's gift for avoidance—for not thinking about unpleasant things right now. Your children are the natural heirs of Scarlett O'Hara: "I can't think about that right now; I'll think about that tomorrow."

If an adult-onset genetic disease runs in the family, and if there's nothing to be done about it at present, or perhaps for years to come, *then there's no reason for your child to think about it today.* And what you're now going to find is that, if you don't push it, your child will be very good at not thinking about it.

It's the default setting for 'tweens and teens: a natural optimism, a feeling of immortality, and an unblinking focus on self. And in the case of genetic diseases, the parent's job is to support, to enhance the child's gift for avoidance. I find that parents, in their efforts to come to grips with the reality of a gene-based disorder that may affect their children, tend to talk about it a lot. And in these cases, I urge parents: Do your worrying, your planning, your information gathering—above all, your talking—*away* from your children. By all means suppress your natural tendency to check, perhaps intrusively, on "how they're doing." *Stay away* from these kinds of questions:

"Are you thinking about this?"
"Are you worried about this?"
"How can I help with this genetic thing?"

Because your job now is to help your children NOT concentrate on the problem.

This Time It's Different

This may be a little different from what I've advised elsewhere in this book. In non-genetic medical situations, I suggest being open— acknowledge, "Yes, I'm worried, and this is what I'm going to do . . ." But with most genetic diseases, *there's nothing you or your child can do right now*. And when there's nothing to be done except wait for the children to grow up, the parent's job becomes to take as much stress off them as possible.

Once again, as a parent diagnosed with a serious, perhaps devastating genetic disease, you are first going to have to come to terms with your own situation before you can help your children. You must work through your own sense of the unfairness, your grief for your own shattered hopes—you must cope with all of this and come to accept it. Only then will you be ready to deal with your children's emotional health and survival.

How much you tell your child depends, first of all, on the child's intellectual capacity at this particular moment. For a preschooler, you probably don't even want to raise the genetic issue—she's not equipped to understand it. On the other hand, a bright eight-year-old, who knows that her grandmother had the same disease, may ask, point-blank: "Am I going to get it?"

Follow Your Child's Lead

At this point, it's probably best to let the child lead the way. You might say something like, "I do have a lot of information about this disease, and I can tell you a lot or a little. What are the most important things you want to know right now?

Whether you're the parent who has the disease, or the well parent dealing with the disease, probably at some point your child will ask a couple of the really big questions:

"Are you going to die?"
"Am I going to get it right away?"
"Am I going to die?"

Or she might surprise you with something utterly trivial: "Is Dad always going to be that funny yellow color?"

Here is where Mike's principle comes in. We aren't going to lie to the children, not even a little lie. But we are going to help them get what they need to know *and then put it out of their minds* until they need to *do* something about it—perhaps years from now.

If your son or daughter persists, really wants to know more than you're giving, you should offer to help him or her research genetics— offer to go online and use some of the reliable websites you'll find at the end of this chapter.

There is one more thing, still being completely honest, that you can offer your child facing a possible future genetic disease:

Hope.

Genetics on the Brink

Genetics is the most explosive field of medicine today. An army of re- searchers, here and around the world, is probing the human genome and its ailments. So far that work has brought immense new under- standing but disappointingly few cures or controls of genetic diseases. The old, simplistic idea that we'll find the gene, fix it, and cure the disease has yielded to the mind-numbing complexity of how human genetics really works.

Nevertheless, in medicine the understanding *almost always* precedes treatments and cures, and today we are at that break point.

When the first edition of this book was published in 1995, HIV/AIDS was an almost invariably fatal disease—once you contracted it, there was virtually no hope that you would survive. Here is what I suggested telling children then:

Be perfectly clear: There is no cure today. Nevertheless, scientists all over the world are working on AIDS, and someday it may well be curable. Next century, next year, next week—who knows?

Today, of course, there is still no "cure" for HIV/AIDS, but it is eminently treatable. Thanks to a cocktail of effective medicines, people with the disease can expect to live normal life spans, and normal lives.

It is perfectly legitimate for you to tell your children the same thing today about genetic diseases:

"Will I get it?"

"Well, this is something that could show up when you're grown up, but we'll probably know a whole lot more about it over the next ten years, including better ways to treat it."

This upbeat "spin" is no spin at all; the next few years and decades are likely to see new knowledge and effective new treatments for even some of the most devastating genetic diseases. You can tell your children that with perfect honesty and so help them put out of their minds a situation that may well change before they have to face it years from now. In Jill Polk's words, "There's no reason for children to worry about this the whole time they're growing up."

They Don't Freak Out

I asked Jill whether parents ever come to her saying, "Oh my God, what have I done? I told my children about the breast cancer gene, the colon cancer gene in our family, and they totally freaked out!" Jill replied that in all her years of practice as a genetic counselor, she has never seen that happen.

Sometimes It Can't Wait

There are, of course, certain situations that will require your child to engage right now, not years from now. One is a condition called FAP, in which a mutated gene causes polyps in the colon that often turn cancerous—in children as young as ten. The prevention is regular colonoscopies to screen the colon and if necessary remove polyps before they can become malignant. In situations like this, the child needs to understand what's going on, and why she must undergo these periodic intrusions. Again, your child's maturity and acceptance will probably surprise you.

I'm working right now with Danielle, a thirteen-year old whose mother died of melanoma—a skin cancer that may have a genetic component. So the dermatologists must watch Danielle continuously, and surgically remove any small skin lesions before they become a threat. She really hates that. But here is what she told me:

"I'm really glad I know a lot about this right now, so I'll never get sick like my mom—so we can keep watching, and make sure nothing gets bad. My mom didn't know about it, and that's why hers got so bad before they found it."

Danielle has, all by herself, put a positive (and entirely correct) spin on what's happening to her.

When It's Time

As important as it is not to burden children with genetic concerns before they need to know them, it's equally important to give them full information when, finally, they must have it. Usually, that will be in the mid- to late teens, when they may be leaving home for college or work, and/or are becoming sexually active. Now they do need to know, ·in detail, what problems may be lying in wait within their genomes. Parents should consider putting together a written packet of material, covering family history, copies of any genetic testing that's been done in the family, and current understanding of the disease. That packet can help a new doctor, in a distant city or campus, obtain an accurate medical history. (Keep a copy of the packet; kids tend to take them, put them away, and forget all about them. Never give a teenager your last copy of anything.)

Even if the children are reluctant to talk about their genetic inheritance, now you must insist. Probably the very worst thing that can happen is to send children off into their new world *without* this crucial information. Jill Polk told me a story that illustrates why. Here's what she said:

Jill's Story: The Terrible Case

One of the hardest things for me is knowing that I might be able to help and not being given the opportunity.

A man was diagnosed at our hospital with diffuse gastric cancer, which can be hereditary. In that form it's called HDGC—hereditary diffuse gastric cancer. As the name suggests, the origin is genetic—mutations in a gene, which can be passed from generation to generation. His cancer was at the final phase, stage four, widespread throughout his system; he basically came to us for hospice care.

But he had two sons, in their mid- to late teens, and he wanted to be tested to see whether his cancer was the heritable type, which he might have passed on to them. If it was, he wanted his boys tested for the genetic mutation that was cutting his own life short. His dying wish was this: "If anything can be done to help my sons not to live and die like this, I want it done."

As it turned out, the tests established that he did indeed have the mutation; his cancer was the hereditary type. That meant that each son has a fifty-fifty chance of having the same mutation. And if he does have the mutation, there is a strong probability—up to 80 percent—that he will develop this fierce, aggressive cancer sometime in early to mid-adulthood; the majority of these cancers appear before age forty.

There's only one known preventive therapy, and it's a terrible choice to have to make.

I gave the results to the father, and he had his wife call me. It was obviously a horrible time for them; the father was now in his final days.*

After I explained the genetic results to the mother, she asked, "If I tell my sons about this, what will you recommend?"

I said I'm not recommending anything; this is a decision your sons will have to make for themselves. But I can tell you that the best, probably the only way to avoid this cancer, when you have the gene mutation, is to have the entire stomach removed surgically before your midtwenties—before the cancer can begin to form.

She was horrified, understandably so. She thought for a moment, then said, "Thank you for the information. I'll call you if there's anything else," and hung up the phone.

I have never talked to her, or her sons, since then. The father died, and the family seemed to vanish off the face of the earth. I think about those two boys often. They will now be in their mid- to late twenties—meaning it could now be too late for the preventive surgery. I don't know whether their mother ever said a word to them. Since neither ever contacted me, I suspect she didn't.

Jill's story raises a central ethical question concerning genetic disease: Who has the right to make these profound, often agonizing decisions? Much as Jill wanted to pass this crucial information—life-or-death information, really—to the two young men, so they could decide their own fates, she could not, ethically or legally, take the initiative. She could not get in touch with either boy without their mother's consent.

The End of Avoidance

What this family's story makes clear is this: There will come a time when you, the parent—perhaps the surviving parent—must end your children's avoidance, must help them confront the genetic realities. When that time arrives will depend on a number of considerations: the nature and time frame of the disorder itself, what is happening in your children's lives, their level of maturity. It's up to you to decide when the time has come. But when it does come, the very worst thing you as a parent can do is NOT help your children confront their genetic legacy.

Putting the Cart (Testing) Before the Horse (Counseling)

Between 2003 and 2009 (the latest year for which we have figures as I write), the number of genetic tests available doubled; today, some 1,900 genetic disease traits can be tested for. With more and more insurance companies willing to pick up part or all of the tab, parents today face some decisions they're not really equipped to make. Two considerations apply, and they're often in conflict:

- Genetically based illnesses can range from a slightly increased possibility of contracting the disease to, in conditions such as Huntington's, a virtual 100 percent certainty that inheriting the gene mutation means developing the illness.
- At the same time, the possibility of effective treatment or prevention varies from zero to pretty likely.

The problem is that when parents arrange genetic testing for their children, the specialist or institution involved usually completes the genetic testing first, and only afterward offers genetic counseling. So the first key question—whether to test or not, and when—is never addressed; by the time a genetic counselor gets involved, the parents (and perhaps the children) already know the results.

My Advice: Get a Counselor Involved First

My own very strong feeling is this: *Before* you make any decision as to *whether* or *when* to test your children, you should get someone like

Jill involved. A certified genetic counselor can explain exactly what you will and will not learn from genetic testing, and where your child's possible genetic problem falls on the scale of treatability or preventability. Essentially, she can spell out a risk/benefit analysis of testing. You can then decide whether or not there's anything to be gained, NOW, by knowing whether your child carries a genetic flaw. Think about how much you want to know, and when you want to know it.

The specialist or hospital you're dealing with for your own illness can put you in touch with a genetic counselor; since it's a certified specialty, you'll have the assurance that you're dealing with a qualified professional who can answer your questions accurately and clearly— even if too often the answer may be, "We still don't know." But do it *before*, not after, you decide whether or not to have your children tested for whatever runs in your family.

(One word of caution. At present, only about a dozen states require that genetic counselors be licensed. To make sure you are meeting with a certified genetic counselor, and not someone trying to sell you genetic tests, ask to see her certificate from the American Board of Genetic Counseling.)

The Worrier: II

So with all that knowledge in our backpacks, let's come back to Susan and her twelve-year-old daughter, Emily—the worrier.

Susan decided that she would indeed have that drastic surgery, the removal of both breasts before a malignancy could develop. Her thinking was straightforward: She wants to see her children grow up, she wants to be there with them and for them, and if this is what it takes, so be it.

And she finally decided to explain to Emily the genetic component, the dangerous BRCA2 gene mutation in the family. Her daughter's very first question: "Does that mean I'm going to get breast cancer?"

Susan and I had done a great deal of advance planning for that question. As a result of that preparation, here is what Susan said:

"Because we have breast cancer in our family, it's always possible that you might get it when you grow up. But I'm going to teach you everything you need to know to minimize that chance, and then, when you're older, we'll talk about testing."

Emily said, "Okay." But then, after a moment's thought, she asked, "Am I going to have to have this operation? How can I find out?" Susan said, well, there's a test we can do now. It's a blood test. Emily (who, like any sensible twelve-year-old, hates needles) said, "Eeew, I don't want to do that."

And that's when Susan pushed the whole thing out of today, into a fairly vague tomorrow. She said, "We don't need to do it right now. You may want it sometime in the future; we can do it then."

For this family, that's been pretty much it. Emily got quite interested in her mom's surgery and the subsequent breast reconstruction, but only in a casual, twelve-year-old way—"What did the doctor say? Do you have to go back to the hospital?" She showed no interest in seeing the actual site of the surgery on Mom. (Interestingly, nine-year-old Spencer *did* want to see—and Susan showed him.)

But basically, Emily's life is going on. She's worrying about what girls her age worry about—boys, other girls, her Facebook page, the mysteries of algebra. What she is NOT worrying about is some potential mastectomy, ten or fifteen years from now.

Success.

JILL POLK'S REFERENCES: GENETICS ON THE WEB

Internet Sources

Genetics Home Reference: ghr.nlm.nih.gov

National Human Genome Research Institute: genome.gov

GeneTests: genetests.org

National Organization for Rare Disorders: rarediseases.org

Your Genes Your Health: yourgenesyourhealth.org

Genetic Counseling

National Society of Genetic Counselors: nsgc.org

America Board of Genetic Counseling: abgc.net

Genetic Alliance: "Making Sense of Your Genes: A Guide to Genetic Counseling": geneticalliance.org/counseling.guide

Alexa Breidinger, fourteen, whose dad died of pancreatic cancer, offers her "tear soup" recipe for other children facing that kind of loss.

14.

Some Other Special Situations

There are a few more special situations—family and medical—that affect how we apply the guidelines from the preceding chapters.

- When the patient isn't a parent
- When the child *can* "catch it"
- When the child is particularly vulnerable
- When the child did help "cause" the adult's medical condition

When It's Not the Parent Who Gets Sick

One nice thing about kids: They love a lot of people.

Parents frequently ask me what they should do when someone who is not a parent, but is close to their children, is stricken with a serious illness, or dies, or goes out of their children's lives in some other way. I may hear that it's "just" a cousin or "just" the mother of a friend: Should we be worried about the children? My answer is yes.

The title doesn't matter: Grandpa, or Nanny, or Mrs. Baxter in the third grade, or Cousin Joe, or Tommy's mommy. If that person has had a strong, loving relationship with your child, and particularly if he or she has been involved in caring for your child, then that person's illness, death, or departure from the scene is going to have an impact—perhaps even comparable to the loss of a parent. And everything we've said about warning signs, about your children's need for emotional support, and about giving and getting help will apply.

(The illness or death of another child—a playmate or sibling—raises questions beyond the scope of this book. Many of the same principles—hospital visits, children's ways of grieving, preparing them for the inevitable, their perceptions of death—will still apply. But there will be additional issues that do *not* arise when the loss involves an adult. If your child loses a close friend or a sibling, you may feel the need of professional help and guidance.)

What If You *Can* Catch It?

One of the reassurances we offered children about parental illness in chapter 1 is, "You can't get it from me." We were talking then about non-contagious diseases such as cancer, for which the reassurance is perfectly true. But where a parent's disease *is* "catchable," we have to modify that message.

We're seeing a resurgence in America of some serious contagious diseases; tuberculosis and whooping cough are good examples.

Children usually begin to understand the idea of contagion, of a disease that is "catching," somewhere in their early school years, around seven, eight, or nine. They know that if Timmy has a cold, and Timmy sneezes near you, you can catch his cold.

Before this age, up through the toddler years, you can enforce any quarantine rules without much explanation: Wear a mask when you're with Daddy; don't touch his plates or utensils; whatever. But when your child is ready, you'll want to explain contagious disease and the rules it requires:

- How the disease is caused: by microscopic living creatures called germs, or by tiny packets of disease called viruses
- How the disease is transmitted: through the air, through physical contact, through blood, or whatever the mechanisms may be

You'll explain whatever rules of hygiene, of quarantine are required. Usually these are very straightforward and easy for children to learn. You'll also tell your children that, of course, there are no absolute guarantees about a disease that's "catching." But usually, if you're really careful, then you're safe. So that's what we'll be: really careful.

The Vulnerable Child

Children with:
- learning disabilities
- developmental delays and disorders

are more vulnerable to all the risks that come with a parent's serious illness, and may have a harder time engaging with the coping strategies in this book. If your child has been diagnosed with ADHD, or falls somewhere on the autism spectrum, or has other, similar problems, he is at more emotional or psychological risk from Dad's illness than another child might be. His attention span, his manipulation of words and concepts, will be different.

So what you the parent, especially the well parent, must do is pull together two different streams of understanding: what you have learned from therapists, other specialists, and your own experience about the unique ways your child's mind works, and the guidelines set out in this book.

Our basics never change: The need for absolute honesty, for never lying to your child in even the smallest way. But how you apply those basics depends on how your special child learns, understands, and copes.

And so it's up to you to modify this book's guidelines to the phrasings and timings that work for your particular child.

If the Child *Is* Involved

Very rarely there will be an exception to that basic reassurance that "Nothing you ever did made me get [this condition]." If a child did have some role in bringing on an accident—shenanigans in the car that caused Mom to crash, or banging into a ladder that made Dad fall off—then a different kind of reassurance is called for.

The child is going to feel great guilt and great fear. He knows he didn't *mean* to make it happen, but it *did* happen, and the consequences now are serious, perhaps lifelong.

What can you say?

You can acknowledge, and forgive.

There's no blinking away the central fact: Something the child did has hurt Mom or Dad, maybe forever. The child knows that. Now he must get past it.

You can tell him, with perfect honesty: Mom and I both know *you didn't mean for it to happen*. We *know* you didn't mean to hurt her. It was an accident. Accidents do happen; that's why we call them accidents.

And second: There is no way Mom will love you any less because this accident happened. There is no way Mom or I would have chosen *not* to have you as our kid, even though she got hurt. Mom still loves you very much. She's not going to come home from the hospital and be mad at you and not love you anymore.

You can't deny the accident, and that's not what your child needs from you now. What he needs is the reassurance of your continuing, unconditional love.

Remember the Circles of Help

Any of these very sensitive special situations may stress your child beyond your own ability to help. Your best guides are the early warning signs in chapter 3 and, should you need them, the widening circles of help described in chapter 4.

With her inspiring picture, ten-year-old Livia Raulinaitis offers the same powerful message as Emily Jones does in this final chapter: Whatever family crises they may face, our children are strong, resilient, and full of hope. With a little help from us, they can and will emerge, even from tragedy, to become the healthy, whole, emotionally secure young adults we want them to be.

15.

Emily's Hero

Throughout this book we've talked about, we've relied on, our children's resilience, the life force that burns so brightly within them. Given the help, the guidance, the unwavering love—above all, the truth—that they now need, our children can, to paraphrase William Faulkner's Nobel Prize address, not merely endure: They can prevail.

When Ron and I were putting this new edition together, I contacted many of the people we've written about, including that remarkable family we met in chapter 10, Brian and Leanne Jones, who, when told that there was no further hope of curing his leukemia, decided that they would not delay: They would give their three young daughters the terrible news at once, and then make all Brian's remaining time an unforgettable celebration of their life together.

Brian Jones died three years ago. When I called Leanne to ask to use their story, she told me their eldest daughter, Emily, now fifteen, had just written about her father's death for her ninth-grade English class. This is what Emily wrote:

MY HERO

"After all, to the well-organized mind, death is but the next
great adventure."

—J. K. Rowling, "The Man with Two Faces,"
Harry Potter and the Sorcerer's Stone,
spoken by the character Albus Dumbledore

A hero is someone who looks death in the face and continues forward to meet it, with dignity and courage. A hero is a person who gets diagnosed with a nearly incurable disease and decides to fight to beat the odds. A hero continues forward when the ugly face of relapse rears its ugly head. A fighter. A cancer patient. Brian Christopher Jones. My dad. My hero.

Hearing a cancer diagnosis is bad enough, but hearing it with three young daughters at home, at the young age of thirty-seven, with so much life left to live, it can be devastating. My dad had his first diagnosis in 2004. He was diagnosed with a form of cancer called leukemia, which mutates the white blood cells in the body. He went through taxing rotations of chemotherapy, while in the hospital for weeks at a time. As the chemo attacked his blood, it ravished his entire body. He was sicker than I ever knew, ever could have imagined. He relapsed in 2005 and 2006. In July of 2006, he was enduring yet another round of chemo and conquering it, when he learned of the reappearance of the cancer. He was given 6–12 weeks to live and what did he do?

He told each of his daughters individually; taking more courage and bravery than anyone who hasn't faced their own death could imagine. We scheduled a trip to Walt Disney World with thirty-eight other people. He lived his life to its absolute fullest, to his last dying breath. That courage, dignity, and complete acceptance of his own death made him my hero. That fight and will to live made him my hero. My dad defined the term hero to a T and he is my hero forever more.

Gabriella Martinez was eight when her dad died at home. Gabriella told me that at that moment, she saw a glowing, golden figure rise from her father in the bed. The glow floated across the room, stopping in front of her. She heard her dad's voice saying "It's okay to cry, but I'll always love you." Then the figure dissolved in a shower of golden sparks. Gabriella's mother, her face buried in her hands, saw and heard nothing. To me, Gabriella's vision embodies the primal link that lets children and parents who love each other stay in each other's hearts far beyond death. Whatever Gabriella saw, it's a vision of hope.

Epilogue

Way back at the beginning of chapter 1, when we were first talking about the need for absolute honesty with your children, I said this:

Your children are affected by everything that happens in the family. The more serious the situation, the more they will be impacted.

In order to help your children, you *must* accept that basic principle. And you do, or you wouldn't still be with me, here at the end.

So we know you are going to be there for your children, keeping an eye on them, watching their behavior, assessing their responses, seeking help for them when they need it.

You recognize that when a child shows negative behavioral or emotional responses to a family medical crisis, it doesn't mean there's anything *wrong* with your child; quite the opposite. It is a signal that the situation, or the stress, or the unknown has *exceeded your child's ability to cope*. Your child hasn't become a bad person, or a mentally disturbed person. He or she is still *normal* and is *responding normally to an abnormal situation.*

As a child life specialist, these are my central beliefs, validated by all my years of work with families like yours:

- Your children are basically good.
- Your children are basically healthy.
- Your children *want* to handle crises in the most positive way possible.
- Your children can stretch their abilities to new and unexpected levels in the face of a family problem.

Nevertheless, when dangerous stresses come into the lives of children, they can produce unhealthy responses.

This book is about helping you and your children develop some *alternative* responses. The aim is for your children to build a whole new repertoire of responses—safe, *healthy* ways of coping with the wrenching, abnormal situation of a parent's grave illness. Whatever transpires now for you, the parents, you want your children to emerge whole, fulfilled, and ready for the rest of their lives.

I am always struck that parenting is so *primal,* locked so deep within our genes. I know the pain parents feel when their parenting is interrupted. I understand the fear that your children might not have you around as they grow up, the fear of the ways your illness or death may impact the rest of their lives. Either parent's serious illness leaves you both feeling so *vulnerable.*

For any family to allow me, a stranger, into its circle, in such a time of vulnerability—to let me come to know the parents and the children, to allow me some input that may smooth the process a little, may reduce the pain a little—this is for me an enormous privilege. Now, by accepting this book, you too have granted me that privilege, and for that I thank you.

And I will ask you the same favor I ask of the families I work with in person. This book is the fruit of their experience; each family has added something to this body of knowledge and understanding. So I would like to hear from you about your own experience:

- What ideas from this book have worked for you and your family?
- What ideas *haven't* worked, and why do you think they haven't?

- What have you learned on your own, dealing with your family medical crisis, that might help other families in future editions of this book, or in my own continuing work with them?

Please write your ideas, observations, suggestions, comments, to me at The Gathering Place, touchedbycancer.org.

Acknowledgments

Seventeen years ago, the following people contributed to the initial version of this book. They all significantly influenced the development of my awareness of the needs of children when a parent is ill, and I continue to hold all of them in the highest esteem.

Many individuals contribute to a project such as this, and they all have my deepest gratitude and respect. But there are a few special people who, over the years, have had a significant role in making a group of random ideas and concerns into first a service and then a guidebook. Michael Kahn and Elliot Aronson showed me that my niche was children, and I am grateful. Extra thanks go to Margie Wagner, who taught me about the relationship between children and health care. The importance of teamwork emerged from the feedback of the early child life staff at Children's Hospital of Los Angeles. The writings of the Association for the Care of Children's Health, and the constant emphasis on parents as partners, made "family-centered care" the core of my work.

More recently, Alice Scesny provided the support and leadership necessary to make good ideas into a real program and keep it going. Thanks to Shirley Gullo and Amy Weiss, nurses who provide a level of patient care and human concern that never ceases to amaze me.

Most important, the tough work was done by the hundreds of

families who allowed us to have a role in their lives. Some of the children who contributed concretely to this book are Jennie Crook, Lea Crum, Sadie Mau, and Jessica Rottenberg, and I will always be grateful that they were willing to share part of themselves in the hope of helping others.

Now, in 2011, there is an additional group of people who have taken the concept of this book to a new and higher level. Many of the suggestions and observations in this new edition are a direct outcome of the work of these dedicated professionals, and I will always be grateful to them!

Most of the new clinical approaches and almost all the family stories in this revised version are the result of the work that I have done over the past eleven years at The Gathering Place, a community-based cancer support center that provides services at no cost to individuals and families touched by cancer. This is an amazing place, truly embodying the values of community, integrity, and intentionality. First I must thank Eileen Saffran, the founder and executive director of The Gathering Place, for her vision and commitment. Children's programs are expensive and time-consuming, and Eileen has never wavered in her dedication to providing services to all members of a family, even the very youngest. Ellen Heyman, program director, has consistently guided me and my colleagues to greater clinical depth and supported our continuing professional growth. And that is no small task, because I work with the best of the best!

Several compassionate and devoted professionals have made significant contributions to the new chapters in this book, including David Deckert, M.D.; Jill Polk, M.S., C.G.C.; Amy Clark, B.S., C.C.L.S.; and Megan Bronson, A.P.R.N., B.C. I thank them for their generous contribution of time and knowledge.

I also want to acknowledge the work of child life specialists across the United States and beyond. Many of you have never heard the term "child life specialist," but these hardworking professionals, located in hospitals and in the community, use their incredible knowledge to help children successfully face some of life's most difficult challenges. If you are concerned about the well-being of a child, think about seeking help from a child life specialist.

Finally, once again, I must thank the many families who not only invited me to walk that perilous path of parental illness with them but then allowed me to tell their stories so that others might find assistance, support, and hope.

—Kathleen McCue

Index